Graham Leona

The Right Reverend and Right Honourable Graham Leonard. *(Western Morning News, Plymouth)*

Graham Leonard

Bishop of London

JOHN S. PEART-BINNS

Darton, Longman and Todd
London

First published in 1988 by
Darton, Longman and Todd Ltd
89 Lillie Road, London SW6 1UD

© 1988 John S. Peart-Binns

British Library Cataloguing in Publication Data

Peart-Binns, John S. (John Stuart)
    Graham Leonard
    1. Church of England, Leonard, Graham *1921*–
    I. Title
    283'.092'4

    ISBN 0–232–51746–0 Cased
    ISBN 0–232–51832–7 Paperback

Phototypeset by Input Typesetting Ltd, London SW19 8DR
Printed and bound in Great Britain by
Anchor Brendon Ltd, Tiptree, Essex

for
Annis
with deepest love

Contents

Illustrations

Frontispiece: The Right Reverend and Right Honourable Graham Leonard.

Acknowledgements

Without the willing availability of my subject and the way he has let me into his mind as well as into his archives there would have been no book. I have read and studied a mass of files, papers and letters as well as every sermon, lecture and address he has committed to paper. Our discussions, whether at London House or at his home in Witney, have been thorough, penetrating and enjoyable. In thanking him for generosity of time and hospitality I also thank his wife, Priscilla, and do so with love and affection.

I have received the help of countless correspondents giving me varying impressions of my subject: Graham Leonard is hard, aloof, prelatical, close and unresponsive, legalistic, remote, lacking in warmth and friendship, ambitious, a dull preacher, genial, warm in personal relationships, soft, an amusing raconteur, compassionate, understanding, innovative and imaginative, good fun, thoughtful, natural, prophetic, an idealist with illusions. Criticism of Graham Leonard's convictions and judgement – some of it strong and strongly expressed – has been of the character of the man, or the functioning of the bishop, but never once of Graham Leonard, *priest*. With any prominent figure, and Graham Leonard is no exception, the public presence differs from the private persona. The image is distinctly not the man and the prelatical caricature is not the bishop. Beneath the surface one finds a man of principle acquainted with compromise, a priest of faith with a malleable heart, and a bishop whose conscience reigns and rules.

Many of those who have helped me, by letter or in person, have asked that they should not be named. It has seemed wrong to thank some by name and not others in these acknowledgements. In any case the list of people would fill a whole page. May I therefore say 'thank you' in fullest measure to all of you. Without *you* the book would be bare and barren. I am immensely grateful for your generosity on paper and for hospitality when we have met.

However, a particular thank you goes to the staff of London House who have been patient with my endless requests for documents, letters, files and press cuttings, and they have plied me with coffee and sandwiches. Nothing has been too much trouble for them.

From the start I decided that I would enter fully into the complex and controversial nature of my subject and present him from the inside out. What follows is the result.

JSP-B

1

A Steady Start

Every man's influence is determined, to an extent that it is difficult to overstate, by the nature of the times in which he is placed. His achievements must always be conditioned by his opportunities, and the manner of his service will be only partly under his own control. Standing, alone, apart and alert, for unbendable beliefs is not strange to Graham Leonard. There is in his stance, but not in his person, more than a touch of Athanasius. Athanasius was deposed and went into exile. He returned briefly but was rejected again and again. His character was as resolute as his theology was sound. He refused to compromise with those libertarians and heretics who denied the true divinity of Christ. He spent the last years of his life building up a new 'party' by whose support orthodoxy triumphed.

Emperors and bishops could not crush Athanasius' invincible stand against heresy. Cardinal Newman described him as 'a principal instrument after the Apostles by which the sacred truths of Christianity have been conveyed and secured to the world'. There is an affinity here with the 130th bishop of London.

Little in Graham Leonard's immediate antecedents give clues to his future. The 'nature of the times' will be the setting that makes the man, proves the priest, and propels the bishop onto the national and world stage.

Graham Douglas Leonard was born on 8 May 1921, the only child of Douglas and Emily Mabel Leonard. His father (born on 26 January 1883), was ordained and at the time one of the regional organizing secretaries of the Colonial (later Commonwealth) and Continental Church Society. This appointment, short in duration, had come after 14 years of curacies in Walthamstow, Tonbridge and Greenwich. In 1922

Douglas Leonard moved to Battersea Parish Church as curate but in charge of St Mary-le-Park, and in 1927 he became vicar of St Michael, Wandsworth Common.

Husband and wife came from very different family backgrounds: he from the well-to-do middle class. His father had been a liveryman in the City. She came from what might be called the competent working class. She did things properly, was good at making clothes and all her standards were high. Emily lived in Walthamstow and it was there that she met Douglas and, after a long courtship, they married on 10 February 1914. She was always a staunch Anglican and the more dominant of the couple. Graham inherited his father's facial features, not least the bushy, well-known and easily caricatured eyebrows. Douglas's work was controlled by a simple, devout piety, which took the form of a warm personal devotion to our Lord and a willing acceptance of the Church of England's formulation of Christian faith and discipline. Theologically, he was a liberal Evangelical and belonged to the Anglican Evangelical Group Movement. This movement, now defunct, was not a half-way house between conservative Evangelicals and Modernists, although it had strains of each in it. It placed more emphasis on the importance of the sacraments than conservative Evangelicals and avoided the unprovable and extravagent speculations of some Modernists.

Douglas Leonard's attitude to the Holy Communion was like that of many liberal Evangelicals, ambiguous. They borrowed from higher Church traditions a number of features by which the dignity and beauty of Communion services were enriched. This arose from their desire for beauty in worship, and by their sense of liberation from the taboos of their stricter Evangelical forebears. No very clear theology lay behind this development. On the other hand, liberal Evangelicals were suspicious of over-emphasizing the Communion. This derived from an inherited prejudice which died very hard, a dislike of anything bordering on the magical, controversies about fundamental Christian doctrines apart from which the Communion was meaningless, and a sense that the typical English layman was happier with Matins than with the Eucharist. He did not sufficiently ask whether they ought to be.

But the Communion was taken seriously. Reception of it

should only come after preparation, something that diminished to the brink of being lost with the coming of the Parish Communion movement. When Douglas Leonard was vicar of St Michael, Wandsworth Common (1927–38), there was a monthly service of preparation for Holy Communion on a Wednesday evening. The Sunday services were typical for a Church of that type and time: namely, an 8 a.m. Communion each Sunday, with Matins (followed by Communion on the first, third and fifth Sundays), and Evensong as the main services. It had never been an Evangelical hothouse. Coloured stoles were worn and the eastward position taken. In fact Douglas Leonard 'lowered' the churchmanship a little.

St Michael's parish was compact, suburban, with little poverty but no great wealth. In 1933 the electoral roll carried 570 names. It was a flourishing Church and Douglas Leonard looked after it with meticulous care. The word 'meticulous' is not accidental for it reflected his first class maths degree from Cambridge. Stanley Howard, his curate, paid two guineas a week for full board and lodging in two rooms on the top floor of the vicarage. He recalls that his vicar was particularly good with men. Badminton was played once a week and the young Graham Leonard learned to play too. He was both good-natured and prone to losing his temper if he did not get his own way. Nothing unusual in that!

However, Leonard was not long in Wandsworth: after a local prep. school he went to Monkton Combe School, near Bath, presided over by one of his godparents, Edward Heywood, who helped to pay for his education. Although his was not a home of financial hardship, money was in short supply. He entered the junior school on the hill top in September 1933 and moved to the senior school in the valley in September 1935.

Although his parents influenced him, they did not do so in a way that has left indelible marks on his character. Monkton Combe however did, for it became something to react against. It was a place for earnest, committed Evangelicals. Indoctrination came through the Crusaders and the Christian Union, which were both more central to the life of the school than its chapel. In one sense this was no bad thing, for the unvaried diet of literalist teaching ensured that there was a basis upon which one could later build, or from which one could depart.

Much wishy-washy teaching elsewhere left no such foundation, so the drift into amiable Anglicanism or pleasant agnosticism was but a short step. Monkton Combe produced real spiritual leaders like W. J. Thompson (bishop of Iran), Maurice Wood (bishop of Norwich) and Graham Leonard, and also people who later rejected Christianity altogether because of its claustrophobic manifestations at school.

Leonard was certainly of studious bent, a boy who applied himself to the subject in hand. There was something unswerving about him even then. He began by specializing in classics but changed in the sixth form to the sciences. As a boy, he had been drawn to the natural sciences. In holidays he spent a lot of time in the Natural History and Science museums in London. He was an omnivorous reader and a carnivorous one too. He was interested in acquiring facts, and chewed whole chunks of books to lodge them in his memory. Writing in the *Spectator* (30 January 1982) he recalled:

> There was never a time in my childhood when books did not occupy a large place in my life. My father had a fair number, which were entirely at my disposal and I made good use of them. I spent hours, for example, with J. G. Wood's *Natural History*, five volumes in half calf, lavishly illustrated with engravings. The last two volumes were devoted to 'Man' and were full of vivid descriptions of the lives and habits of even the remotest tribes. The effect on me was comparable to that described by Keats in his poem *On First Looking into Chapman's Homer*.

He admitted that while his stock of knowledge increased, 'I gave little attention to considering the purpose for which it was to be used or how the various subjects were to be related'. Data only becomes information if it is used intelligently and correctly.

The Evangelical atmosphere of his school, less so of his home, did not satisfy him. It may have touched his heart, but it neither excited his senses nor satisfied his mind. If religion is wholesome it will have an effect on every part of one's being. Leonard remembers a mission in Battersea Town Hall in the 1920s. The Church of the Ascension, Lavender Hill, a well known Anglo-Catholic citadel in South London, hosted a Mass with a procession and an address by the vicar,

Fr. Beckingham. There, in the procession, was a Cross, lifted high with taperers, banners and incense. It was the first time he had seen or smelt incense. There was something joyous about the occasion. Somehow he thought it right. What surprised him was that members of the Salvation Army, near them in the congregation, kept shouting 'hallelujah', rejoicing in the Gospel message of Fr. Beckingham. When he mentioned this to his mother and asked questions, he received no answers. She preferred not to discuss the matter. On one occasion when he was in London he went into Brompton Oratory. He was stunned by the glory within. Here again was a feeling of fear and awe, of something mysterious. He had known nothing like it but again he knew it was right.

By the time he left Monkton Combe, where he became senior prefect, Leonard was a mature and serious person, but there was nothing solemn about him. Canon Mark Kennaway, rector of Cardynham Bodmin, who had known Leonard at school, says that 'He seemed to stand, with quiet confidence, alone: one never thought of probing.' There seemed to be a self-sufficiency about him. He was respected by his contemporaries but although he took part in most normal school activities he was never the centre nor the leader of a group. He had an excellent singing voice and sang in the choir, and if he cannot be accused of blowing his own trumpet he was effective with the bugle in the band as a member of the Officers' Training Corps [OTC] in which he became under-officer.

Although ordination was already in his mind, he wanted to take a degree in science. He managed to get a place at Balliol College, Oxford, and arrived in 'that sweet city with her dreaming spires' in the Trinity term of 1940, entering the Honours School in Natural Science. This was not a time when Oxford could bestow its best gifts: war was in the air, severely restricting normal university life. In his first term Leonard was the college representative for OICUU, but that marked the end of his organized Evangelical commitment. He was ready for a step away from the amenable Evangelicalism of his father and the starker brand of his school. It was appropriate that one of the stable stepping stones was a book, *Belief in God*, the first volume of Charles Gore's trilogy *The Reconstruction of Belief*. It was the book Leonard chose for his

Spectator article on 'A book in my life'. This book gripped Leonard's mind and changed it:

> I think I then became aware of four truths which have grasped me ever since. First, he spoke of the 'coherence of Christian doctrine'. Any 'article of faith' is in Gore's words 'a component in a living whole' which provides a philosophy of life applicable to all created activity, and of which we cannot select only those parts which are congenial. Secondly, I learned that while a man must never be asked to believe what appears to be contrary to his reason, the truths which God has revealed about himself will always surpass his intellectual capacity and can never be encompassed by it. If a man supposes that they can be, he will be in danger of believing in a faith of his own invention. Thirdly, I became aware for the first time of the sacramental nature of life in Christ and the Church, at least. By that I mean recognizing that in the New Testament the Christian life, as incorporation into Christ, is given by God through the sacraments and sustained by them. It is not simply the result of a human act of apprehension whether of mind, will or emotion.
>
> But, above all, Gore gave me a vision of God, in his infinite splendour and goodness, to be worshipped and loved in awe and obedience, a vision which those who knew him saw in Gore himself and which was summed up in the words he murmured as he lay dying: 'Transcendent Glory'.

He realized how lopsided and partial was the Evangelical emphasis on the need for redemption and their scandalous neglect of the doctrine of Creation.

Leonard's time at Balliol, of which he was elected an honorary fellow in 1986, was brief because of the war. During the Second World War potential officers intending to go to university were encouraged to do so for a period before undertaking officer training. Specially shortened Honours courses were provided on condition that such undergraduates would, if possible, return after the war to complete their normal full course. Some scientists, judged to be potentially useful, were, by decision of joint recruiting boards, allowed to stay during the war for their normal full courses. Botanists, like Leonard, were not on the whole part of this category, but he was allowed to stay for an extra term after his twentieth birthday to complete his course. He dived into his work with customary zest and concentration, completing the whole Schools course in four terms. He arrived at the laboratories at 9 a.m. each day, worked throughout the day and studied again at night. He needed some recreation, decided on athletics, and was invited to run in the 220 yard hurdles for the Oxford University Centipedes. There were many acquaintances, but no close friends. He was sociable but self-sufficient. His reading extended to poetry and philosophy, preferring the 17th-century poets and T. S. Eliot. Herbert Read interested him.

Religion at Balliol was deadly. There was no chaplain in college and the only course on the menu was morality served by the master of Balliol, A. D. Lindsay. Leonard did not go on the church-sampling circuit, but often attended the university church which, under its vicar T. R. (Dick) Milford, offered cultural depth and some theology with bite in it provided by visiting preachers. Leonard was one of many (and not only of his generation) deeply affected by William Temple who conducted a mission to Oxford in 1940. He remembers Temple breakfasting with the undergraduates at Balliol: his extraordinary ability to bring people to discuss religion unselfconsciously was very evident. It was the 'whole-ness' of Temple that was so powerful, unusual and compelling. Bishop George Bell wrote that 'William Temple had all the vividness and swiftness of a flame. It was like a flame that he spread through our whole firmament, filling every corner of it with a new splendour. It was like a flame that communicated warmth and light to all who saw or heard him.' Temple is still the most quoted English churchman of this century. Despite a temporary eclipse, he is also the most important. It would be faithless to say 'We shall not see his like again', but it needs all the faith we have to believe that we shall.

Leonard joined the Army at the beginning of the war, taking advantage of a scheme by which members of the OTC who had certificate 'A' could enlist as potential officers being released when they were old enough to be called up for service. Leonard, the under-officer, remembers going to Bristol with another boy to enlist. Such men were required to spend a short while in the ranks before going to their

Officer Cadet Training Unit. So when he was called up in 1941 he went first to Norton Barracks, Worcester, being promoted fairly quickly to lance-corporal in view of his service with the OTC. The prospect of ordination was kept steadily in view and in Worcester he became friendly with the rector of St Andrew with All Saints and St Helen, W. R. Buchanan-Dunlop, who gave him a room and a key for any time he was in Worcester. Leonard eagerly took the opportunity for reading, research and study.

After six months at the OCTU on the Welsh coast at Barmouth he joined the 4th Battalion of the Oxfordshire and Buckinghamshire Light Infantry, which was then stationed on the outskirts of Woodhall Spa, Lincolnshire – next to a bomber airfield from which Lancaster bombers took off pretty well every night, making the Nissen huts rattle. Soon after Leonard joined the regiment in 1942 he became signals officer and then adjutant and company commander. John Bradburn, adjutant when Leonard arrived, remembers him as a very agreeable companion in the mess; he was knowledgeable and talkative. Bradburn also recalls that Leonard's 'hobby, in such spare time as was available, was exploring the local woodlands in a quest for different varieties of fungi'.

Leonard absorbed much during these years as he watched the way in which people *commanded*. Some commanding officers looked like pre-war 'Blimps', but they knew how to lead men. The relationship between officers and men, leaders and led, still fascinates Leonard, and he thinks the Church has much to learn from the military example.

In 1944 Leonard was seconded to the Ministry of Supply to work as a military experimental officer in the Army Operational Research Group, where he remained until the end of the war. Captain Leonard was posted to the Research Section attached to the School of Infantry, first at Barnard Castle and later Warminster. This was a suitable place to be because it brought him under the influence of a good priest, Charles Gordon Tulloch Colson, vicar of Warmister and gave access to the library of St Boniface College, Warminster (a missionary college until 1948 when it was leased to King's College, London). Thus Leonard was able to continue his reading.

There had been one further development during these war

years which, together with his priesthood, changed his life and was of supreme importance to him. This is best introduced by retracing the narrative to Balliol and Botany. When Leonard went to Balliol Dr A. G. Ogston (later president of Trinity College, Oxford) was in charge of all biologists. He saw Leonard regularly, arranged for his tuition at classes, got tutors' reports on him and notes that he 'saw him as a capable student, though not an outstanding one; an easy and pleasant member of the college society, though not a leader in it. Personally, I liked him, and still like him – though I do not at all like his theological views'.

It is Professor A. R. Clapham who introduces the other development. He was demonstrator in the department of Botany; the professor and head of department was T. G. B. Osborn. Clapham shared with the professor all the botanical teaching other than mycology and plant physiology, and spent three full days of every week in the lecture room and labora-tory. Professor Clapham recalls:

Two of my earliest pupils were Graham Leonard and Priscilla Swann. They occupied adjacent chairs in the morphological laboratory and were clearly closely acquainted. I remember them as deeply interested and hard-working students, talking in a free and friendly way on botanical and other topics and displaying their fami-liarity with the surrounding countryside during our field excursions. I early became aware of the breadth of their intellectual interests and also of their shared religious feelings.

Those who did the shortened course successfully were given an honours degree without being classified, so it will never be known what class Leonard would have achieved if he had been able to study for the full three years. Priscilla was, however able to do so and was awarded a first in the Schools in 1943. By this time she was no longer Swann but Leonard.

2

A Sense of Direction

Once they encountered one another there was no hope for them! Yet Vivian Priscilla Swann had every good reason to be cautious. Her father had been a distinguished fellow of Gonville and Caius, Cambridge, but had died when she was three years old. She and her elder brothers, Michael Meredith (now Lord) Swann and Hugh Sinclair (Tim), were brought up by their mother. It was a difficult and precarious upbringing and made Priscilla doubly aware of the importance of father and mother in any family if stable, happy and fulfilling relationships are to have a chance of being secured.

Priscilla was 18 when she met Graham Leonard at Oxford, they became engaged and were married in St Benet, Cambridge, on 2 January 1943. The vicar, the Revd J. O. Cobham (later archdeacon of Durham) officiated, assisted by Leonard's father. Priscilla had been prepared for confirmation by Michael Ramsey (later archbishop of Canterbury) during his brief tenure of St Benet's church. After leaving Oxford they established a home in Cambridge although Leonard himself was still serving in the forces. There are two children of the marriage, James (born 21 December 1944) and Mark (born 10 February 1947). Leonard was released from military service on 9 November 1945 ready for training for the priesthood. Married ordinands were not the most welcome of students and one with a child even less so. Leonard entered Westcott House, Cambridge, with a well-stocked mind and a clarity of purpose. His vocation to the priesthood had become clear and henceforward he never wavered.

A contemporary of Leonard's, Ivan H. Whittaker (later chaplain of St Michael's School, Otford), recalls the Westcott of 1945–6: 'There were thirty men at Westcott House and as the number was small and built up gradually, and inherited no living tradition, the men became immediately involved in the work of creating one, and every one had his part to play. It was a time dominated by the experience of war and about to be overtaken by the experience of peace.' There were many different groupings at Westcott particularly concerned with intellectual and academic questions of theology. One new grouping developed which met regularly for tea in room D4 and was concerned with Christian spirituality and the Catholic heritage of the Church. Leonard was a member.

His short time at Westcott was one of the only really unhappy periods of his life. Leonard's major criticism of Westcott was the lack of a sense of being under authority – the authority of God by which we are judged. What distressed him was the feeling of superiority engendered by the house, the *noblesse oblige* of Anglicanism. 'We do it this way here' was a phrase that summed it up. It was all rather gentlemanly with a clubbable atmosphere and a special language used by members of that club. Was this studying for ministerial leadership rather than training for the priesthood? How serious was it? There was supposed to be a tint of High Church colouring in the house's make-up: not too much of course.

Leonard's disappointment with the training at Westcott meant that he was keen to move to a parish. He was made deacon in December 1947 and ordained priest on 19 December 1948 to serve a title at St Andrew, Chesterton, Cambridge. His bishop was Harold Edward Wynn of Ely, who had served all his ministry in Cambridge colleges before becoming a bishop in 1941. He was a good and quiet man, and of definite Catholic churchmanship. Despite lacking the capacity to inspire, Wynn was a good pastor, but found the care of the Fenland parishes a crushing burden.

St Andrew's was the parish in which the Leonards had their home. The vicar, J. A. V. Wallace (from 1934 and through the war years), was a committed pacifist and caused consternation in the parish when he refused to allow the bell to be rung to celebrate the end of the war. The parish was on the outskirts of Cambridge and retained a certain half rural, half urban atmosphere, with a population of between 8000 and 10 000. The Sunday services comprised 8 a.m.

11

Communion, 9.30 sung Eucharist, 11 Matins and 6.30 p.m. Evensong with full choir.

Outside academic terms at Westcott Leonard had been at the church's daily Eucharist and during the long vacations of 1946 and 1947 he would often take Evensong during the week; and the parish registers show that he preached (still a layman) a few times at Evensong on Sundays. He also joined the choir during vacations and there is a photograph of him with the choir football team. Mr Alfred Francis has memories of Leonard at St Andrew's:

> He commenced his parochial duties with great enthusiasm and I always remember him as a fresh complexioned and well-scrubbed, well-dressed (always black suit and never without a clerical collar) young cleric dashing around the parish on a bicycle. I think he first cycled around with cassock and biretta on but found the cassock such an encumbrance that he had to give it up! He was dedicated to pastoral work and spent an enormous amount of time visiting the sick in their homes, patients in hospitals and the (then) infirmary and of course members of the congregation.
>
> He formed study groups which met every week, started an amateur dramatic society and also a parochial breakfast after the sung Eucharists and days of obligation if they happened during the weekdays. Leonard had almost finished his diaconate when the vicar announced that he had accepted the living of Sedbergh in Yorkshire. He left the parish on Sunday 14 November 1948 and Graham was left to carry on until a new appointment. From then until 19 December (when he was ordained priest in Ely Cathedral) he had to find any priest either parochial or collegiate to say Mass for him daily.
>
> On Monday 20 December 1948 he said his first Mass at the Lady Altar in St Andrew's church at 7.30 a.m. There were sixteen persons present including his wife and his mother and father. Fr Davies from Little St Mary, Cambridge, was the assistant priest and I served the Mass for him. What his dear old father thought of it all I do not know. He was a good old Evangelical and must have been out of his depth at the service. Graham used the English

Missal. From that day on I do not think Graham missed saying Mass every day.

A new vicar was appointed, Basil Roberts Buchanan, then vicar of Bloxham in the Oxford Diocese, and he was instituted at St Andrew, Chesterton, on 4 May 1948. For almost six months Leonard had been running the parish on his own. But, as Alfred Francis remarks, Buchanan was a very different incumbent from Wallace: 'Buchanan was a strict conformist to the *Book of Common Prayer*, without any deviation whatever. Graham and Basil were poles apart where theology was concerned but nevertheless got on well together as vicar and curate.'

It was inevitable that new vicar and old curate would soon part company. In September 1949 Leonard moved to the parish of All Saints, St Ives, in Huntingdonshire, and was put in charge of St Peter, Oldhurst and St John the Baptist, Woodhurst. The vicar was Alexander C. Lawson, who had moved to St Ives after a 14-year curacy at St Mary Magdalene, Oxford. The Leonards did not settle here although he insists that he learnt much about being a priest from Fr Lawson; and after only four months he moved to Stansted Mountfitchet, Essex.

The bishop of Chelmsford, Henry Albert Wilson, who retired within a year of Leonard arriving in the diocese, was one of the bishops Leonard admired. Theologically and doctrinally they were far apart. Leonard was however attracted to the independence of Wilson. He had never been a popular bishop either in the national Church or in the diocese of Chelmsford. He was a man who had made up his own mind about issues – and he had a good mind to make up! He had written some useful books and to his 30 years in parishes could be added 21 as a bishop. Wilson was never frightened of being a lone wolf or of unpopularity. The desire for popular approval revolted him for it destroys individuality and corrupts the moral sense.

There were two churches at Stansted, St Mary and St John, which were served alternate weeks by vicar and curate. The vicar was Canon John Harrison Barrow, who had a strong interest in education. He had been an organizing secretary of the Society for Promoting Christian Knowledge. He was also vice-chairman of the Royal School of Church Music. The churchmanship was described as Prayer Book Catholic. It was at Stansted that Leonard's interest in religious education was kindled and set alight. He was also gaining a reputation for teaching the faith with an equal emphasis on word and sacrament. He had never wished to be part of the Anglo-Catholic merry-go-round with its external ritualistic observances more in evidence than its evangelistic fervour. It should be mentioned that Leonard never served in any of the well-known Anglo-Catholic parishes, nor did he wish to. When he was seeking a parish of his own his stipulation was: 'Country parish. Population: up to any size as long as it remains a village; mixed population. Location: anywhere in England – preferably Chelmsford Diocese. Churchmanship: Prayer Book Catholic'. He noted his 'interests' at the time as English illuminated manuscripts and sports. As early as 1950 his name was beginning to appear in print in short articles, and he wrote anonymously too: for example, he contributed the notes on 1 and 2 *Thessalonians* for the Bible Reading Fellowship for August 1950.

Henry Wilson of Chelmsford retired in 1950 and was succeeded as bishop by Sherard Falkner Allison who, although not to Leonard's taste as *pastor pastorum*, was anxious to keep him in the diocese of Chelmsford.

In 1952 Leonard was proposed by the bishop of Colchester (F. D. V. Narborough) for the living of St Mary the Virgin, Ardleigh, which was in the gift of the lord chancellor. He accepted the offer with relish. It was a church with an interesting historic past, little life by 1952 and a future almost wholly dependent on the new priest. Leonard was instituted on 18 September 1952. Ardleigh had a total population of approximately 2000. The parish church was an ancient foundation (with tower and porch of about 1500). Most of the church was rebuilt by William Butterfield of All Saints', Margaret Street, fame and some of his ornate style was introduced into Ardleigh. It was appropriate that the Oxford Movement, or Catholic revival, found solid roots in Ardleigh and the movement's best fruit was tasted there: not the kind that is alluring from without but has little nourishment under the skin; nor that which has a hard core but little else. Leonard has always been suspicious of those who either hug religion to themselves or use it for their own purposes. There is no escape with real religion. A famous forebear was Canon T. W. Perry, a notable Tractarian and friend of T. T. Carter, Arthur Stanton, and A. K. Mackonochie. Perry was the founder of the Church Protection Society which became the nucleus of the English Church Union.

Prior to Leonard's arrival in Ardleigh, the parish had declined and its religious temperature was low. The incumbent from 1935 to 1952 was W. A. Parker Mason, a bachelor, reclusive by temperament, not young, not in good health. His interest was history (he was a fellow of the Royal Historical Society) and he was happier in that sphere than in the parochial round. Moreover, he had the bad fortune to succeed a popular man who, when he retired, stayed in the parish.

When Parker Mason died, the parish asked for a young priest, preferably married. They got one and almost more than they bargained for. Here was a man who was a mixture of dynamite and fresh air – but always, and everywhere, a priest. Of that no one has ever been in doubt. It is the priest who is sometimes an evangelist, a preacher, a teacher. It is the priest who administers the sacraments and leads the people of God in worship. It is the priest who has the responsibility of training individuals in holiness that they may live to the glory of God and be able to fulfil their calling as members of the Church, to take their part in bringing all life under the sovereignty of Christ. It was Leonard the parish priest of Ardleigh who knew that his main task was to turn people's eyes (not sway their heads) until they were firmly fixed on God in worship and to teach and help every member of the Church to grow in holiness.

How was he to do this? The reflections of some of his parishioners describe this better than commentary. Mrs Barbara Erith, who had lived through the previous regime, writes:

The services and general tone of worship altered at once and congregations grew rapidly. Graham has a very nice voice, both speaking and singing, and that added to a very striking presence, making the worship very impressive. There was a natural air of authority about him which always made me think of St Matthew's comment on our

Lord, 'He taught as one having authority and not as the scribes'. He commanded attention by just being himself.

Leonard was never a priest who cultivated sanctuary manners, which tend to erect a barrier between them and their people. Leonard was and is a natural priest.

Another parishoner, Howard Wright, was president of the local branch of the British Legion for which Leonard was chaplain. It had been the custom to hold a Remembrance Sunday service jointly with the Methodists, marching to the church service; the Methodist minister would preach, and minister and priest shared the recital of prayers between them. Mr Wright notes that 'Graham Leonard put a peremptory stop to all that. To him, the Methodists were dissenters from the form of worship practised in the Church. They were welcome to attend but not to officiate in any way in a Church of which they did not approve. There were hard feelings, but the integrity of Graham Leonard was respected.' Moreover, Leonard attracted people from nonconformity and those on the other side of what might be called the Christian fringe, by an uncompromising exposition of the faith. Teaching, teaching and more teaching came from the pulpit. His popularity had nothing to do with pulpit flamboyance or tricks of oratory. Quite the contrary: the pulpit was ancillary to the altar and not a platform from which a preacher could 'sway the multitude'. Leonard mistrusted then, as he does now, the wrong use of the pulpit.

Even at this early stage of his priesthood a few constants were emerging. There was about him a quixotic honesty which was the reason for his steady refusal to 'run in harness', or perhaps it is truer to say, his constitutional inability to do so. He was provokingly, almost grotesquely, conscientious. He would insist on careful explanations when the one thing needful seemed to be unity of action. Gradually people learned to value his approval the more for its deliberately scrupulous character, but at first they were moved to surprise. Nothing remained the same following Leonard's arrival. He immediately resumed the full range of services which had been customary in the parish church, and in the Crockleford Mission in an old school building on the outskirts of the geographically large parish. This meant at least six services every Sunday with daily celebrations of Communion and other and special services at regular intervals.

A combination of colour, joy and awe came into worship. If the focus of worship was God, the locus for worship should not be neglected. The painted walls and ceiling were still stained from the original oil lamps which had long been replaced. This would not do. Leonard led a working team for cleaning and renewing the building. All kinds of items were needed to beautify and dignify the church. Suddenly there was a stream of anonymous donors and by the time Leonard left Ardleigh many alterations had been carried out. A big event in the parish was the rededication of the peal of eight bells on 5 February 1955. A note on the service sheet records that the foundation of this 'peal of eight' was the pre-Reformation tenor bell. (The fine-toned bell was cast by Robert Burford about 1415 and is still in its original condition. On the shoulder of this 13¼ cwt bell is inscribed, 'Sum Rosa Pulsata Mundi Maria Vocata'.)

Leonard was soon known by everyone in Ardleigh, not least because of his persistent and constant visiting. His pastoral care for the sick and the dying was sustained and loving. He very quickly showed himself to have a gift for spiritual direction and in the confessional. Everyone was encouraged to have a rule of life, and while Leonard set the guidelines he helped many individuals in adapting these guidelines to suit their particular needs and way of life.

A priest of Leonard's convictions is bound to have 'enemies'. Lady Thurlow wrote to the bishop of Chelmsford (Falkner Allison) asking whether permission to use the 1928 Prayer Book for the Communion service had been given. Leonard had introduced a Parish Communion Book without authorization. As it was so widely used he could not think formal authorization was necessary. The real fuss was over the Gloria, which Leonard omitted in the penitential seasons of the Church's year as had been customary at the churches in which he had served before Ardleigh. Moreover, 'I feel that anything which marks off these seasons and leads to a deeper realization of the nature of sin is desirable, especially in these days.' Leonard was concerned with the matter of authority. On the one hand he was prepared to come to an agreement in the matter as it was not anything about which he felt strongly and he had promised canonical obedience to his bishop. On the other hand if Lady Thurlow, or people like her, who seemed to want to run everything they come into contact with, got their way by appealing to higher authority, Leonard's position would be untenable. Leonard received the bishop's authorization for the Parish Communion Book, 'although I cannot officially authorize the omission of the Gloria, as you will realize'.

There was another major difference in the parish during Leonard's time. The vicarage became an open house, with parishioners welcome after services for coffee and social contact. Mrs Barbara Erith adds:

> Priscilla was a wonderful support to her husband. She did much to make the church more beautiful. She made a huge pair of damask curtains lined and inter-lined to go across the west arch. How she managed to handle them I never knew, as they were tremendously heavy. The vicarage was open to everyone at any time of the day and there was always a warm welcome for everyone, and the house, which is a very beautiful old one, looked lovely whilst in her care. It contrasted sharply with my memories of it during the life of the previous incumbent who was looked after by a dragon of a housekeeper, known as 'public enemy no. 1', and who opened the door a crack to one if a visit became necessary. The poor old vicar only had a newspaper for a table cloth and the house was dreadfully neglected and cold.

Let the excitement of Ardleigh under Leonard be recaptured by Anne Bayley (now a professor of surgery in Zambia and an authority on AIDS, but in 1952 about to leave her home in Ardleigh for university at Cambridge):

> He plunged into rehabilitating a 'middle' churchmanship parish with immense energy and enthusiasm. I marvel now at the rate at which he introduced changes and his total certainty that the outward and visible signs of his strong Catholic faith should be adopted immediately. As an 18-year-old uncritically delighted by every new development, and only in the parish during vacations, I imagine I missed or ignored the opposition but I think it was overcome by

his youthful and infectious *enjoyment* of what he was doing. Dull, dreary, dutiful Matins gave way to a sung Eucharist; a makeshift 'choir' of enthusiasts huddled in the chancel (which was the only reasonably warm bit of the church) to learn hymns with cheerful tunes, Merbecke, and (later) bits of the Missa de Angelis. The sacramental theology, Mary as the Mother of God, a Catholic view of the Church, came naturally with the hymns and, as soon as practical, we changed from *Ancient and Modern* to the *English Hymnal*. Graham has a beautiful singing voice (which he loved to use, I think) so we had strong leadership and learned quickly. He made no bones about parallels in relationships between man and wife, and between God and his people. I remember him saying to my father once, in connection with the strange practice (previously unknown) of a daily Eucharist, 'You don't kiss your wife once a week do you?' – or words to that effect. He kissed *his* wife often, unselfconsciously, in greeting or reassurance as he returned to the kitchen for the next mug of coffee after a session in his study, or a meeting. . . .

I think Graham knows he has a voice which people enjoy listening to, and occasionally shows it, but there was always one place where his voice became plain and completely unselfconscious: at the words of consecration, said with intensity of attention.

In 1953 we had various celebrations for the coronation in the village on a cold, windy, grey day which contributed nothing festive. Graham provided, in my recollection, a good deal of leadership and we started off with a vigil of prayer the previous evening before the sacrament. On coronation day I suppose there was a service, which I don't recall, but I do remember Graham in black cassock with patriotic red, white and blue ribbon round his felt black clerical hat in the village street as we processed – the *pièce de résistance* was the dragon composed of choirboys sorted into diminishing size under a paper carcase, with St George protecting a frozen maiden (me) from the dragon.

Family life, open house at the vicarage, much visiting, the human warmth and self-discipline to use pastoral opportunities, dignified *and* enjoyable worship, a sense of humour and an infectious chuckle, enjoyment of ordinary pleasures (his pipe, rum and orange on a cold day), commitment to the ordinary life of a country parish and a spontaneous appreciation of people, maturity (I think) beyond his age – these are my recollections of 1952–5.

Anne Bayley is not alone in remembering lived-in kitchens, mugs of coffee, usually at least one large cat, a wooden table, physical, social and spiritual warmth. Priscilla was around. There was often a family meal to share and talk ranged widely.

It was difficult to contain a priest of Leonard's energies and abilities within the confines of parish and diocese. He was becoming well known in a number of different spheres: education (he was on the schools council), Church order (shades of controversies to come), the spiritual life (he had a large number of people whom he directed and who used him as their confessor, and retreats and quiet days found in him a stimulating conductor). Although highly regarded as a preacher at Ardleigh, views on his style, or lack of it, have varied over the years. Anne Bayley has some observations of contrast between the spoken and written word:

> I have always been puzzled because the heart and 'punch' of what Graham says so well in sermons and private conversation does not, for me, come out in what he writes, which neither speaks with his personal voice nor (for me) conveys a message. In personal *letters*, yes, but not in public writing, and this seems a strange limitation.

> Three terse instructions spoken in 1963 or 1964 when I was questioning the existence of God for the first time were matter of fact and practical but immensely influential. 'Question presuppositions': the most generally applicable (and quotable!) piece of advice I have ever been given; 'Hold to reason'; 'Hold to the sacraments'. He was unsurprised that faith should seem to me then unreasonable; he was unperturbed, unconcerned to hurry the process of rethinking, probably more concerned that my need for security would make me take short cuts back to half belief.

Although Leonard belonged to some specifically Anglo-Catholic organizations he did not spend his time in such circles.

In 1954 the Church of England Moral Welfare Council recommended to diocesan bishops the necessity for a campaign for education in marriage and family life. A conference was called in the diocese of Chelmsford and one result of it was the setting up of a small working party to prepare a report. The working party was chaired by Canon William F. P. Chadwick (then vicar of Barking, later bishop of Barking) and Leonard was its secretary. The report reads like pure Leonard. It started with the fundamental theology behind the Church's attitude to marriage, sex and family life (its opening words are 'In the beginning, God'). It went on to show ways in which parish priests could be helped in educating adolescents (Leonard wrote the portion entitled 'The Preparation of Adolescents' although much of the report bears his mark), couples coming to be married, and parents. Of all dioceses, Chelmsford was the first to prepare and publish its report.

It was only a matter of a short time before the priest who had been instituted less than three years ago would be called elsewhere. Would it be another and more challenging piece of parochial work, or movement into a specialist ministry? Leonard was fitted for either. The answer came when in 1955 the bishop of St Albans (Edward Michael Gresford Jones), who was also chairman of the Church of England Moral Welfare Council, invited him to be Director of Religious Education in the diocese of St Albans.

3

Christian Education

Leonard's new duties were formidable. He was charged to oversee the whole field of religious education in the St Albans Diocese and initiate schemes for the advancement of education; to aid and support the work of the further education, youth, schools and children's committees; to act as youth chaplain; to collaborate with and aid the work of the adviser on children's religious education. His appointment was announced in February 1955 and in May he was made an honorary canon, taking the stall of St Benedict. If his ministry was going to be an itinerant one he realized the importance of having a good home base and an altar. They moved to a house in Maple Road, Harpenden, in the parish of St Nicholas. He celebrated there or at one of the daughter churches when he could. People found him approachable and friendly provided that they did not expect a hearty hand shake. The 'modern' habit of shaking hands with the people as they left church he found objectionable.

Within a few weeks he was assimilating a vast amount of information relating to education in the diocese, and within six months he had prepared a report suggesting lines of policy which, subject to the bishop's approval, he intended to pursue. In September 1955 he arranged a retreat, which he conducted, for those going up to university, medical school or training college in the autumn. He knew what he wanted and how to achieve it. Leonard's 'determination' arises from his religion. Canon Geoffrey L. Edwards, a parish priest in the diocese of St Albans at the time, writes:

> I knew nothing of him prior to his appointment as Director
> of Education in the diocese of St Albans and was instantly
> impressed when I met him. I recognized at once a priest

22

who was enthusiastic about the Catholic faith and a man who was likely to make a success of anything that he undertook.

One of his immediate tasks was to promote the work and influence of the Church schools. The diocese had been fortunate in having a great lover of the schools in Cuthbert Thicknesse, dean of St Albans (1936–55), who had fought hard to 'save' the schools from surrendering, but the task was enormous. Many of the schools were 'hanging on' in old buildings with modest resources to improve them and there were murmurings that we should be better without them. Indeed I had been advised by a senior diocesan official that I should do well to dispose of ours.

Graham brought two things to bear on the situation. First, there was his own priesthood; he must establish a base with an altar where he could say Mass. Secondly, there was his clear vision of the immediate task to which he brought adroit business efficiency and administrative skill. I recall Canon Demant once saying that if a man got the ultimate issues of life settled he was free to concentrate on 'other things'. It struck me that Graham's personality demonstrated this truth. A brief conversation in the vicarage drive convinced me.

Leonard was like a dynamo about the diocese, and absorbed facts like blotting paper. He seemed to know a great deal about a large number of people. His memory was extraordinarily acute and woe betide the parish which fell below the high mark in religious education. Report followed report, which always led to action. The whirlwind was too much for some priests who were a little awe-struck at Leonard's progress. There was such assurance. In the end, if not in the beginning, those who stood up to him gained his respect and affection and it is they who saw the priest first and the director of education second. Canon Geoffrey Edwards has further memories:

We used sometimes to laugh about Graham and the telephone. He was always elusive, rarely back at his desk at the time when one had been told to ring him. When he returned he would tell you that he had come straight from 'the ministry' as it then was. This phrase came to be bandied about among the clergy with chuckles. We used to think that he took a mischievous delight in these expeditions but they certainly achieved results. A visit to Curzon Street where the powers that be lived in those days would reveal that he was on your side. He knew his civil service and how to manage it. He was aware that to achieve anything worthwhile you must be in contact with those who make decisions at a high level and with those who implement them. Mr Klein would tell us that it was not possible to do what we asked. Graham would leap in and say 'but Mr Klein, you are wrong about that, you will recall that in the case of x and y it was decided that the managers were entitled to act in that way!' References to sections of the '44 Act by number were on his lips at any moment. His penetrating mind and scientific training were always evident.

On 13 July 1957 the bishop of St Albans offered Leonard a residentiary canonry in the cathedral, to be held so long as he remained director of education: 'But I must add I hope you'll accept the offer as some recognition of your hard and effective work since you came here and for making time somehow or other to help many people with their problems – and some of the problems have been tough! Don't overwork and may God bless you daily. I should be interested to hear Priscilla's comments on the first part of the last sentence.' He left the stall of St Benedict for that of St Amphibalus, the name of a martyr closely associated with St Alban. There was an extra joy in accepting this appointment, for it brought Leonard in closer contact with his friend of like mind but different manner, the sub-dean of St Albans, Douglas Feaver, later bishop of Peterborough. Leonard liked this unusual man who had an incisive mind and brilliant powers of expression.

As he travelled up and down the country on preaching and retreat engagements Leonard was surprising an increasing variety of people. He surprised ardent educationalists who found themselves being challenged about the priority of evangelism. He surprised those Anglo-Catholic priests who were pious and priggish, who thought a talk about confession or

24

spiritual direction would be soaked in the language of some divine mystics. Instead, this was what they might receive:

> It is not especially devout to use in our private devotions the idiom of a hundred years ago, yet in the books for that purpose we still find verbose prayers in phraseology which seems quite unreal to people today. I would like to make it clear that I am not referring to the language of the Prayer Book, but to such phrases as 'reaping the sweetness of holy consolation' which do not spring spontaneously from 20th-century lips. Reading extracts from the Don Camillo stories will teach confirmation candidates a great deal about praying. . . . Do not confuse direction with the giving of specific counsel to deal with a crisis. There is all the difference between the advice we give in order that people may grow in holiness, and the specific counsel we give to the person who comes to see us with an urgent personal problem. . . . We must be direct and definite. To talk of 'availing yourselves of the sacrament of penance' means virtually nothing to most churchgoers. If you speak, whether in the pulpit or in private, of going to confession, you must give precise instructions as to exactly what the penitent is to do.

Leonard surprised groups who invited him to speak on such subjects as, 'Can social work be effective without religion' Did they expect Good Samaritans 1957 style? Leonard soon put them right. Social work was the means of increasing the individual's capacity for exercising free will. Leonard always faced the problem of evil in man, and often spoke of six evasions of this problem: (1) *The scientific approach.* Scientific progress will make all things well in time, (2) *Determinism.* 'Nerves', 'glands' etc so influence and determine man's behaviour that personal responsibility is taken from him, (3) *Relativity.* No absolutes of good and evil; all things relative. (4) *Shift of responsibility* from the individual to a corporate society. (5) *Pietism.* Religion divorced from life. (6) *Activism.* A lack of penetrating thought leading to greater activity as a substitute for it. He liked the phrase, 'Evil pays spot cash; virtue on a credit basis'.

Leonard managed to combine great activity with penetrating thought. Within two years St Albans people were saying that the diocese would not hold him. He had made an early impression on other diocesan education officers: in 1956 they attended a course in St Albans. Archdeacon C. W. D. Carroll attended from Blackburn: 'He was on his home ground and his enthusiasm was infectious. He showed us some examples of schools which had been up-graded and of new schools where new design techniques were used.'

In his dealings with the Church 'centre' Leonard had much to do with the National Society. Founded in 1811, it was the Church's only society for advancing religious education in schools of all kinds. Church schools were its main concern, of which there were over 8000 in England and Wales, containing in 1959 one million pupils. Although independent the Society was associated with the Church of England's Board of Education and its general secretary was paid half by the National Society and half by the Central Board of Finance. Robert Wright Stopford (later bishop of London) was general secretary from 1952–55 and was succeeded by Canon Roland Ralph Bailey who died suddenly in 1957. It was not entirely surprising that Leonard was appointed to succeed Roland Bailey in March 1958. He kept the house at Harpenden and became a commuter.

The general secretary of the National Society was also secretary of the Schools Council of the Church of England Board of Education. The relationship between the society and the Schools Council was a difficult one. The chairman of the Schools Council was Roger Plumpton Wilson, bishop of Chichester. He remembers Leonard to be

> tireless in energy and [one who] faced the demands of travel up and down dioceses. He also had the clarity of mind that could grasp both principles and details. All this helped him to be a good negotiator both with dioceses (and their bishops) and with the Department of Education who continually found him on their doorstep. . . . He showed them, what has been more evident since, his clear and firm adherence to his conviction about Christian faith and conduct. His singleness of mind has met with opposition, and criticism, but it has always been honest, clear and therefore stimulating.

It was through Leonard's skill that both the National

Society and Schools Council realized that they had separate and important roles to play. Leonard propogated his message by writing articles for periodicals, being interviewed by the press and what seemed like a stream of engagements. He was a reviewer of books, a reader of manuscripts for several publishers; and lectures and speeches, as well as sermons and retreat addresses, were legion. There was a freshness about them and each was carefully prepared. A good phrase might be used several times. He was now very well known. The number of new people who approached him for pastoral care and spiritual direction was increasing all the time. It was often difficult for Leonard to do this outside the parochial network. Yet this distinctly priestly work was essential to his well being.

He was not always aware of the impression he made on others. Mr B. L. Thorne was legal adviser to the National Society: 'I remember the first time Graham Leonard came to see me in my office in the Sanctuary, Westminster. He was wearing one of those wide brimmed Spanish style hats favoured by High Church clergy. He looked rather severe and I wondered how we would get on. I soon discovered his sense of fun and we became great friends.'

As chairman of the Board of Education, Robert Wright Stopford, then bishop of Peterborough, was able to leave much important work to Leonard and when, in 1959, the government statement on Education had to be produced it was Leonard's mind and hand behind the Church's response to it. The archbishop of Canterbury (Geoffrey Fisher) congratulated Leonard by letter (12 June 1959): 'It is really a very fine piece of work not so much for the advantage which it brings to the C. of E., though that is considerable, but for the fact that you have delivered the Churches and the political parties from a miserable and unedifying renewal of conflict. It is pleasing to think that the initiative and the leadership all along has, thanks to you, come from the C. of E.'

In fact his responsiblity for liaison with the Government, in particular for piloting the Education Act 1959 through Parliament, was one of his chief legacies. The Act raised the grant paid by the Minister of Education towards the cost of works on the aided schools from 50% to 75% and also introduced a new grant of 75% payable towards the cost of building secondary schools to provide for children in primary schools existing at the time the bill was introduced into Parliament. The financial relief to the Church was very considerable. The bill was introduced as an all-party measure, and this agreement was reflected in the spirit of the debates. Earlier debates on Church schools had been acrimonious. The debates surrounding the 1959 Act represented a great change of attitude. Other Leonard legacies were a series of studies he initiated on problems of Christian education and work on the agreed syllabuses of religious education for use in county schools.

Leonard was a *great* general secretary. He did not always inspire affection. He always had a clear grasp of the concept of education and of the implications and complications of the 1944 Act. He found the way for future general secretaries to have an easy access to the minister and to the principals in Curzon Street. Austerity combined with a magnificent grasp of his job tended to make his peers full of admiration tinged with a little jealousy. He dressed differently from them and he was ruthless, but none of them would have questioned the wisdom of his appointment or the success he made of it.

After four hectic years with the National Society Leonard was not exhausted, but he was ready for different work within the framework of a diocese. The bishop of Chichester had tried to lure him to that diocese. In 1961 when the important parish of Leeds fell vacant Leonard was top of the list, and although the experience of having four or five curates to train would have been good for him, and good for them, the duties of a vicar of Leeds would not have satisfied him. They may have exasperated him. Robert Stopford had been translated from the see of Peterborough to that of London in 1961. The archdeacon of Hampstead, Hubert John Matthews, was retiring in 1962. He was also leaving the living of St Andrew Undershaft with St Mary Axe in the City of London, where he was rector. The bishop of London was responsible for appointing the archdeacon, and the dean and chapter of St Paul's Cathedral for appointing the new rector. Could Leonard be persuaded to move? He might even wear archdeacon's gaiters and a rosette on his hat, for this was still the Church of Fisher, and one which Leonard does not decry.

What Stopford offered, Leonard accepted. He was still only

40 but now by title 'Venerable'. His previous bishop, St Albans, had been suffragan bishop of Willesden, the area covered by the archdeaconry of Hampstead. To some extent an archdeacon can take his choice as to where his main labours lie. Hampstead – and in a short while Willesden – would soon know the force and direction of Leonard's labour.

4

The Pastoral Archdeacon

His first words to his archdeaconry recorded that 'It [was] good to be part of a diocese again and I am looking forward to doing a pastoral job concerned with the life and work of the parishes'. That makes it clear where the thrust of his work and energy would rest. The functions of an archdeacon include the temporal administration of ecclesiastical property, the induction of parish priests and the admittance of church-wardens to their offices. They are more concerned with drains than brains, parish share than pastoral care, faculties than worship. If a new type of heating is introduced the archdeacon must know about any risks to the chimney flue; are parish records kept meticulously and safely? Is the vicarage conducive to reasonable comfort and family life, hospitality and study? Or is it a barn of a place in which the constant task is to keep doors shut, the rain out and heat in to give a modicum of comfort? Are the sacred vessels looked after and kept in a place of safety?

Such questions are the lot of any archdeacon and it may be wondered why he should be in priest's orders. If he stuck to his statutory work there is no need for an archdeacon to be a priest. It is since 1662 that he must be a priest. Previously he was in deacon's orders yet as a result of his close and regular contact with the bishop (after all he is the 'bishop's eye') he acquired what was almost a right of succession to the episcopal throne.

Leonard was well equipped to master the temporal nature of his new work and that he did very speedily. He was inquisitive and probing as he went about the parishes. Suspicion of the new man 'poking his nose into all our affairs' quickly receded as it was realized that his priority was strengthening the body of Christ which was built up in the parishes. In his visitation charges to churchwardens, Leonard reminded them that they held office within the Church in order that the Church as a whole would be able to fulfil its purpose in the world. The responsibility of the laity was worship, witness, service and giving. 'It is the churchwardens' responsibility to ensure that the lay people are given every assistance so that they can worship God *properly*. That adverb covers a very wide range of matters.' This approach did not always find receptively gleeful ears. Here was an archdeacon bringing religion into the business of being a churchwarden. That was going a bit far. But Leonard was as persuasive as he could be provocative. He was keen for any opportunity to meet the laity in the archdeaconry and there were manifold opportunities for him to explain his policy, convey his convictions and impart something of his vision. This he did with distinct success.

Leonard's work was not made easy because of his relations with the suffragan bishop of Willesden, George Ernest Ingle. They covered the same territory, taking in the rural deaneries of Enfield, Hampstead, Harrow, Hendon, Hornsey, St Marylebone, St Pancras, Tottenham and Willesden.

There was something ominous about Ingle's letter to Leonard on the latter's appointment: 'Naturally, the archdeacon and I work very closely together'; this suggested a meeting. Unfortunately the bishop of London had not consulted his suffragan about the appointment of Leonard. When Leonard went to see Ingle at his flat near Baker Street, the initial reception was distinctly frosty: 'Who are you? I don't know you!' And it was not until Ingle realized that Leonard knew his brother-in-law in Norfolk that the frost melted: 'Why didn't you say so?' It was never a happy duet. As men they were too dissimilar, a fact compounded by age and the generation barrier. Ingle was made deacon in the year that Leonard was born.

Ingle had made his mark as a housemaster at Felsted School and later as vicar of St John the Baptist, Greenhill, Harrow, before becoming suffragan bishop of Fulham with jurisdiction over northern and central Europe in 1949. He had been a hardworking priest with a passionate concern for individuals and social justice but cared little for order and tidiness. He had acquired a reputation for being both ener-

getic and impulsive, not a person to plan a course of action
or weigh consequences. By the time Leonard worked with
him he had become a little cranky in his views and blustery
in manner, not a bishop to be trifled with. He was of the kind
that thought all Anglo-Catholics were homosexuals and all
Evangelicals had marital problems. Sometimes there was
extraordinary behaviour, as when, for example, he arrived at
a parish in Tottenham for a confirmation. He was actually
at the wrong church, meeting the wrong priest, but the priest
was told that it was *he* who was in the wrong place!

One of the most satisfying aspects of Leonard's new work
was that of having his own church and altar, even if it was
a City church. The church of St Andrew Undershaft is the
parish church of the united parish of St Andrew Undershaft
with St Mary Axe. The church of St Mary Axe was demo-
lished in the 16th century. Leonard published a short illustrated guide to St Andrew Undershaft in which he wrote:
'The number of resident parishioners is very small but the
church has close connections with the Baltic Exchange and
with Lloyds, both of which are in the parish and which
provide towards its upkeep. For many years the secretary of
the Baltic Exchange has been one of the churchwardens.'
Despite the few residents there was really a 'Church' and
family.

The Eucharist was celebrated regularly and on Sundays
the faith was taught in a consistent way. Phrases stuck in the
minds of some of those attending, encouraging them to want
more: 'The Holy Eucharist stands midway between baptism
and the consummation of all things'; 'One of the besetting
sins of the Church is to expect people who are not Christians
to behave as if they are'; 'Humility springs from an acceptance
of reality'.

Although Leonard never shrank from dogma he would
never impose this on people. They must find their own way,
use their own minds, be guided by their own consciences. It
was disconcerting for some enquirers who approached
Leonard to find that they were not given little packages of
specific instructions all neatly tied with dogmatic tape. He
was not an Anglican personalized version of the Catholic
Truth Society. He was both symbol and sign, pointing away
from himself. Small groups looked to him as a source of

teaching, inspiration and hope. There were some very interesting groups, both formal and informal, which Leonard
organized. One of them, the Institute of Education group, met
over three years. This was an experiment in group direction.
Leonard was clear that it had to be content in confining itself
to general issues, for example, the background of Christian
prayer rather than actual methods of or difficulties in praying.
Leonard was concerned that he should not be regarded as a
repository of wisdom. He was happy to be a guide but not
an oracle. However, questioning was everywhere, and during
Leonard's time as archdeacon a number of issues concerned
him deeply.

On Sunday morning, 17 March 1963, Leonard opened *The
Observer* and read the article by John Robinson, bishop of
Woolwich, 'Our Image of God must Go'. This was not a title
of Robinson's own choice any more than was *Honest to God*,
which the article summed up. But the contents of each were
all his own. *The Observer* article unleashed such anger in
Leonard that he went straight into his garden and taking a
spade he dug and dug and dug to near exhaustion. At least
the garden benefited from *Honest to God*.

Leonard was filled with anger for it seemed as if *Honest to
God* had struck savage blows at Christ and his Church. He
read and liked some of Robinson's works, notably *The Body*
(1952), and later, *Redating the New Testament* (1976). *Honest to
God* was different. It was a book containing what seemed to
him to be heresy and written by a bishop! Much of its thinking
was muddled and pen had gone to paper too soon. Robinson
should have either produced a much more careful book or
put it out as a starting point for discussion among theologians.
Leonard saw the aim of the book not merely as the reiteration
of theological truth in contemporary language (which in fact
it was not, for some of the writing was difficult and obscure)
but a fundamental rethinking of basics. Leonard regarded
Honest to God as the mess that envelops the Church when it
has no sound philosophy – a view which he still holds. One
of the great deficiencies in too many of today's priests is that
they have no philosophy and no sense of history, so they
adopt the philosophy of the moment. That leads to thinking
and writing that is theologically unripe and pastorally inept.
Why was the book written? There were probably certain

psychological personal reasons, but Leonard suggested to groups and audiences that among the ostensible ones there was (1) a deep concern for the outsider who could not make sense of traditional religious language and experience, that (2) Robinson himself discounted religious experience as commonly understood, and regarded it as undesirable. He considered (3) that the way in which Christian spirituality had been presented as the negative way, was a violation of human personality which was unacceptable to modern man; that (4) the Church had failed to stress the God-given nature of the Christian life and equated religion with the search for God, whereas Christianity is rather God's search for us; and that (5) the true doctrine of the Incarnation, by which manhood was taken into God, had not been taught. For this reason Robinson seemed unable to accept the 'scandal of particularity' as applied to God, namely, that a particular historical event could have eternal significance. The Church had failed to present the biblical doctrine of baptism and the Eucharist, thus causing a radical dichotomy between the religious and the secular. These were all reasons, according to Leonard, why *Honest to God* was written. The book was confused and confusing when it was not deficient and heretical. Robinson's assumptions were wrong.

Leonard's views soon became known, but in public his main concern was how the Church was to answer Robinson. In one sense it meant redoubling his efforts at sound teaching. He grappled seriously with the question of history and biblical criticism. He read voraciously, discussed widely and exposed his own thinking at theological conventions in Oxford and elsewhere. He took every opportunity of proclaiming the *God given* nature of Christianity. He was always working out a Christian spirituality in the terms of the affirmative way, insofar as we become Christian we become more truly human. Leonard was concerned that the Church should develop a Christian mind, in short that it should think theologically. He had little patience with the unthinking critic. He once described himself as an orthodox radical which is an apt description but not a label. He has always penetrated into the orthodox position to see the fulness and richness of the whole gospel of God which he believes is something that far surpasses our imagination.

By his utterances, Leonard had established himself as a man who thought theologically and acted sacramentally. He understood the world in which he lived in sacramental terms. He was interested in some of Teilhard de Chardin's thinking, particularly that contained in *Le milieu divin*. The means chosen by our Lord to communicate life to people were sacramental: baptism and Communion. Both these ways had been used before; our Lord took what already existed and gave it new meaning as he did when he took our human nature (with the real difference that human nature had been misused) and without denying it made it wholly transparent to the will of God. He does this also with water, bread and wine. St Paul understood and taught this, that all created things are for the glory of God.

There were still calls upon Leonard for speeches, articles and papers on education and, from further back, on science. A booklet on *Science and Religion* was published in 1958. It was well received and of as much use to the Christian who had little knowledge of scientific method as to the scientist who was willing to study the relationship between Christian thought and the conclusions of modern science. In 1962 he was asked to give a paper in the education section of the annual meeting of the British Association for the Advancement of Science held in Manchester. The major theme was 'The Unity of Knowledge: a new dynamic for the schools'. The object was to counter the growing fragmentation of knowledge by showing the interrelatedness of the different disciplines of the mind. The speakers were David Daiches on 'Reason and Imagination'; George Kitson-Clark on 'The Use of History' and C. P. Snow on 'Science and Human Values'. Leonard was asked to make up the quartet with a contribution on science and revealed religion. The annual meeting was provided with a wonderful all-round view of God, man and nature to sustain the audience in the struggle against the growing insularity and materialism and provincialism of education in so many places.

At a Church Union conference on Faith and Unity at Canterbury Hall, London (September 1962) Leonard asked if there could be some sacramental fellowship beyond that of baptism between separated Christians. His paper 'Intercommunion in the Context of Catholic Order' shocked some of the audience. In the first part of his closely reasoned paper Leonard argued that if intercommunion between separated Churches is accepted before unity is achieved, it would seem that further developments would lie in the sphere of jurisdiction only, with the implication that the divisions among the Churches were questions of authority only. But prayer for unity is not just prayer for authority. Leonard could not accept current suggestions for intercommunion with non-episcopal bodies, or the arguments on which they were based. One of his main arguments was that visible unity must be achieved by a death to our separations and by a willingness to accept the cost of our membership of the one Body which is expressed in the episcopate. The listeners purred with approval. But Leonard is not predictable. This is part of his strength, not an element of weakness. He made a suggestion:

> What I believe is needed is a bold anticipation of the visible unity of the one Church which involves penitence for, and a repudiation of, our existing divisions but which does not involve judgment on the status or regularity of the separated communions. Let a bishop, I hope that it might be the archbishop of Canterbury, announce that he will, as a solemn act of prayer for visible unity and of penitence for our divisions, celebrate the Eucharist. Let him say that he will do so not as an Anglican but as a bishop of the universal Church, as representative of that unity which we share and which we seek to express visibly. It will help to make this clear if he uses not the Prayer Book rite but a rite of the early Church or the South India rite. Let him say that it is open to all baptised Christians to offer and to communicate freely and without any judgement on the communions to which they belong. But let it be made clear that anyone who takes part is thereby declaring that he acknowledges the sinfulness of separation and that the way to visible unity is by death to our separations to the life of the one Body. No one will be accepting Anglicanism for it will not be an Anglican act. No one will be accepting prelacy, or any of the later accretions of episcopacy, for the bishop will be acting in the true exercise of episcopacy as president of the Eucharist and as the symbol of unity. I think I should make it clear that because it would not be

an act based on the mutual recognition of our existing separations and because it recognizes the true function of episcopacy, the celebrant would always be a bishop in the apostolic succession.

The secretary of the Church Union (F. P. Coleman) was not pleased: 'I still believe it would be an improper thing for a bishop to act in the way you suggest.'

Archbishop Ramsey wrote to Leonard (2 October 1962):

As to the concluding part of your paper in which you commend a possible course of action by myself or other bishops, I would say this. I think that the kind of service which you commend would be entirely possible and desirable so long as the ideas which you criticise in your earlier pages were clearly excluded from our policy. Provided that this is made clear then I think the sort of action you propose could be a legitimate and perhaps very helpful kind of economy. My fear, however, would be that in the present situation the action would have its significance obscured by other actions which go on of the undiscriminating sort based on the bad theology which you criticise. That, of course, may not be a reason against doing the thing if it is inherently a good thing to do, but I should be concerned about the true significance of the act being obscured.

Leonard was verbally attacked ('Is he sound?' wondered a fellow Catholic). He remained impenitent about the propriety of his suggestion. To one critic he wrote: 'I am pretty certain that some of the utterances of St Cyprian and St Augustine must have produced rather similar comment. As to the wisdom of putting it forward publicly, I have decided on one thing and that is that in future I shall be guided by my own instincts and not by the advice of others, however eminent. The factor to which they all gave most weight in advising me to put it forward was that Catholics had to demonstrate that they were concerned not to adopt a purely negative position.'

Leonard was enjoying his busy life as priest and archdeacon. And, perhaps to his surprise, he was popular. The clergy realized he was a priest who cared before he was an archdeacon who chastened. He was also a fighter. He had had experience of officials and officialdom (and knew the difference between the two) when he was general secretary of the National Society. Being an archdeacon pleased and suited Leonard and increased the possibilities for puncturing inflated bureaucracy. He liked nothing better than taking on some department in battle – civil service, local council or ecclesiastical committee – which thought themselves to be omnipotent and untouchable. He had to be his own eyes rather than the bishop's eye, for his relations with the bishop of Willesden were formal rather than friendly, and the bishop of London was a far too busy man.

Leonard had settled with his family into 2 Church Road, Highgate. To many clergy and laity it was like the best kind of vicarage door, always open. A constant flow of people, and not only those with problems, found their way to Highgate. The Leonards liked giving and receiving hospitality. He had embarked on this work in 1962. In 1964 the bishop of Willesden died.

5

Being a Bishop

There is a French proverb that 'Fools invent fashions and wise men follow them'. The 1960s was a decade which gave some substance to that proverb. Tradition which had grown musty by complacency was thrust aside and novelty was enthroned. Tradition used to mean the proper preoccupation of the living with the dead. Now it meant the morbid preoccupation of the living with the living.

The shallower aspects of fashion were immediately recognizable and significant but it took time for the full impact of fashion on social behaviour and intellectual theory to become evident. The word 'pop' entered the vocabulary. It soon became the key word for a whole culture in this country. 'Pop' sounded as harmless and fizzy as lemonade. In steadier times it would have been harmless, for particular enthusiasms hardly add up to a culture. But the 1960s was a time of history's traffic jams, when all manner of vehicles, including the economic Rolls Royce, the political van, the scientific ambulance, the literary and musical caravanette and the Church bus all arrived at the cross roads at the same time. Suddenly, to a background of music, everything seemed to change direction.

Was this all froth on the surface? Britain has a deep strata of conservatism. It may change a great deal but leaves many of the old values still intact, in a different place and slightly exacerbated by the disruption. The 1960s *were* different; a retrospective glance shows that some of the wholesome as well as the diseased aspects of our life have vanished and not reappeared.

The Church of England bus was caught up in this jam and didn't know how, or was unwilling, to extricate itself. It was driven by an unlikely person. From the untimely and unfortunate death of William Temple in 1944 until 1961 the bus was driven by Geoffrey Francis Fisher as archbishop of Canterbury and he had the best bus-conductor possible for most of those years in Cyril Forster Garbett, archbishop of York. Leonard looks back to the Church under Fisher as being healthy. Of course he winces at the excessive amount of time spent on reforming canon law, but taking the archiepiscopate as a whole he sees it as an important and stimulating one.

In January 1961 when Fisher resigned as archbishop, there was compressed speculation as to who would succeed him. 'Compressed' because the announcement of his successor came two days after the public notice of his resignation. Arthur Michael Ramsey was translated from York to Canterbury. In 1958 he had written of the bench of bishops: 'My own guess is that the criticism history will make of our mid-20th-century episcopacy is its tendency to be 'of a type', lacking the marked differences and clashes of individuality which, in a period a little earlier, assisted the Church's vigour of mind and appeal to the community.' He was not reckoning for the 1960s when he might have wished for less colourful and awkward bishops. Yet as an umbrella observation he was right. History may also note, comparing Runcie's bench with Ramsey's, that the latter appears distinctly strong and variously distinguished. Frederick Donald Coggan's translation from Bradford was announced at the same time as the Canterbury nomination. This duo was thought to be one of Harold Macmillan's conjuring tricks, a perfect combination, the one balancing the foibles of the other in each direction. It was not a conspicuously successful combination, as the runaway Church of the 1960s may witness.

London too had a new bishop: Robert Wright Stopford. Organization, manipulation, innovation by stealth, and hard work brought him to London. In 1964, the year in which Stopford was appointed chairman of the Anglican–Methodist Commission, he had to find two new suffragan bishops for Kensington (to replace Edward Roberts, who had become bishop of Ely) and Willesden. Leonard's name was rumoured for Kensington. Surely it was too early to consider moving him and he was too young to be a bishop, only 43. So Stopford imported his former archdeacon of Northampton, the 53-year-old Ronald Cedric Osbourne Goodchild, for Kensington. The same arguments were valid for Willesden. Any reports from the Willesden–Hampstead area that filtered to Fulham Palace reflected a different spirit in the archdeaconry, restrained and firm leadership and pastoral care of clergy. Stopford had recognized Leonard's maturity, beyond his years, when he put him in at Hampstead. He had had every reason to witness and admire Leonard's brain and energy at the National Society. He was not keen on his Catholic churchmanship, but it seemed all of a piece with Leonard's conception of his priesthood. It was there as a whole, not an extravagent and showy part of him, to be flaunted at High Church events. In any case, Evangelicals liked this archdeacon of firm faith with a capacity for friendship and pastoral direction. Moreover, he lost himself in his priesthood rather than losing his priesthood in himself; thus he was never in danger of becoming a producer who projected himself. There is risk in any appointment, and there were certainly risks if he appointed Leonard. Stopford was already aware of Leonard's views on the issues which were, or were about to be, on the Church's agenda in the next decade. On most of them Stopford took a different view from that of Leonard, but he had to appoint a new bishop of Willesden taking into account local needs. A suffragan bishop may never rise to diocesan level.

In August 1964 Stopford took the plunge and saw Leonard. Would he be bishop of Willesden? On 5 August he wrote to confirm that he was proposing to submit Leonard's name to the queen. On 6 August Leonard replied, 'I am very happy to agree to this'. On 14 August the Prime Minister (Alec Douglas Home) communicated the queen's approval and the public announcement was made on 19 August to a very great chorus of rejoicing. Letters poured in to Leonard's home at Highgate (and it was a blessing that the appointment did not necessitate a change of home). The letters of congratulation or commiseration – for are congratulations the correct sentiments to express? – came from such an array of people with different interests that they reveal Leonard as still independent, however much some cotories, cliques or organizations sought to claim him as their own. It is understandable why the clergy were glad. One wrote: 'You came into the diocese at a time when the iron had entered into my soul and I

41

was deeply unhappy and distressed. And perhaps without realizing it you, by your approachability, kindness, friendship and support . . . helped me to find my feet once again'. The laity, who had found Leonard a priest with a 'sure touch' whose vision was as steady as his teaching was firm and invigorating, rejoiced. All the same, there was a feeling that Willesden would be a junction rather than a terminus. A lovely misprint in the *London Churchman* for September 1964, noting that Leonard was preaching at St Paul's Cathedral on 13 September, listed him as the archbishop of Hampstead. Leonard's ecumenical friends were pleased too. John Huxtable, Secretary of the Congregational Church of England and Wales, was happy, 'but it will make dissent that much more difficult'.

Leonard was fortunate in his episcopal wardrobe by gift and by design. He had worn a buttoned-down cassock as a priest. This was regarded as High Church or Roman! He wondered if he should change his habit now he was about to become a bishop. No. Why should he? He did not want to do anything that might give the impression that he would trim his sails now that he was a bishop. Episcopal dress has always interested him. He enjoys wearing purple, sometimes looking like an out of date Roman Catholic bishop. There is something charming, even amusing, about his boyish inability to resist a preoccupation with getting things outwardly, as well as inwardly, right. Leonard simply enjoys it; he does not flaunt it and he does not use it to emphasize his rank.

The consecration was fixed for the feast of St Matthew, Apostle and Evangelist (21 September 1964), in St Paul's Cathedral. The archbishop of Canterbury (Ramsey) was chief consecrator. The sermon was preached by Leonard's friend and theological sage Eric Lionel Mascall, then professor of historical theology in the University of London. They were to be in and out of many a theological and doctrinal skirmish together in the ensuing years. Professor Mascall pointed to those twelve men whom Christ called, trained, commissioned, equipped and then *sent* – not just to be persons who would act instead of him, but persons through whom he himself would act. That is what Leonard must hold before him. The anthem sung whilst Leonard was putting on his rochet before being presented to the archbishop contained words which might have been Leonard's own prayer:

> O Lord, increase my faith, strengthen me and confirm me in thy true faith; endue me with wisdom, charity and patience, in all my adversity, sweet Jesu, say Amen.

In view of the future of the 1960s and '70s and the tumult of the '80s, when Leonard had to rely on his consecration vows, it is worth setting down the words used at his consecration:

> Receive the Holy Ghost for the office and work of a bishop in the Church of God, now committed unto thee by the imposition of our hands; in the Name of the Father, and of the Son, and of the Holy Ghost, Amen. And remember that thou stir up the grace of God which is given thee by this imposition of our hands: for God hath not given us the spirit of fear, but of power, and love, and soberness.
> Give heed unto reading, exhortation and doctrine. Think upon the things contained in this book. Be diligent in them, that the increase coming thereby may be manifest unto all men. Take heed unto thyself, and to doctrine, and be diligent in doing them: for by so doing thou shalt both save thyself and them that hear thee. Be to the flock of Christ a shepherd, not a wolf; feed them, devour them not. Hold up the weak, heal the sick, bind up the broken, bring again the outcasts, seek the lost. Be so merciful, that ye be not too remiss; so minister discipline, that you forget not mercy: that when the chief Shepherd shall appear ye may receive the never-fading crown of glory; through Jesus Christ our Lord. Amen.

Because there was much controversy in the Church at large during the time he was at Willesden, this chapter is devoted to Leonard as bishop of the Willesden area. A successor to himself as archdeacon of Hampstead was appointed: Hubert Arthur Stanley Pink. Pink was 59, himself a former general secretary of the National Society and a person with whom Leonard could work.

Leonard saw his chief work as simply being a bishop and being seen to be a bishop, which was a new experience for the area. He went out of his way to meet people in the places where they lived. He has a prodigious memory for *people* and their individual circumstances. As he became a public and controversial figure the people in his area still received primary claim on his time. Prebendary Kenneth Toovey was then vicar of St Martin, Ruislip (which came into the new Willesden area in 1970), and has this memory:

> Two families from my own parish had a night out at the 'Talk of the Town' restaurant where you can enjoy a show while dining. Both families – husbands and wives – had been fairly recently confirmed by Bishop Graham who happened to be invited out to the same place on the same evening. He spotted them on the other side of the restaurant, made his way over to them and said 'I am sure I have confirmed you recently. I can't quite recall at which church, but I am delighted to see you'. The families were thrilled. The show they were to see paled into insignificance alongside this greeting, and the fact that their bishop remembered them and knew them.

Examples of this kind are legion. A lady from Willesden who happened to be at a church book shop near Westminster Cathedral at the same time as Leonard, was called by her name, and he asked after other members of her church.

Nonetheless he was concerned at the amount of time he spent in parishes for confirmations and other 'single' services. Was this the best use of his time? Was sufficient time spent with the clergy and the laity, separately and together? What could be done about it? Leonard decided to embark on regular parochial visitations – a practice which he has continued throughout his episcopate in Truro and London. He recruited one of his priests, the Revd Reginald Ames, vicar of St Edmund the King, Northwood Hills, to assist with the preparation. By these visits it was possible to get the feel of a parish in a way which is impossible in a visit for a single event. The bishop got to know the laity at work and in their homes. Leonard was accompanied throughout by the incumbent and one or both churchwardens, which gave opportunities to discuss the parish.

Reginald Ames adds some notes about these 'action-packed' days:

The bishop carried the sacrament to the sick – speaking quietly and in a most comforting manner – often laying his hands in healing. Every committee in a parish met him for a session and he was very adept at giving himself completely, switching from subject to subject – always building up the ministry of the vicar. There was sometimes a working lunch with the treasurer, secretary of the PCC and wardens. There was checking too – random visits just knocking at a door to ask the name of the local vicar. I watched him join in bathtime with children and prayers at their bedside with young parents in a most natural family manner. I am sure that he felt completely at home with them – no 'effort' no 'talking down'. Met PCC, celebrated Communion and ended the day with his charge to the parish – straightforward and from the heart. Always building up, always encouraging; left the parish by 10 p.m.: a mini mission. Visited schools, colleges, factories, hospitals, and knowing that the day had been planned to pack in as much as possible was disciplined over time, responding to my 'it is time to go' with a rueful smile. Sometimes he would say 'I need half an hour in the midst of the day to be at so and so, please fix it' and my job was to 'fix it'. Once we had to go to a parish where the vicar had taken his own life. Here he dealt with worried and distressed people and officials in the midst of a busy tight scheduled day, then back to the parish visitation carefully not taking the sorrow from one place to another – his distress was real and taken to God. Another day to a hospital to annoint a dying priest; such compassion yet a direct and loving preparation of a spiritual sort to meet the Lord.

He trusted me to do the job – and he answered for any mistakes made – a really professional approach to his 'bishoping' a tender-hearted, self-giving man conscious of his responsibility to God for his clergy and people. Not afraid to give clear guidance, not shirking the difficult interview, but always lovingly concerned, and constructive.

Another priest recalls an incident during a parish visit:

We had one lady over 100 years old, who was not a very easy person to get on with. She was standing by her garden gate when the bishop came along. Her greeting to him was a snort, and the comment, 'You look too young to be a bishop'. The lady then proclaimed that in her ancestry in mediaeval times was an archdeacon who, in those enforced celibate days, yet was father to one of her ancestors. The lady seemed rather proud of the fact, to which Bishop Graham gently retorted, 'Well, my dear, time does not excuse sin'.

It is little wonder that Leonard advised his successor, 'Don't overdo them [pastoral visits]. I started with a whole day and a half day each month but that nearly killed me and I stuck to one whole day a month. They are most exhilerating but also exhausting and I found it necessary to keep the evenings before and the mornings after as free as possible. Parochial or pastoral visits have become commonplace today, but at the time they were introduced by Leonard at Willesden they were innovative.

Leonard could be challenging in his sermons and addresses. The focus was always on God and the locus was always the Church. Preaching at the inaugural service of the episcopal area of Willesden in St Stephen's, Ealing, on 24 October 1970 he indicated the marks which he looked for in the Church. They were of course those which are found in the Church in the New Testament.

I look for men and women of faith, for priests and people who have the courage of their convictions, living in obedience to the truth as revealed in Christ. I look for priests who know themselves to be and live as stewards of the mysteries of God. I look for love – a love of real warmth and joy – in our relations within our common life together. I look for love which has for its motive not its usefulness to us or the comfort which it gives us but the desire to give honour to God. I look for parochial church councils and synods in which the members, as they deliberate, will be moved supremely by one desire that in all that is said and done God may be glorified. I look for priests and people, men and women, who honour and glorify God by faithfulness in taking their place Sunday by Sunday in the Christian assembly. I look for men and women who, in the Eucharist, obeying our Lord's command, show forth his death until He comes again, proclaim the glory of God and his love for mankind and are nourished in fellowship with him. I look for priests and people, men and women, who are concerned to honour and glorify God by expressing the relationship in continuing prayer – adoring, loving and interceding for those among whom they live and work. I look for those who are willing to leave things in God's hands not believing themselves to be indispensible and to give time in the adoration and contemplation of his eternal majesty and holiness for his sake.

Leonard led from the front. He had been charged at his consecration to 'feed' his flock. But how? Clearly by sermons in the parishes and at confirmations. Was there something more substantial he could do? A wonderful opportunity materialized. The London Diocesan Union of the Church of England Men's Society, still a force in 1969, wanted a teaching mission. As initially conceived by them it was impracticable. Would Leonard help? Yes, but only on condition that it took place in his own area – what a way to inaugurate the Willesden jurisdiction! Who should attend? After discussion with Leonard it was agreed that four lectures would be given by him. The evangelistic content of the lectures was not designed for those outside the Christian Church but was a heart-searching for personal commitment from those who were the acknowledged leaders in their parishes. What did they as professing Christians really believe? Because belief ultimately guides behaviour and not the other way round there was the title 'Belief begets Behaviour'. This was evangelism *plus*. There was an emphasis on the theme that each Christian should be able to give a reason for the hope that is within him, and the *plus* – according to the teaching of the Church.

Would people attend? It is a measure of Leonard's stature and popularity as bishop (and to the credit of the planners) that not only the largest available hall in the Willesden area (Acton Town Hall) was booked, but was packed each Monday in January 1971. Some one thousand church leaders from the parishes, who had paid a fee of ten shillings each, attended each week to hear Leonard teach about God, Christ, the Holy Spirit and the Christian way of life. 'What is the eternal Gospel which we are to proclaim and by which we have to live? What are its implications for our attitudes and behaviour?'

Leonard's approach has not changed. It is one of the particular duties of a bishop to teach the Christian faith and especially to help those who are Christian to understand more fully what God has told us about himself and his world and to see and accept what it means in terms of the way they live. But why does that matter? Would it not have been a better use of their time if these people had been trying to do something about the appalling problems in the country and the world? Leonard's answer then and now is a firm no, because in the last resort Christians must be concerned with both symptom and cause.

And when it comes to causes, it is our beliefs that determine how we act. Of course, other things, such as our background, our make-up which we inherit, our environment, all affect our behaviour. But one of the characteristics of man is that he asks 'Why'; he has been given the ability to reason, to think, to act responsibly and not simply to be at the mercy of all the different pressures which bear upon him. What we believe determines what we regard as important: how we spend our money; whether we take account of the needs of others or just try and grasp as much as we can for ourselves.

The lectures were delivered in a crisp, astringent, unsensational and direct style and people thirsted for more. The style is important. Leonard is an emotional person, easily moved to tears. He wants to speak to minds, not to sway hearts. Mass evangelism frightens him. The thought of people being swept off their feet disturbs him. For one horrifying moment at Acton Town Hall he realized that people were eating out of his hands and he could have fed them with anything and, metaphorically speaking, been carried shoulder-high to the applause and adulation of the multitude. That vision frightened him and he is ever careful, perhaps too careful, but erring always on the side of extreme safety, not to fall into the trap which makes heroes and devils of people. As Plato said, 'People who are good at setting people free are also good at enslaving them'.

This is always the difficulty with leadership. For both as

word and as *idea* it is too closely associated in the traditions of national life and to some extent in the Church with the formation and direction of 'parties'. How could it commend itself to one who so consistently feared and detested the spirit of partisanship, however much partisans sought to claim him as their own. A growing respect for the wisdom and justice of his 'rule' would be more acceptable to him. And this came not least as a result of his never patronizing or talking down to people. He provoked intelligence by expecting it, by taking it for granted in everyone and on all occasions. Of course, such an approach will misfire on occasions and people will find little for them to grasp.

Well timed for the post-Acton follow-up in the parishes was Leonard's first full-length book, appropriately dedicated to Priscilla, *The Gospel is for Everyone*, which was the archbishop of Canterbury's Lent Book for 1971. A few sentences from the archbishop's foreword will illustrate the theme:

> It is a book to ponder and to spend time in doing so. Its theme is that we should be better Christians, more Christ-like, more good, more saintly than we are. But we do this not by struggling to follow an ethical example so much as by receiving a gift and realising our true status. While like all human beings we strive to justify ourselves to ourselves and to others, unconsciously ruled by all manner of thoughts of status in relation to the world around us, it is God who gives us our real status as his sons, and our Christian life is its faithful acceptance. Here is the meaning of Gospel, Church, sacraments, worship, prayer, practical Christian ethics. This book helps us to see many moments in our lives as illustrations of the true relationship. It is wide ranging in its applications while it retains a rare simplicity of theme.

A more potentially contentious innovation was the revival of the pilgrimage to the shrine of our Lady of Willesden where a figure of the Black Virgin had been installed in Willesden Parish Church. The pilgrimage drew people from all over the area and provided a focal occasion with a unifying effect. Evangelicals joined in whole-heartedly. Leonard did not minimize the part played by our Lady, but avoided the more extravagent forms of devotion. There was a long-standing tradition, evident in some of the older parishes only, of parochial isolation. The pilgrimage did a good deal to overcome this.

Although Leonard was not a bishop with a blueprint of ideas that he would stamp on his area, neither was he a pragmatist. There were five main areas of policy on which he concentrated: (1) welding the new area and making it conscious of its identity although he had treated his 'jurisdiction' as an area, almost a separate diocese, from the moment he became its bishop; (2) the deepening of the spiritual life of both clergy and people; (3) parochial visitations; (4) the selection and pastoral care of ordinands; (5) the deepening of understanding of the Eucharist in parishes. At first Leonard wanted an effective area synod, but he abandoned the idea when he realized that such a body would lack teeth, and would have no statutory existence. Further, it would simply and intolerably multiply meetings for people who would almost certainly be on the diocesan and deanery synods.

He also developed a habit of visiting clergy chapters regularly to discuss priestly discipline and the spiritual life. Small groups of clergy, old and young together, were invited to his house for schools of spiritual direction. When he conducted informal discussions for the clergy on matters pertaining to their priesthood he created an atmosphere of intellectual directness and sincerity, extracting from each in turn the very best of which he was capable. Irrelevance, which is the chartered libertine of such occasions, withdrew abashed at his presence. Spiritual commonsense and reality were evident. These occasions were not all sunshine and light. Leonard worked himself very hard and expected his clergy to work hard too. Not all the clergy liked him, some disliked, even hated, him, others were afraid of him. Basically, as a man, he was shy and not easy to get to know.

But when one knew him as man *and* bishop the portrait changed, became more vivid and colourful. What does one see, now as then? Certainly the definiteness, courage and integrity are there. One of the most telling television encounters of this period was a long conversation or debate between Marghanita Laski and Leonard. Here was a real match of minds and convictions. It made compelling viewing as these two intelligent people, one a believer, the other not, slipped beneath the surface of prepared positions to examine and explore one another's convictions in a courteous, friendly but firm manner.

What else is in the portrait? Restrained emotion, a holding back in case it is unleashed; a fighter too, though caring. Look into the eyes and one sees compassion arising from the priest on his knees and at the altar. Also a feeling of isolation over some of the issues confronting him and the Church at this time. And again, there is the aesthetic spirituality of the priest. Something else – a sense of humour and a boyish sense of fun. Leonard had a chaplain, at first part-time and then full-time (in every sense) at Willesden – Robert C. Jennings, now rector of St Mary the Virgin, Hayes. He is able to illustrate this part of the portrait. First a note about Leonard's *apparent* impulsiveness with regard to appointments:

> The bishop offered me the post 'at a moment's notice'. His wife had been visiting the parish to open the autumn fair, and when having a cup of tea afterwards, she remarked how overworked he was, and had had to spend part of the weekend at home in bed, between addresses at a pre-confirmation weekend. My reaction was 'if there is anything that I can do. . . ' That evening, the bishop telephoned and said 'When can you start?'. I began working with him the following week; at first one day a week, then three, and finally five. I was given a curate to cope with the parish work. Finally, I became full-time.

He goes on to relate a few incidents, out of many, which illustrate Leonard's sense of fun:

> He could be very human, and has a good sense of humour when relaxed. When my leg was in plaster, he wrote the episcopal signature on the plaster under the name 'Noot' (Derek Nimmo was starring in 'All Gas and Gaiters' at the time). He (at a party) also persuaded the then bishop of London (Robert Stopford) to put his signature on the plaster. No mean feat! At another time, during a hot spell when, unusually for him, he had taken off his cassock and was wearing a pair of shorts, he stood on his head. Something had gone particularly well and he was bubbling over with enthusiasm . . .

In church I have known him have a fit of the giggles when something has amused him, especially if there was some clergyman trying to be very correct and proper. Both he and I were practically helpless on occasions, trying very hard to disguise the fact. A very amusing occasion was a smart institution in Hendon. The car arrived at the church gate where there was a scout guard of honour drawn up, all at attention and saluting. The back door of the car was opened and the bishop expected to emerge. Imagine the surprise when the 'bishop' got out, went to the boot and produced the bags. The bishop was in fact driving, and I was in the back (although I did drive him about a good deal, after bullying of him by Mrs Leonard). He took a while to get used to being driven in his own car by others. In my car he was fine from the start.

The bishop on one occasion – being ill with flu – could not go to an institution. The clergyman concerned was summoned to the bedside where the bishop put a stole on over his dressing gown. I don't think he put his mitre on! Occasionally, to summon me, when in procession, the bishop would either hook his crozier into my collar, or tap me on the head with it.

In 1972 Leonard, with his wife, went with a party from the area on a pilgrimage to the Holy Land. Mrs Joan Oakley JP, widow of the former vicar of Willesden, has a memory of this:

He was the most wonderful leader. He made the Bible come alive for all of us. Because he was, who he was, he was allowed to celebrate Holy Communion in many of the Jerusalem churches. I will always remember the evening services in his room at the various hotels overlooking the Sea of Galilee, or the Walls of Jerusalem. When we visited the Dead Sea, he enjoyed bouncing my husband up and down as he floated on the salty water to show that it was impossible to sink.

Earlier in this chapter I referred to Leonard's primary task as that of being a bishop and being seen to be a bishop. He seemed always to be about the area even when he was away or abroad! This is a measure of the impact he made on the area as well as on the Church. Never was there any doubt of who he was or what he stood for. He bore the heavy wooden cross for part of its long journey through the streets on Good Friday. These were ecumenical occasions. When the first civic service was held for the newly chartered borough of Brent, Leonard preached on the relation of Church and State, and Church and civic authority: 'The civil authority deals with people as they are, whereas the Church's task is to change human nature.' He was asked to speak to secular groups on religion – and religion is was they got. The East Willesden Young Conservatives Organization (26 April 1965) heard, not a recital of the country's problems or the Church's agonies, with a veneer of Christianity in the message, but a challenging talk on the relevance of Christianity and the boldness, courage and breadth of vision needed for Christians if they were to try to catch a glimpse of what St Paul called the 'gathering together in one, all things in Christ'.

A matter of major importance was that of ordination candidates. The number of ordinands was considerable and increased over the years. Leonard reckoned to see every accepted ordinand every six months. He appointed a director of vocations who saw all potential ordinands in the first instance and reported to Leonard when they were ready for a selection conference. In an article on 'The Episcopal Care of Ordinands' (*Ministry*, Autumn 1967) Leonard explained something of his methods. Pastoral care belongs not to the bishop alone but is shared with clergy and laity.

> The local worshipping congregation, however, has a responsibility both in the selection and in the continuing pastoral care of an ordinand. It is for this reason that I require that a candidate must have been a regular member of a worshipping community for sufficient time to enable the churchwardens, as representatives of the laity, to speak as to their opinion of his suitability. This practice had an unexpected result. Some churchwardens openly admitted that for the first time they realised that ordinands came from the parishes!

Leonard made it clear that the bishop accepts the responsibility for the candidate through every stage and he must have personal knowledge of each man:

The object of a selection conference is to make recommendations to the bishop, who must then make his decision. How can this appear to be any other than a formal rubber-stamping if the bishop has not already come to know a candidate before he goes to a conference? How can he advise a man about his choice of theological college if he has not kept in touch with him during the time at university? How can he decide on the right parish for the man in which to serve his title if he has not seen him regularly while at his theological college?

Leonard was chairman of the Clergy Orphan Corporation, chairman of the board of governors of St Edmund's School, Canterbury, St Margaret's School, Bushey and the College of All Saints, Tottenham. He was a member of the council of Church training colleges and the recruitment committee of the Advisory Council of the Church's Ministry. In 1968 he was appointed chairman of the Church of England committee for Social Work and Social Service, being responsible for the policy with regard to social work and the theological basis of it. He was responsible for initiating the Institute of Christian Studies at All Saints', Margaret Street, of which he became the visitor. He was chairman of Wel-Care in the London Diocese, whose success depended upon cooperation between parish priest, local authority, local doctors, schools and deaneries – just the kind of mixed group Leonard enjoyed. It is as a result of none of these activities that he was propelled into the national and international headlines.

If there was a disappointment for Leonard during the Willesden years it concerned the deepening of understanding of the Eucharist in the parishes. He felt he had achieved least in this respect. The great majority of parishes had a parish Eucharist or Mass, but many worshippers had little understanding of its meaning. Leonard's practice of instituting incumbents and confirming in the context of the Eucharist and of always celebrating as the main feature of a parochial visitation with an instruction about the Eucharist helped. What concerned and distressed Leonard was that in too many parishes the Eucharist was seen as a natural rather than a supernatural occasion.

When Willesden became an 'area' in 1970 the archdeaconry

of Hampstead was lost to the new Edmonton area and a new archdeaconry of Northolt was created for Willesden. Roy Southwell, vicar of Hendon, who was appointed as archdeacon of Northolt, comments that

> It was a curious feature of the nine years or so that Graham occupied the suffragan see that he was generally loved in his area and in the diocese, but beyond that he became increasingly the butt of criticism and dislike. This was on account of his firm convictions about the significance of the catholicity of the Church of England and the perils which he saw ahead in such matters as the scheme for Anglican–Methodist unity. There was little doubt that those who thought as he did looked more and more to his leadership.

And so to his first major confrontation with the Church of England and Anglican communion establishments, archbishops included.

6

To every man's conscience ...

Official conversations between the Church of England and the Methodist Church commenced in 1956 under the joint chairmanship of George Kennedy Allen Bell, a former bishop of Chichester, and the Methodist Harold Roberts, principal of Richmond College, Surrey. The Anglican members represented different traditions and theological positions within the Church of England. Membership changed over the years and in the eleven years over which one commission or another met only three members remained constant: Harry James Carpenter, bishop of Oxford; Lionel Meiring Spafford du Toit, at first vicar of St Mary, Windermere, then dean of Carlisle; and Eric Waldram Kemp, fellow and chaplain of Exeter College, Oxford.

An interim statement was published and received a cautious welcome by most people. There was a hint of the way the commission was thinking when reference was made to the plans of Church union worked out for Ceylon and for North India and Pakistan: 'In these it is explicit that no one is being required to repudiate his previous ministry'. How then could a form of unity be brought into existence through an initial unification of the ministries on an episcopal basis? A few years later the Churches found out, when in February 1963, *Conversations between the Church of England and the Methodist Church: a Report* was published. The eleven Anglican delegates were unanimously in favour of the proposals whilst on the Methodist side there were eight delegates in favour and four dissenters.

The chief thrust of the report was a scheme of reunion in two stages. At the heart of stage one was a service of reconciliation bringing about full communion without union. Each Church would be able to receive the sacraments in one

56

another's churches and priests/ministers would be able to
officiate in either Church. It was proposed that the Methodist
Church would accept episcopacy in continuity with the
historic episcopate, and the practice of episcopal ordination
for its ministers in the future. During the period of full
communion all kinds of important matters would have to be
settled including the future of relations between the Church
of England and the Establishment, the synchronizing of the
two administrative systems, the future of both private
patronage and the parson's freehold, the fusion of diocesan
and district structures, the willingness of Methodists to accept
episcopal confirmation, the future of ecclesiastical plant and
of liturgical practice, and the best use of finances to promote
the faith. When these and other questions were answered and
settled there would be stage two – the full and complete act
of final union.

The report was referred to the dioceses. The way in which
diocesan opinion was sought and assessed was haphazard and
unsatisfactory. There was neither order nor precision in the
way questions were asked and answered. But the variation
was small compared with the different methods of recording
decisions adopted by the dioceses. It was left to the whim,
calculation or discretion of the bishop as to how any voting
figures were published. If more time and care had been
devoted to the phrasing of the questions, the way in which
diocesan consultation and voting took place and a uniform
way of assessing opinion and conviction been agreed, perhaps
some of the agonies of the ensuing years could have been
avoided. However, in May 1965 the convocations of the provinces of Canterbury and York considered that the reports
from the dioceses constituted sufficient approval of the main
proposals embodied in the report of the conversations between
the two Churches, and 'despite reservations and questions in
many quarters' that they enabled the Church of England to
enter into negotiations with the Methodist Church. A joint
Commission was appointed to carry this work forward and it
was under the chairmanship of the bishop (Stopford) of
London and Dr Harold Roberts.

What was Leonard doing at this time? It is important to
appreciate that he was not a proctor in convocation and thus
not a member of the Church Assembly. His voice could not

be heard directly in either place. Any influence he would have would have to be outside the central councils of the Church. This does not mean that he was not meeting those people who inhabit such places. It was already known that he was a sceptic of the proposed scheme of reunion, yet most desirous of pursuing the quest for unity. He had been involved in informal (yet official) discussions on some of the legal problems raised by the service of reconciliation, which as it stood was illegal because of the Act of Uniformity of 1662. Parliamentary approval would be required. Over some discussions on 24 January 1964 between Anglicans, Methodists and lawyers, Leonard pointed out that in the Church of England ordinations and consecrations were to titles. It was not possible for a man to be ordained priest, or consecrated bishop, in abstract. If this principle were ever conceded the result would open the door to the *episcopi vagantes* of the Middle Ages, or to a practice of the Celtic Church where bishops were kept in reserve and were brought forth only for the performance of special episcopal acts. Leonard feared that unless the practice of ordination to a title was introduced at stage one, not only would this danger be present, but also the new practice would play into the hands of those extremists who thought of ordination as an isolated act in which some sort of magical element was present.

Leonard was attending meetings of a body called 'Towards Anglican–Methodist Unity', chaired by Dean Robert (Robin) Woods of Windsor. On the appointment of the new commission in 1965 this body died and in its place rose the Anglican–Methodist Council for Unity. Leonard was invited to join the council by Bishop Falkner Allison of Winchester. Its purpose was the promotion of the unity of the two Churches at the local level. It was not intended to be propagandist: certainly not a pressure group holding public meetings. The words of the invitation suited Leonard: 'Rather, its work will be devotional, in the preparation of prayers and other exercises in the deepening of unity. It will be educational in clarifying those principles which have official sanction but may still perplex many people. The council will also be concerned to encourage all forms of joint activity, especially at local level.' Leonard accepted and attended the inaugural meeting in the Jerusalem Chamber, Westminster

Abbey on 18 March 1966. There were 14 Anglicans and 14 Methodists, plus the joint chairmen – the bishop of Winchester and the Revd Dr Maldwyn L. Edwards.

Leonard only undertook to serve on the council on the clear understanding that it was representative of various shades of opinion about Anglican–Methodist unity and was to disseminate opinion and encourage discussion but was not necessarily committed to what the commission might produce. There appeared to be variety on the council, but perhaps not as much as the titles, positions and backgrounds of some of the members might suggest. Professor Margaret Deansly could be relied upon to understand Leonard's position and so, in theory, could the Revd F. P. Coleman, secretary of the Church Union. The Revd Colin Buchanan (London College of Divinity) was an Evangelical who was to cooperate with Leonard in the future, but these were early days of beginning to know one another. The bishop of Liverpool (Clifford Martin) was an experienced ecumenist, while the Earl of March and Miss R. Christian Howard were radical voices in the making.

It soon became clear that there was a groundswell of opposition in both Churches which could not be ignored and which could not be subdued nor sterilized by negotiations. There would be splits in the Churches. Leonard shared the unhappiness of many Anglicans about a scheme that was likely to create yet another dissenting body. He considered there was a new spirit in the ecumenical movement, moving away from the idea of 'negotiations'. Opposition was gathering from many individual Anglo-Catholics and Anglican Evangelicals as well as Methodists, from the *Voice of Methodism*, the Methodist Revival Fellowship, the Church Union and the Society of the Holy Cross. But the Anglican constituency which was ignored at the promoters' peril was the ordinary Church member who remained comparatively unmoved. From rarefied heights reports and answers descended to questions that had never been sent up in the first place. People in the pews had as little understanding as they had over the vital diphthong of Nicaea.

Leonard did not make the mistake of the promoters. Admittedly, his conscience was paramount, but he knew what was being said in the parishes. The temperature of the water was hardly lukewarm. However, he, like the rest of the Church, awaited the result of the negotiations. In using that word he had put his finger on what was to him a fundamental flaw, namely, that the plan was conceived as a matter of negotiation. This was the way of an organizational merger, not the way of Christian unity.

In 1967 the Anglican–Methodist Unity Commission published an interim statement, *Towards Reconciliation*, which showed the commission's approach to the central doctrinal questions of priesthood and ministry, scripture and tradition, and the sacrificial aspects of Communion, and set the revised draft of the service of reconciliation and the draft of the ordinal in the context of that approach. At a conference of representatives of Catholic societies of the Church of England, Leonard was asked to convene a group of representatives of these societies and a few individuals to prepare a response. Leonard prepared his own draft comments on *Towards Reconciliation* which became the working paper of the group which met at the Convent of the Sisters of the Resurrection of our Lord in Friern Barnet on 20 July 1967. This group became known as the 'Bishop of Willesden's Conference'. The conference made some additions and amendments to Leonard's paper, and it was agreed that it should form a pamphlet which was privately printed and published as *The Unity of the Faith* on 1 September, 1967.

The key to understanding *Towards Reconciliation* so far as the Anglican–Methodist commission was concerned rested in the fact that it left open a wide area of liberty of interpretation. Indeed, when the conversations began, the Methodists agreed to enter into them on certain conditions, one of which was 'That the same liberty of interpretation of the nature of episcopacy and of priesthood would be accorded to the Methodist Church as prevails in the Church of England'. *Towards Reconciliation* took this principle and applied it to other matters as well as episcopacy and priesthood. Advocates of the report pointed to the sweet reasonableness of such a principle. Were not the differences of interpretation within Anglicanism reflected in all the Churches? The report sought to establish as a basis for union; in the words of Dean du Toit of Carlisle: 'Differences of interpretation within invariability of practice' which, he said, 'is the price we pay for such unity as we now possess'.

What of the service of reconciliation? It had always been the intention that the service would be for the reconciliation of *Churches* and only of *ministries* as belonging to the Churches. The equality of the ministries was emphasized by the words, 'We welcome you as fellow presbyters with us in Christ's Church' at the reception of the ministers of each Church after the silent laying on of hands. The question of ambiguity was dealt with in this way: the declaration which would be made involved a willingness to receive what God may desire to give. This implied an openness of interpretation which the service was specifically designed to meet. Earnest enthusiasts of the scheme emphasized that for any kind of unity, variety of interpretation would be required and if this is what ambiguity meant then it was a price worth paying. Variety of interpretation mattered because God had made everyone different. A divided Church was the worst ambiguity of all.

Such arguments made Leonard hot under his purple stock. Alterations had been made to the original proposals, but as was made clear in *The Unity of the Faith*: 'This service of reconciliation is (a) still ambiguous in the wrong sense and demands doctrinal agnosticism for participation with a clear conscience; and (b) concerned with the relative status of the two bodies and not with unity.' For these and other reasons the members of Leonard's conference made clear that 'We do not feel that we can, in conscience, take part in the service of reconcilation, as the proposals stand'. How often those searing words, 'in conscience' were going to surface, and how unwise were Leonard's opponents in minimizing their importance. They would come to realize what the words meant.

During 1967 the Anglican–Methodist Unity Commission was taking note of a growing volume of criticism and they particularly acknowledged the former archbishop of Canterbury (by now Lord Fisher of Lambeth), who one columnist suggested 'may be the front man for a considerable number of prominent Anglicans whose official positions require them to appear to be favourably disposed towards union with the Methodists' – a thought more ingenious than accurate, others included the Revd Professors G. W. Anderson, C. K. Barrett and E. L. Mascall; the Revd Colin Buchanan and Revd A.

H. Simmons (Master of the Society of the Holy Cross, who was responsible for the pamphlet *Truth, Unity, and Concord?*), and Leonard himself. Mascall and Leonard sent joint notes and some of their suggestions were incorporated in the revised service of reconciliation.

The draft ordinal and service of reconciliation were slightly amended as a result of comments received. The commission deposited its final report in two volumes: *The Ordinal* and *The Scheme*. The Revd Dr James Packer, warden of Latimer House, Oxford, and a leading Anglican Evangelical, was unable to sign the report because he could not accept a service of reconciliation which could in any way be construed as ordination. At this juncture it is worth showing the respective strengths and organization of the two Churches at this time. The 'strengths' may be theoretical, but they indicate hidden reserves:

The Church of England	*The Methodist Church in Britain*
27 435 000 estimated members	2 100 000 members
9 887 000 confirmed	701 306 communicants
20 084 places of regular worship	11 539 places of regular worship
17 814 clergy	4 371 ministers
6 981 full-time lay workers (men)	150 full-time lay workers (men)
3 193 full-time lay workers (women)	350 full-time lay workers (women)
Governed by bishops, clergy and laity in Church Assembly under the Crown and Parliament.	Governed by conference, elected annually.
Divided into two provinces, Canterbury and York, and subdivided into 43 dioceses.	Divided into 46 districts, and subdivided into circuits, averaging 20–30 circuits a district.
Part of a world-wide Anglican Communion in which the Church of England strongly predominated.	Part of a world-wide Methodism in which British Methodism did not predominate.

The final report was insufficiently different from what had gone before to change minds. If anything, it stiffened opposition.

The advocates had every avenue, administrative and financial, open to them. The opponents, not yet united amongst themselves, had to establish their own presence by their own efforts. Two diocesan bishops were already vocal opponents: John Moorman of Ripon and Cyril Eastaugh of Peterborough. They were joined by others when the time came for voting. Again, it should be emphasized that though Leonard had a big following and was well known in 'official' circles, he was as yet outside them. Anything he wanted to impart to a wider audience had to be done by himself. But he had unexpected and influential allies – the Press. There is a risk that people at 'the centre' – and not only the ecclesiastical centre – think their enthusiasms and reports will be shared by a wide constituency, which is not always the case. People can be manipulated when they cannot be persuaded. The convocations and Church Assembly can speak for the Church of England; no, they *are* the Church of England. It is easy to slip into this way of thinking.

Yet the Church is not like that. The people in the parishes were not obsessed about Anglican–Methodist Unity. They were not much interested. The secular press had never teemed with enthusiasm about the proposals. When the original conversations were published in 1963 only the *Guardian* and the *Daily Mail* gave them a friendly reception. *The Times* was chilly, *The Daily Telegraph* lukewarm and the *Daily Express* freezing. The *Daily Mirror, Daily Herald* and *Daily Sketch* refrained from commenting editorially. So when Leonard wrote personal letters to editors of newspapers in June 1968, asking if they would send representatives to a Press conference on 14 June at the Howard Hotel, Westminster, the reaction was immediate and encouraging and some of the editors pledged their support for Leonard's views. He was seen as someone with the Establishment forces against him and needing encouragement.

Leonard put out a statement which riled advocates of the scheme from Archbishop Ramsey down. His language and convictions were clear, and his accusations were direct:

The report is suspect in general and in particular with
regard to the honesty of what it advocates. The proposals
for reconciliation involve an intentional ambiguity which
makes the prayers of the service of reconciliation irrelevant
or irreverent. Many of us cannot see how, with a clear
conscience, we can take part in prayers to God which are
deliberately disingenuous. This is not a matter of a fine
point of theology – it is a matter of common honesty. We
believe that true Christian unity can only be achieved with
the help of the Holy Ghost, the Spirit of Truth, and that
this is completely incompatible with any deliberately determined disingenuity. . . . The proposals, as they stand,
present a device to escape reality and a formula to avoid
clarity. Far from achieving true unity, they will cause
further divisions.

By June 1968 the advocates had become alarmed at the
extent of the disquiet which was being revealed. By his
activity and swelling publicity it was realised that Leonard
was rapidly becoming the focal point of opposition and Evangelical opposition was joining forces with him. But it was not
merely Anglo-Catholics and Evangelicals, although they were
substantial and sufficient in themselves to supply a brake.
Priests and laity who would not own a partisan label moved
towards Leonard too. They felt the greatest distress in having
to take up a position, and one of opposition, but there was
no alternative other than a timorous silence. If only Leonard
and his tribe could be shown to be extremists – unbalanced
and unrepresentative, with no spirit of tolerance. That was
the rub. The real danger was that toleration masquerading
as charity would slither into indifference to truth. A so-called
charity which disregarded truth and principles was at best
sentimental and at worst amoral.
  Leonard's opponents began to realize that it was dangerous
to enter into combat with him unless they were well armed,
protected and prepared. He did not let his opponents get
away with the unproven allegation, the throw away remark
or the unsubstantiated opinion. An example of Leonard's
approach in battle relates to an address given by Canon
Bernard Clinton Pawley, a residentiary canon of Ely
Cathedral, at the Ely Diocesan Conference on 18 May 1968

in which Pawley warned people that, 'the bishop of Willesden
is misinformed about the attitude of Rome to this question'.
Leonard wrote to Pawley on 11 July saying: 'I think I can
only be misinformed if an official pronouncement has been
made by the Vatican, of which I am unaware. Please let me
know if, and when, an authoritative statement was made.'
There was no immediate reply and Leonard sent a reminder
on 17 August which brought forth a white flag of surrender
from Pawley (21 August), 'Even now after a considerable
search, I cannot find the document on which I based my
original assertion that "the bishop of Willesden is
misinformed. . .".' Even adversaries admitted that Leonard's
logic was irrefutable. Occasionally in debate his logic was like
that of Enoch Powell, tense in its construction and remorseless
in its advance.

Bishops whom Leonard might have expected to have
agreed with him, if not to have been closely allied to his
cause, choked him with disappointment. The scholar bishop
and moral theologian Robert Cecil Mortimer of Exeter said
he would certainly be intending to ordain the Methodist
ministers but did not think it mattered what *they* thought
was happening. In a nutshell there was the most alarming
manifestation of ambiguity. What mattered to Leonard was
the intention of the Church not of the individual.

If the views of the bishops of the Church of England were
beginning to be made known, what of the Anglican
communion? Soon they would know, for the Lambeth Conference met from 25 July to 25 August 1968. There was
tension in the conference when it came to consider the terms
of the resolution on the Anglican–Methodist proposals. The
Lambeth Fathers were being asked to pronounce on the theological adequacy of the service of reconciliation in achieving
its declared intentions of reconciling the two Churches and
integrating their ministries. Some bishops were frank enough
to say they had not studied the report at all; it had not been
made available to the whole conference. Leonard's was the
strongest voice raised in objection. He made it clear that
opposition was not confined to Anglo-Catholics and extreme
Evangelicals:

There are many that fall between these categories and you

can't ignore us. If I could endorse the scheme, now at this very moment, and with a clear conscious face my Lord in prayer, I should do so with the greatest of joy. Nothing would give me greater relief at the present time. I don't want to be unduly personal, but I think some speak as if we were wicked people, dragging our feet, unwilling to go forward prompted by the Holy Spirit. . . . If you knew what it is like to live day by day with the ache of knowing that you can't see your way to go through with it, I think they would perhaps understand us a little better. . . . We are concerned here with a formal act between two Churches that will have permanent significance. We are concerned because we believe that the Catholic norms . . . are not antiquities to be preserved for their own sakes but given by Christ so that the Church may grow in obedience to that increased fullness.

The bishop of Peterborough, Cyril Eastaugh, moved a blocking motion. After some procedural confusion, the conference returned to the subject the following day when the archbishop of Dublin, George Otto Simms, acting on behalf of the steering committee, introduced an alternative to the conference section's own resolution. 'This conference welcomes the progress made since 1952 towards unity between the Church of England and the Methodist Church in Great Britain along the lines recommended by the Lambeth Conference of 1958, and hopes that the Churches will be able to proceed to full communion and eventually to organic union.' This was ill received by bishops who wanted the conference to express a firm view and Archbishop Coggan, who, as a member of the steering committee had helped with the wording, changed his mind overnight. The bishop of Peterborough would have withdrawn a motion of his own in favour of the Dublin alternative. A rare lighter moment in the debate came when the bishop of North Queensland, Ian Wotton Allnutt Shevill, supported Peterborough's suggestion that the motion 'be not put', saying that the situation reminded him of a conversation between Big Ben and the leaning tower of Pisa: 'Big Ben is reported to have said to Pisa, "You haven't the time and I haven't the inclination." We from Australia have the inclination to pass the resolution but we don't have the time to study it properly.' Instead, the suffragan bishop of Jarrow, Alexander Kenneth Hamilton, moved an amendment which placed the emphasis on what the section of the conference considering the scheme had said. It became the motion of the conference and was passed after a speech by the metropolitan of India (Hiyanirindu Lakdasa Jacob de Mel). He warned the conference against adopting a 'parliamentary dodge' in the conduct of the debate, and called the Dublin resolution 'a toothless, bloodless, colourless thing. I am surprised that this emanated from Ireland: don't they still like a fight? It is an easy and despicable way to treat our Methodist brethren, who have been left dangling for the past ten years'.

> I hope people here will think of the effect this kind of cavalier behaviour will have on the status and prestige of the Anglican communion. Some of the elder brethren here have some experience in these matters and are not so confined as many others would believe. We cannot act in this hasty and irresponsible way. A little more of this behaviour, and the Anglican communion will get such a magnificent reputation for double-talk that we will become utterly disreputable. Our very honour will be challenged. People will see that, when we get down to the real thing, we find an opportunity to slide off. We have this reputation of talking with sweet reasonableness but it is a different matter when the challenge comes.
>
> Some think that more time is needed to study the scheme. But why not be ready to trust the judgment of a good representative committee? You can let North India and Lanka go through, but when it comes to a touchy point, it is said, 'We haven't had time to study it'.
>
> If you want peace, then you must pay the price and, if you want unity you must pay the price also, not by bargaining but by listening to the voice of the Holy Spirit. It is an evil thing to dispose of Anglican–Methodist unity in the way that has been suggested.

It is said that he sat down to the most thunderous applause of the conference. It was a speech of vigorous defence or unexampled vituperation, depending on one's view. De Mel was on record as saying that the Church of England was enthusiastic for reunion anywhere else other than in England or, as he put it, 'to the last Indian'. A Roman Catholic observer remarked afterwards that 'The Lambeth Conference was saved from the black hole by Calcutta!' The final and amended published resolution was as follows: 'The conference welcomes the proposals for Anglican–Methodist unity in Great Britain and notes with satisfaction the view expressed in the report of section three that the proposed service of reconciliation is theologically adequate to achieve its declared intentions of reconciling the two Churches and integrating their ministries.' Section three on 'The Renewal of the Church in Unity' had as its chairman the metropolitan of India, and the chairman of the sub-committee reviewing current schemes was the bishop of Oxford (Harry Carpenter) who had been joint chairman of the original conversations.

Leonard was not the only bishop to be sick at heart with de Mel's speech. The bishop of Peterborough countered the suggestion that the speech had been a personal triumph. Quite the contrary,

> It was in fact not a speech which should be heard in any civilized assembly, let alone an assembly of Christians. It was a torrent of abuse, insult and hysteria – a rabble-rouser . . . [but] it certainly succeeded, and, if there could have been anything more sickening than the speech itself, it was the tumult of applause with which it was received. This classic instance of mass reaction and non-thought was utterly disillusioning about the judgment of the conference.

The furore came in the closing stages of the conference. Leonard was again not alone in informing the archbishop of Canterbury (by a handwritten note) that after such a speech he could not attend the final service of the conference in St Paul's Cathedral, at which the metropolitan was preacher. The archbishop penned a reply to Leonard (23 August 1968):

> I saw today your little note saying why you were not coming to St Paul's on Sunday. I can indeed understand your feelings, as I thought the Metropolitan's speech castigating those critical of the Anglican–Methodist report was deplorable, as has been every piece of innuendo about the motives

68

and convictions of any group of 'dissentients'. A number of people have spoken of their pain at the Metropolitan's speech.

I can the more share your feelings as I have myself sometimes felt a bit wounded by *your* own suggestions from time to time that if we think well of the Anglican–Methodist plan we must be *dis*honest or at least be conniving in a dishonest procedure. So acutely had I felt this (though I don't think this has occurred during the conference) that I was intending sometime to tell you of my feelings. So I take this chance of doing so. My view of the 'integrity' of the main features of the 'A–M' proposal is based upon such theological and moral judgements as I am able to make, and I have felt it a bit much when a bishop has to tell some of his brethren – including those who rejoiced to lay hands on him at his consecration – that they are by implication dishonest!

But the last thing I want is to start a debate. I only am telling you something of my feelings, while having the utmost sympathy (in this present episode) with *yours*. I like to think that you know how very considerable is my theological agreement with you about very much. And I have had real gratitude for your contributions to the Lambeth Conference, not least this afternoon when you made a good resolution on prayer better still, and added some most pertinent comments.

Leonard replied:

I was deeply touched that you should find time to write to me personally. I greatly appreciated your letter which not only made me feel that I could be present at St Paul's this morning but that I should go. I am thankful that I did. I am very sorry if anything I have done or said should have been regarded as having personal implications. I have tried very hard to make it clear that I was concerned with the document as presented for discussion and not with the people who produced or support it. In my failure in this respect I ask forgiveness.

The archbishop suggested they should meet after the holidays. Of Leonard's letter he wrote, 'Not for a moment do I mean that the criticism of a document of proposal necessarily has personal implications – it is only the use of certain *words* which has.'

The interview was in the event at Leonard's request and took place in October 1968. When they met, Leonard explained his reasons for being unable to accept the scheme, and told the archbishop that if it were accepted he would have to disassociate himself from those who implemented it and would feel bound to do what he could to provide for those clergy and laity who could not, in conscience, take part in it. He had not given great emphasis to this publicly as it could have been interpreted as holding a pistol to the heads of voters, in the shape of a threat of schism. But he wanted to let the archbishop know that those who thought that, when all the arguing and pamphleteering had ceased, the dissenters would fall into line in Anglican fashion were very much mistaken. Leonard stated as clearly as possible that when those whose episcopal ordination was in doubt were permitted to celebrate the Eucharist in Anglican churches: 'a breach will have been made and one basis of the Anglican settlement destroyed. Those of us who remain will regard ourselves as continuing faithful to our present formularies which all the Church of England clergy, including the bishops, have solemnly declared to be "agreeable to the Word of God".'

The archbishops of Canterbury and York had not taken a particularly active part in the Anglican–Methodist debate during its earlier stages. They were criticized for not giving a lead and afterwards it was said if they had done some rallying the scheme would have gone through. There is no evidence for that point of view.

Leonard was now coping with a phenomenal amount of correspondence. Letters poured in and some of his careful replies are several pages long. It was as if he were leading the total opposition to the scheme single-handed. His considered comments on the final report were published by him in a short booklet *To every man's conscience*. . . (1968). Nearly 20 000 copies were sent out from his home. He covered moral, theological and practical issues. It is a cogently worked booklet in which he removed brick after brick from the scheme until all that was left was a service of reconciliation based on faulty reasoning with ambiguity for a heart. There was no lifeblood in it. It was merely a scheme, and one in which Leonard could not participate. All the while he was putting his opponents on the spot yet they still thought that the scheme could somehow be forced through the Church's councils.

Leonard cannot be said to have been confident that the proposals would be defeated. What would he do if they were accepted? He knew that his conscience would not let him change his mind. He was acquainted with Orthodox and Roman Catholic opinion. Archbishop Athenagoras (Greek Orthodox) wrote to Leonard on 14 December 1968:

> The Orthodox Church firmly believes that the threefold ministry of bishop, priest and deacon is an essential element in Church order. Hitherto the Church of England, in the preface to the ordinal in the Book of Common Prayer has explicitly and unambiguously affirmed its acceptance of this three-fold ministry. This clear acceptance on the Anglican part of apostolic Church order has been a primary factor in the special relationship which has come to exist between Anglicanism and Orthodoxy. If the Church of England ratifies the Anglican–Methodist scheme in its present form, this will constitute, I am afraid, an abandonment of the principles affirmed in the Book of Common Prayer; and I also fear that the special relationship between our two communions will be seen as seriously impaired'. . . . The Methodist minister is in a similar position to an Orthodox sub-deacon; he has received charismata from the Spirit, but he has not received the grace of the priesthood. This should be clearly stated in the Anglican–Methodist reunion scheme.

Leonard's experience of the Roman Catholic Church was greater than his knowledge of the Orthodox. And his friend and collaborator, Eric Mascall, was well known and respected in Roman Catholic circles. Shortly after the final report was published the Roman Catholic bishop, scholar and former Anglican, B. C. Butler, wrote to Mascall expressing surprised interest in the proposed ordinal but disquiet with the scheme:

> I fear that the report, if accepted, will give *de jure* rights to Protestantism; and that this will in fact (according to one's point of view), either compromise a position which has hitherto been substantially intact, or give fresh endorse-

ment to a compromise which is already existing. From the point of view of Anglican–RC relations, and indeed from the wider point of view of the future of the movement towards universal Christian unity, I should deplore this. I need hardly point out to you that sacramental forms which in one context of official doctrine are 'valid' can be invalidated by removal into a different (official) context.

There had been one other development with historic implications. Leonard was at a reception given by the apostolic delegate, Archbishop Hyginus Eugene Cardinale, to mark the anniversary of the pope's coronation. Cardinale said he would welcome a talk with Leonard 'to discuss our many problems', and suggested that he might take someone with him. It was an alluring invitation and an important private meeting. Cardinale, titular archbishop of Nepte, who was technically apostolic delegate to Great Britain, Gibraltar, Malta and Bermuda (1963–9, before moving to be papal nuncio to Belgium and Luxembourg and the European Economic Community), quickly made his mark in this country. It was not an easy position to hold in a country that still had lingering suspicions about the real intentions of the 'scarlet woman'. Cardinale showed an acceptable face of the Roman Catholic Church that was changing fast.

Leonard took Eric Mascall with him for lunch and the conversation on 17 July 1968 at the apostolic delegation. They were received with exceptional cordiality. Gifts were exchanged and Cardinale said he would send Leonard's pamphlet on the Anglican–Methodist report to the pope. If anyone needed a tonic for an exhausted spirit it was Leonard. The meeting gave him more than a tonic. What would happen and what would the Roman Catholic attitude be towards Anglicans who could not participate in the Anglican–Methodist scheme if it were passed? Leonard was as clear over this issue as he was to be over other issues in the future: that is, that he, with others, would not wish to leave the Church but rather remain, insisting that they were the true Church of England. There would have to be a settlement over such matters as endowment funds. Cardinale said that if a body of Anglicans found themselves bound to stand out and stand firm, maintaining the Catholic standpoint, there should be no difficulty over them being in communion with the Roman Catholic Church.

The time for voting was drawing nigh. Those against the proposals had to fight to have a fair hearing in some dioceses and at great cost to themselves – spiritual, physical and financial. The convocations of Canterbury and York met in May 1969 and agreed that there was sufficient doctrinal agreement for the Church to proceed to stage one. This was self-delusion and soon the truth of that remark would be evident. There was a referendum of clergy in June 1969. They were asked 'Will you take part in the service of reconciliation to inaugurate stage one?' The voting was as follows: yes: 9642; no: 5621; abstentions: 243. The House of Laity (Church Assembly) met on 7 June 1969 and voted on the motion that final approval should be given to the inauguration of stage one. Their voting figures: for: 115; against: 105; abstentions: 1.

On 8 July 1969 the Methodist Conference met at Birmingham and approved the scheme by a majority of 76%. The Church of England had decided that, for itself, it must have 75% approval. On the day the Methodists met in Birmingham the joint convocations met in London. It was referred to as the most momentous decision of the century for the Church. The speeches were of a high standard, but it is doubtful if any of them changed voting intentions. Voting by houses, the results were as follows: Upper House of Canterbury, 27 for, 2 (Peterborough and Leicester) against – 93%; Lower House of Canterbury, 154 for, 77 against – 67%; Upper House of York, 11 for, 3 (Ripon, Carlisle and Sheffield) against – 78%; Lower House of York, 71 for, 34 against – 68%; total vote: 263 for, 116 against – 69%.

That should have been that. Not a 'no' to Christian unity, but a 'no' to the scheme. But a supposed saviour for the scheme was at hand in the shape of the General Synod. With the material of the old Church Assembly, if ever there was a case of trying to make a silk purse out of a sow's ear this was it. The General Synod would be the Great Deliverer. It was clear the scheme would be reintroduced.

Indeed in the autumn of 1969 the archbishop of Canterbury was telling advocates of the scheme that he shared their feeling that the non-acceptance by the convocations damaged the Church's credibility and had left it in great frustration. But he encouraged the idea that it would be better for the proposals to come again to the General Synod after its inception and he even went so far as to say that he did not think it would be at all bad to have one clear issue that might be prominent in the elections for the Synod because otherwise those elections might have no clear issue, only misleading party labels as a guide. Nothing should be done until the General Synod had been born. If it was brought back to convocations the risk of another setback would be disastrous and would encourage those in the House of Laity who wanted to make it a laity versus clergy issue by alleging that the views of the House of Laity were again being bypassed. It is strange that even Archbishop Michael Ramsey had inflated and unrealistic expectations of the new General Synod.

Meanwhile, the volume of noise against Leonard and other vocal opponents was loud and clear. 'Let the dissentients tell us what their scheme is' asked the archbishop of Canterbury. Why did not these 'wreckers' produce a scheme of their own? The challenge provoked a unique endeavour and achievement. Since 1968 there came together two groups of people each opposing the scheme from different vantage points – the one Catholic, the other Evangelical, and for different reasons, but each seeking to be obedient to God's truth in their situation. The Evangelicals were Colin Buchanan, who served with Leonard on the Anglican–Methodist Council for Unity from 1966 to 1969, James Packer, who had signed a minority report when a member of the commission, and Edward Michael Bankes Green, principal of the London College of Divinity (later St John's College, Nottingham) who was a consultant at the Lambeth Conference and participated in the section on which Leonard served. The Catholics were Mascall and Leonard.

Buchanan and Leonard published an article 'Intercommunion: some interim agreement' (*Theology*, October 1969) and in record time Buchanan, Mascall, Packer and Leonard (Green was not able to participate fully for reasons of his own timetable) produced a 214-page book, *Growing into Union* (1970). Reaction to the book was fast and furious. Six leading Methodists – B. S. O'Gorman, R. E. Davies, Dr H. Roberts, E. W. Baker, Dr T. K. J. Leese and Professor W. R. Hindmarsh, criticized it in the *Methodist Recorder* (4 June 1970) and the *Growing into Union* team rushed to publish a pamphlet in reply (25 June 1970).

In *A History of the Church of England 1945–1980* (1984) Paul A. Welsby writes waspishly of *Growing into Union*: 'It was unfortunate that the tone of this work was arrogant, polemical and even absuive and that the authors displayed such self-satisfaction with the rightness of their views. . . . Fundamentally . . . the whole concept of the local 'piece by piece' approach was regarded as untheological, highly divisive, and productive of little more than a form of congregationalism.'

This comment must be based on Welsby's own assessment. *Growing into Union* was received with interest and reviewed with care, although not necessarily with agreement. The debate in the book was kept at a high level. Catholics and Evangelicals had dropped their defences and shared both their disquiet and their aspirations. Each had fundamental convictions which could not be moved or negotiated. There was no pragmatic cutting of the corners of principle. The primacy of theology and integrity guided their deliberations. Such statements offended those who did not think that this mixed and unlikely foursome could come to any substantial agreement. Moreover, if they were offended by such an approach it was because it was a reproach to their own failed attempt to face issues within the Church of England before they embarked on discussions with Methodists. And it must be remembered that the negotiations had been conducted against internal turmoil within the Church.

The authors wrote that 'In our doctrinal discussions, we tried to use our variant heritages as Anglicans constructively rather than centrifugally, and instead of digging into entrenched positions from which we then agree to differ we have laid together foundations which will bear the weight of the practical programme we are now to erect upon them. We do not attempt to 'contain and subdue' supposedly ultimate doctrinal cleavages by means of equivocal liturgical uniformity.' What was special and different about *Growing into Union*, which is still quoted today? It was not another scheme. The authors advocated a one stage procedure, the nub of the matter being expressed in the following way: '[we would recommend] the simple expedient of inaugurating a

75

united Church in a piecemeal way territorially, leaving the existing denominations to exist alongside each other in every place where conscience, even untutored conscience, might so decree. This is the conclusion, novel in the history of English ecumenical discussion, to which we have come. This will do justice to the various principles on which we wish to build far better than any other procedure which has suggested itself to us. And it is a principle which, if novel in England, has some precedent in South India. As South India is the only existing union in which Anglicans have joined, we may well look cautiously in that direction for help.'

If ever there was a movement from the roots upward this was it. There would be no union between whole Churches but between local churches. Joining together on a 'one plus one' basis, the churches thus joining would become the first diocese of the united Church. The archipelago would gradually become a landmass. As more churches joined, more dioceses would be formed. In that way the Church would grow. Such a vision was open to critical appraisal which was received in abundance. As an adventure of faith it was daring even if it was not easy for even friendly critics to see how this would work out in practice. But it was not a scheme and the authors did not see it as *the* way but *a* way that was worthy of exploration. Of course, the threefold ministry was to be retained. They wished to admit to communion after baptism. Although there would be a 'confession of faith' at a later stage in the presence of a bishop this would not be confirmation as the Church of England knew it. Such matters were not decisions but firm footholds for the adventure. Alas, the authorities were keener to reintroduce their own scheme rather than respond to the challenge contained in *Growing into Union*.

The General Synod in February 1971 passed a motion asking that the recently rejected scheme be 'clarified' but, in the archbishop's words, 'not amended'. A small group was appointed to prepare a document of clarification to accompany the presentation of the Anglican–Methodist Unity Scheme for discussion at the General Synod in July 1971. Buchanan, Packer, Mascall and Leonard met the group on 13 May. The leader was the dean of Worcester, Eric Waldram Kemp, who was to become an ally of Leonard's in the future but who was now on the opposite side. The other members were the dean of the Court of Arches, Sir Harold Kent, Canon Paul Welsby and a prominent lay member of Synod, Oswald Clark. The president of the Methodist Conference was also in attendance. As the group could not affect procedure, only 'clarification', it was a friendly but fruitless meeting.

In September 1971 the *Growing into Union* authors addressed and circulated a published open letter to members of the diocesan synods of the Church of England. On 3 May 1972 at a specially convened meeting of the General Synod the Anglican–Methodist unity scheme was debated. The archbishop of Canterbury was trenchant in demolishing the opponents' case and reminded the synod that they had just voted that the North Indian reunion scheme was sound. 'What kind of God is it who is willing and able to answer the prayer with laying-on of hands in the North India scheme and is not willing to answer the prayer in the Anglican–Methodist service?'

The archbishop's reference to North India is interesting and, strangely for him, was not quite on target. The Act of Unifcation in the North India scheme said that 'The uniting churches affirm that the intention of the rite is clearly and unambiguously set forth in the prayers to be used together with the Declaration and the Formula'. Leonard agreed with the lawyers of the legal board (Chancellor Wigglesworth and David Carey) that whatever else might be said in the scheme, the decision must in the light of that affirmation be made on the basis of what the rite said, and it was clear that the intention was to produce priests or presbyters in the three-fold order. There was a sharp contrast with the acknowledged ambiguity of the service of reconciliation. Another difference with regard to North India was that the union had happened with a restructuring on an episcopal basis which again was in contrast with the Anglican–Methodist scheme which gave bishops to Methodists without requiring that they should be enabled to function as such.

At Church House, Westminster, on 3 May the question remained. Would the house fall down under the demolition hammer? It was a day of drama and a moment of decision. When the vote came it was as follows: bishops, 34 for (85%), 6 against; clergy, 152 for (65.5%), 80 against; laity,

147 for (62.8%), 87 against; total vote: 333 for (65.8%), 173 against. The scheme had failed again. Many people were devastated. For Leonard it was a matter for relief rather than for rejoicing. He had become a figure to hate as well as to admire as for most people it was clear that Leonard had won. One person threatened to throw a stone through his window if the scheme were defeated. When it was, he did. Even then he was on the wrong side as the stone was thrown through the window of 2 Church Road, Highgate; Leonard had moved to 173 Willesden Lane.

7

A Runaway Church

Leonard's name was by now familiar to people all over the country. He was regarded as Catholic and conservative, but rarely as reactionary. Never could he be described as a back-woodsman. When he was invited to address gatherings or preach sermons, people were usually surprised, and disappointed if they expected fire and brimstone. Always he brought minds to bear on the cross which 'points to the sovereignty of God, his moral demands and his boundless love'. He never spoke down, but preached directly. His style was constant but the message in the framework was varied. To this extent he took into consideration whether he was preaching to a parish in his area to whom he was Father in God and probably well known by the people, addressing a mass meeting on a contentious issue, or preaching a university sermon.

Leonard was always worrying at the way in which the Church made the contemporary and therefore the transitory, the criterion for its action. Moreover, the mind of the Church was being affected by the wrong kind of secular thought, and was lagging behind the best thinking of the world. The Church's thinking was being done in small groups which produced reports. It was an era of policy by working party and salvation by committee. Enough was produced to occupy the Church for several decades. The Gadarene rush for reform proceeded. Sample the issues raised by only a few of the reports which appeared between 1964 and 1970: 1964: *The Deployment and Payment of the Clergy* (The 'Paul' Report), *Crown Appointments and the Church*; 1965: *Alternative Services* (First and Second Series), *Abortion: an ethical discussion, Decisions about Life and Death: a problem in modern medicine*; 1966: *Women and Holy Orders, Government by Synod, Putting Asunder, Fatherless by Law?*

79

The law and welfare of children designated illigitimate, Sex and morality (British Council of Churches), *World Poverty and British Responsibility* (BCC); 1967: *Partners in Ministry, Diocesan Boundaries (London and the South-East of England), Police: a social study*; 1968: *Intercommunion Today, Theological Colleges for Tomorrow, Ascription or Assent to the 39 Articles*; 1970: *Man in his Living Environment, The Fourth R.*

There were also reports issued at regular intervals to stimulate discussion from the various boards and councils of the Church, including two from the Advisory Council for the Church's Ministry which attracted attention – *The Ordained Ministry* (1968) and *Specialist Ministries* (1971). Neither must it be forgotten that this was the era of The New English Bible. The New Testament had been published in 1961. There were campaigns, movements and discussion papers: 'The People Next Door' (1967) was frothy.

Moreover, serious discussions were taking place with the Roman Catholic Church. The first two reports from the Anglican–Roman Catholic International Commission (ARCIC) came in 1971 (the Eucharist) and 1973 (the ministry). There were official conversations with the Lutheran Churches and joint doctrinal discussions with the Orthodox Churches. This was a runaway Church with no strategic planning and no coordinated thinking.

In selecting Leonard's reactions to only three of these subjects is to show aspects of his thinking which have remained constant. Incidentally, on the question of theological colleges, he held that no principal should be appointed who had not been a parish priest. In 1965 this would have meant that the following – and there are more – would not have been theological college principals: Robert Runcie of Cuddesdon; Peter Walker of Westcott House; J. Stafford Wright of Tyndale Hall; Michael Hennell of Ridley Hall; Cheslyn Jones of Chichester; J. P. Hickinbotham of St John's, Durham, and Derek Allen of St Stephen's House, Oxford.

When *Sex and Morality* was published (1966) Leonard read it carefully and thought it so confused and in places contradictory that he wrote to each of the incumbents in his area about the report. Among the defects he listed the following:

(1) It fails to represent faithfully the relationship between

80

Law and Grace as expressed in the Gospels. Our Lord came 'not to destroy the Law but to fulfil'. The aim of Christian proclamation and pastoral care should be to enable people to fulfil the Law spontaneously and generously. We are not yet in heaven and until we are we need the Law to give us the framework in which we are set free to learn to love. It is strange that this freedom-giving quality of the Law is not recognized as of general application when in one instance of a voluntarily accepted discipline, that of celibacy, the freedom which results is explicitly recognized.

(2) It appears to regard the adoption of the 'no rules' attitude as essential to 'get inside the painful dilemma in which many of the young and not so young find themselves and utter words which express genuine interest and concern' to quote from the comments of Monica Furlong in the *Daily Mail*. But insight and concern are not enough as anyone who has really tried to listen is aware. Listening is the first and essential stage, but the Christian must have a positive and creative contribution to make.

(3) It takes little account of sin and of the redeeming power of our Lord. I find much in the report about people; I find little of the triumphant yet humble confidence in the grace of God which runs through the New Testament. As I have written elsewhere 'the real problem is how do we take the needs of the world seriously and yet proclaim the needs of redemption. For the individual it is the problem of knowing that one is forgiven and yet recognizing the need to grow in holiness. "Neither do I condemn thee" – forgiveness is offered freely by the grace of God, yet it is based on an acceptance of the fact of sin; "Go and sin no more" – the acceptance of forgiveness must be shown in growth in holiness and the fruits of the Spirit'. The problem is solved not by the abolition of sin but by its recognition and by the acceptance of the forgiveness of God.

(4) Reference is made in the report to the fact that the founder of the Playboy and Bunny Clubs preached the dogma 'sex is fun', yet was disconcerted at being asked at what age his own daughter would be allowed to apply the doctrine. Much of what is said in the report sounds all right when applied to people in general but gives little

practical help when it is an individual person who is concerned.

(5) The most serious defect seems to be that the report pays too little attention to the teaching of our Lord in the Gospels and puts too much weight on present day philosophical and sociological thought. There is an extraordinary reluctance to accept that the New Testament regards adultery and fornication as sinful. It may be that we have failed to present the teaching of our Lord in a clear and compassionate way but I do not believe that we are being faithful if we regard such teaching as having to be adapted to suit the needs of the world at one particular moment. If we do try to do so I believe we make nonsense of the Gospels.

The bishop of Willesden's conference looked at the 'Paul' Report (1964) and *Partners in Ministry* (1967) in January 1968 but there was too much work to be done on the Anglican–Methodist proposals for much progress to be made. Leonard appreciated, even advocated, reforms, but once again the Church was not digging deep. Leslie Paul had produced a report according to his terms of reference. He assumed that he knew what the clergy should be doing. He adopted certain criteria by which to judge the effectiveness of the work they did. He made recommendations which would, in his judgment, have made it possible for the work as he saw it to be carried out more effectively. Leonard noted:

But nowhere as far as I can discover does he consider whether the work which the clergy do is the right work or whether their conditions of work require that they should spend their time doing things which they should not have to do. If the latter were the case the remedy would lie in removing the necessity and not in making it easier for them to do that particular work more effectively. Are there things which the 'under-employed' should be doing and cannot or will not do? If so, why? Are there things which the 'over-employed' should not be doing?.

When the thoughts of the 'Paul' Report had been digested and incorporated into *Partners in Ministry* with firm recommendations for the Church, Leonard was concerned that the relationship between bishop and clergy was in danger of being altered. A 'diocesan ministry commission' was an inappropriate substitute for the intimate pastoral care and initiative which belongs to a bishop in deciding which priest can best be placed in any particular parish. While the 'parson's freehold' may be abused, it was not something that should be abolished without adequate security of tenure being assured. The fair distribution of clergy throughout the country indeed needed attention, and clergy were often too 'choosey' as to where they would like to be in contrast to the expressed wishes and direction of the bishops. The reformists wanted to throw off the shackles of the past. *Partners in Ministry* was part of their panacea for the radical reorientation of the Church. As always, Leonard looked at the proposals theologically. Nothing and nobody should come between a bishop, as father in God, and the clergy under his care. The relationship is precious and would be seriously impaired by *Partners in Ministry*.

The third example of Leonard's reaction to developments in the 'runaway Church' concerned the new and alternative services. A Swiss Reformed theologian, Von Allman, wrote a book on *Worship* (1966) which Leonard found helpful. In answer to the question, 'Is the Eucharist necessary for Christian worship to be truly Christian?' Von Allman gave three reasons for the answer yes: (1) it is essential because Christ instituted it and commanded the Church to celebrate it; (2) the Eucharist is as necessary to preaching the sacrament of the Lord as the Cross is necessary to the ministry of Jesus. A liturgy without the Eucharist is like the ministry of Jesus without Good Friday; (3) the Eucharist is necessary because it enables us to mark the difference between the Church and the world in a way which is not subjective, self-centred and moralizing, but objective. Leonard realized that the relationship between doctrine and liturgy was delicate and complicated. He recognized the difficulties but did not think the alternative services had completely overcome them. Leonard judged changes by the extent to which they accorded with the truth of revelation and not by the extent to which they were found helpful or expedient. Leonard constantly affirmed that 'The purpose of our communication of the Gospel is that men may be brought into fellowship with God in Christ.'

In his close and regular contact with Evangelicals, Leonard was encouraged by the way in which they were coming to a real understanding of the centrality of the Eucharist. In fact this was when the old divisions began to disappear and also a time when they were superseded by a more fundamental division. The heart of the new distinction was this. On the one hand there were those who accepted the revealed nature of the Christian Gospel, the need for redemption and the dimension of eternity. On the other hand, there were those who saw religion primarily as a human activity, which was justified insofar as it was seen to lead to a solution of the world's problems as understood on the world's terms. That is the distinction at its starkest. It is not quite as simple as that, but will suffice in this context. Answering some questions on the revised services, Leonard said;

I believe that disquiet about the new service is not always reactionary but arises from a proper sense that the element of mystery is lacking. It is important to educate people to judge whether changes are made to embody new understandings of revelation or are the result of our being conformed to the thinking of the world.

We have to face the fact that some people object to the Eucharist because it is so simple and direct. This should not surprise us in the light of *John* vi: 60–66. We must, of course, do all we can to instruct our people in the meaning of the Eucharist but we must not assume that they will all, therefore, accept it readily. The desire for Matins sometimes comes from a basically wrong attitude to the Church. Such an attitude views it more like a shop or a place of entertainment than the house of the family of God – you go there to get what you like or what you want. At the same time we must appreciate that people have preferred Matins because the 8 o'clock [Communion] has been a monologue by the priest with virtually no opportunity for the people to take part. We must proclaim the centrality of the Eucharist as was clearly recognized in the report of the [National Evangelical Anglican] Conference at Keele [University in 1967], and we must make it the central service. People will not believe our proclamation if we do not act upon it. At the same time we must seek to understand those who find it hard to accept. The Keele Report makes it clear that this is not a matter of churchmanship, but of being rooted in the scriptural revelation. . . .

I believe that we need much more flexibility in the evening. Simple services advertised as instruction, followed by informal prayers, meet a real need. Enquirers can and will come because they don't feel that they will be expected to know what to do. Perhaps I should add one warning. Some clergy seem to lose all sense of fitness and time with informal or extempore prayer. In one church in my area, the intercessions at Series 2 took ten minutes. We need more discipline not less if we are to use our new freedom properly. I'm sure that our laity need much more instruction. The complaint so often made is: 'We are always being told what to do and never how to do it'. We must tell our people how to pray, how to read the Bible, how to take part in the Eucharist, and so on. One small, but not unimportant point. At a recent synod of clergy and laity in my area, a great desire was expressed for a simple office which could be used by the laity to enable them to pray with the Church. Morning and Evening Prayer, with the present lectionary, are not suitable for this purpose.

There were two unhappy periods in Leonard's life. One was the time at Westcott House; the other occurs now. It began with a letter. Leonard was connected with the Company of Compassion which helped its members to overcome the problems which arose from separation or divorce. He was able to meet the new moralists on their chosen battle ground, and win. They, the secular Christians, were concerned with making society more loving, with picking up pieces and putting balm on the wounds, claiming that the causes could not be controlled. The wicked Church must learn to be more accepting, more caring. There was another aspect which they declined to see, but Leonard thrust it before them:

If the Church is to be truly the accepting society, it will be even more a mixed society than it is. It will have to accept those who cannot accept others, which means that it will still be open to the charges that are brought. It will have to accept those who are muddled, who are narrow-minded, who have got the wrong ideas about sex, who are puritanical. It is because of this that we have to distinguish between the individual and the Church. The Church, as such, cannot say 'You need not love', but individual Christians must be prepared to accept those who cannot see the need of loving. By doing so they do not condone 'not loving', though the world may think that they do. It is because of this that the Church distinguishes between what it is in itself accepted by God with all its flaws, living under God's mercy, and what it is in the eyes of the world.

The contrast will always be there as long as the Church is concerned with the world. What matters is that the Church is inspired by the love of God, who to accept us as we are was in Christ reconciling us to himself, the cost of which is seen in the cross.

These were words ending his address at the annual general meeting of the Company of Compassion on 1 May 1965. For years the Mothers' Union had been under great pressure to widen its membership to admit divorcees of communicant status. There was talk of having full members and associate members. The first for those who upheld the permanence of marriage in their own lives, the other for those who accepted the principle but could not witness to it in their own lives. The central secretary of the Mothers' Union, Mrs C. Llewellyn-Davies, wrote to Leonard on 27 September 1967 for his advice. With such letters, then as now, people either have to wait some time for a considered reply or be content with no reply of substance at all. What Leonard takes seriously he takes a great deal of time over. In view of what was to come he might have been wiser to have replied quickly and crisply. Instead, he wrote a four-page letter in reply on 28 February 1968.

I believe that some of the difficulties you are experiencing stem from the fact that the Mothers' Union attempts to be, at once, two things which are, I believe, fundamentally incompatible. On the one hand it seeks to be a society which stands for a particular truth and exists to witness to that truth in the life of the Church. In this respect it might be compared, say, to the Confraternity of the Blessed Sacrament, which exists to stand for certain truths about the Blessed Sacrament. No one is compelled or expected to join it, and it has clear rules for those who want to do so. The Mothers' Union, however, is also in practice regarded as a society for all mothers in the Anglican communion, which Anglican mothers have almost a right to join.

If any society intends, or is regarded as intending, to cater for all Church people then it cannot be more strict than the Church itself. It must accept as its own basis for discipline the rules of discipline which exist in the Church. If any society intends to stand for a particular truth or practice it is fully entitled to do so, and can lay down its own conditions provided they are compatible with permissible belief or practice in the Church, but it cannot complain if people do not join it, or if a society catering for similar people, but without such restrictions, wishes to establish itself. Of course, the nature of the society must be recognized by the Church as well as by the society itself. I have always regarded it as perfectly permissible and reasonable for a parish not to choose to have a branch of the Mothers' Union, but quite intolerable for a parish to want to have a branch on terms which are incompatible with the central objects of the Mothers' Union. I would, myself, regard the existence of a society which stands for and witnesses to our Lord's teaching on marriage as always desirable and increasingly necessary within the Church.

Leonard loves to take an issue, examine its strengths and flaws, strip away any historical or theological accretions and see what is left, the raw material. As with 'issues' so with 'organizations'. He wondered if the Mothers' Union should undergo drastic reorganization, perhaps into two separate branches, one the 'Fellowship of Marriage', or the 'Christian Marriage Society' which would also be open to men, witnessing to the sanctity of marriage: 'I cannot see why divorced men or women who undertake not to remarry should not be admitted. . . . they do not forfeit their communicant status. It would seem quite illogical to debar them while admitting those who have not been confirmed and are, therefore, not communicants.' Another society might be called the 'Christian Family Union' which would concentrate on the second and third of the objects of the Mothers' Union, awakening in all mothers a sense of their great responsibility in the training of their children; and seeking by example to lead their families in purity and holiness of life.

Leonard's letter produced an immediate meeting between the central president, Mrs Ronald Hallifax, Mrs Llewellyn-Davies and Leonard. Before the end of April 1968 he had agreed to be the chairman of a commission on the objects and policies of the Mothers' Union. It became known as the bishop of Willesden's commission. The amount of evidence that was collected from all over the Anglican World was vast. Membership was 429 000, of which 308 000 were in the British Isles. As a society since 1876, working to strengthen, safeguard and promote Christian family life on the basis of the life-long nature of the marriage vows as taught by the Church, it had been a force to be reckoned with. In some parishes the MU was a formidable and occasionally forbidding body. It was right to have another look at its basis. Unfortunately there were some tensions amongst the commission members. Eruptions developed and on more than one occasion Leonard thought he should resign. The possibility of agreement was at first remote, then it vanished altogether. By the time the commission's report was published in June 1972 there was a spirit of acrimony rather than of harmony in diversity, such a different atmosphere from that to which Leonard had grown accustomed with Evangelicals. The report *New Dimensions* ran to 292 pages, plus index, and included in its appendices a lengthy comment by Leonard on the report of the archbishops' commission *Marriage, Divorce and the Church*.

The Mothers' Union was being recommended to amend its constitution but the commission was divided as to the extent to which it should do so. Leonard, and two other members would restrict the membership of the divorced to those who had not remarried. Four members would go further and, at least in Britain, make membership open to all women who, in good conscience, supported the objects of the society. One member was unable to accept the redrafting of the objects and recommended one object: to strengthen and support Christian marriage and family life. There *were* matters on which the commission agreed but they were matters of detail rather than substance. Leonard presented the report to a meeting of nearly 300 members of the MU Central Council in Manchester in June 1972. When he had accepted the chairmanship he had no idea of the magnitude of the task. It had been an arduous, time-consuming haul and a thankless task. Now anyone, married, divorced or remarried can belong to the Mothers' Union.

The Lambeth Conference of 1968 had not been a time of great joy for Leonard either, and not only because it was clouded by the Anglican–Methodist issue. Nonetheless, he had been one of the conference's most frequent speakers.

It is interesting that these years of the runaway Church were presided over by Michael Ramsey. Superficially, it may be thought that Leonard would be a Ramsey devotee. That is not the case. So what can be said of the relationship between Ramsey and Leonard? There was much in Ramsey's thought that Leonard respected. Ramsey was a theologian of the first rank, with a mind that was off-centre. His earliest book *The Gospel and the Catholic Church* (1936) is still quoted. Since he died on 23 April 1988 there has been a heady rush of laudatory comment, little short of hagiographical hysteria. His death has been used as an occasion to compare him with the present occupant of St Augustine's chair. On a personal, theological and spiritual level the contrasts are chasmic. But that is the man, thinker and pastor. What of the archbishop, for it is the archbishop with whom we are here concerned? The most perceptive obituary appeared in the *Church Times* (29 April 1988) and, although anonymous, it was in fact written by the late Ronald Ralph Williams, sometime bishop of Leicester. He wrote: 'He was undoubtedly one of the greatest men to hold the office of Archbishop of Canterbury, although . . . this is not quite the same thing as saying that he was one of the greatest Archbishops of Canterbury.'

On the Anglican–Methodist Scheme, Williams considers rightly that the mistake was to have brought the scheme forward for the second time of asking. After praising Ramsey's contribution Williams says: 'There were, however, many other aspects of the matter which Ramsey was either blind to or preferred not to observe, notably the solid core of opposition, which showed no signs of diminishing. Everyone must form their own opinion as to whether he was wise to commit himself body and soul to a scheme that was controversial

from start to finish.' Again,'He could be incredibly difficult
in personal conversations. . . . Many who knew him well can
recall moments when it was utterly impossible to get him into
gear and to inaugurate any conversation at all.' Leonard
knew what it was to be on the receiving end of the silence,
to go to Lambeth Palace to seek advice, for example, on the
Mothers' Union commission report, to enter the presence,
receive the silence and depart.

In Ramsey there were unlikely combinations: intellectual
arrogance and spiritual humility, courage and cowardice, an
inability to communicate with people and an ability to have
students eating out of his hand. He did not like his views
being questioned and appeared to have little time for the
mental weight of his fellow bishops – Ian Ramsey of Durham
being a particular exception. Many bishops stood in absolute
awe of him, few could get near him. Leonard was not an
admirer. Ramsey's mind was too subtle for him. How could
the author of *The Gospel and the Catholic Church* preside over
the runaway Church of the 1960s? Ramsey's observations on
such issues as Robinson's *Honest to God*, his advocacy of the
'Paul' Report and later of *Partners in Ministry* and the part he
played in the Anglican–Methodist debate convinced Leonard
that Ramsey had changed his theological position. The
Church's policies on major moral and ethical issues of that
decade were uniformly liberal and accepted, encouraged or
even initiated by Ramsey.

All the activity which occupied so much time, a correspondence that could have kept three secretaries busy, a public
profile which meant that he was constantly in the news would
have been unendurable but for the support of Priscilla, his
daily Mass and his experience in the parishes. It was there
that he saw a quiet and strong growth in the life of the
worshipping community by which the Gospel was proclaimed
to the glory of God. *That* was what mattered.

8

Moving on, or off?

The Willesden years had been gruelling ones. In ordinary circumstances Leonard should have had a diocese of his own by about 1970. But the circumstances were far from ordinary in view of the Anglican–Methodist debacle. It was generally felt that Leonard's prominent part in toppling the scheme had cost him a diocesan bishopric and he himself felt that he had been deliberately passed over. Here is paradox. In his curacies, as a parish priest and at the National Society it was considered that Leonard was 'going places'. He was thought to be, and appeared to be, a man with ambitions, and in the Church that usually means moving towards the purple. A man of both purpose and ability should have found it easy to mount the ecclesiastical ladder, rung by rung, with care and calculation. By his actions Leonard had shown himself careless of the way he trod, yet still he climbed. He neither muted his convictions nor minded his manners. This is not to say that he was clumsy. He did not stumble upon controversy by accident. He knew when and when not to hold his peace and keep his counsel.

The future prospect did not look bright. Leonard had offended against the archbishops and most of the occupants of the bench of bishops. Torrents of abuse were often thrown in his direction. For example, after an article in *The Times* in July 1969 over Anglican–Methodist relations in which he had questioned the theological perception of those who could absorb the deliberate ambiguity in the service of reconciliation he was said to be haughty and wholly prejudiced. 'Do cut out the humbug!' wrote one priest, 'In accusing those who disagree with you as lacking in theology, or acting in an expedient manner, you have shown yourself to be insensitive and perverse.' A bishop fulminated, 'Do I understand that you say we can have no unity until the majority have, by acclamation, accepted the theology of the minority, and in this case your side of the minority?' Was he daring to attack people of the distinction of the archbishop of Canterbury and scholar-bishops such as Ian Ramsey of Durham and Robert Mortimer of Exeter? A man of lesser principles would have muted his convictions.

If Leonard would not be silenced or be persuaded to conform he could at least be kept in his place, at Willesden. Moreover, in 1970 he was too young at 49 to move to a diocese. Such an expressed opinion hardly stands up when one considers that Mandell Creighton was 53 (1897), Arthur Foley Winnington-Ingram was 43 (1901) and Geoffrey Francis Fisher was 52 (1939) when appointed to London and none of these men was bound by the present retirement ruling of 70. Further, the archbishopric of York went to 44-year-old Cosmo Gordon Lang (1909) followed by William Temple who was 47 (1929) and Arthur Michael Ramsey was only 51 when he went to York. At the other end of the scale, Frederick Temple was appointed to Canterbury at the age of 75.

If Stopford had been ten years younger and remained in London would Leonard still have been at Willesden? Still the question persisted. What could the Church do with Leonard? His judgement might be questioned, but never his ability. His pastoral credentials for higher office were recognized. Nonetheless he was swimming against the tide. He was attempting to repel the waves of progress which were carrying the Church along into unchartered waters.

Another ploy by his detractors was to call him an extremist. Was he really an Anglican? Did he not lend his presence and his signature to extreme Anglo-Catholic organizations? Was there not a smack of triumphalism – and a receding Roman triumphalism at that – about him and his vesture: mitre, crozier, gloves and gremial? He did appear very much as an Anglo-Catholic, in an historical party sense: that distinct brand of Anglican which, often despite protestations, exhibits an introverted, self-conscious, idiosyncratic version of Catholicism. It was also the distinct brand which produced Catholic sages of the past such as fearless fighter Frank Weston, bishop of Zanzibar. Such fighters were also men of deep spirituality. And it must not be forgotten that the criticism does not make sense when it is known how well regarded he was by many leading Evangelicals.

This was not a man becoming prelatical, but a prelate with the poise and dignity belonging to his office. There were other considerations too. A future bishop of London might have his obedience, but would he have his support? He could become a rival focus for diocesan unity, or disunity, not by deliberate intention but by a swell of assent from people inside and outside his area. If all seemed negative in England, it did not mean that a call elsewhere could not be heard. In 1969 he was asked to stand for election as bishop of St Andrews, Dunkeld, and Dunblane, in Scotland, following the appointment of its bishop, John William Alexander Howe, as secretary general of the Anglican Consultative Council. The clergy voted for him but the laity did not.

In March 1969 the bishop of Bunbury, Ralph G. Hawkins, senior bishop of the province of Western Australia, wrote to see if Leonard would allow his name to go forward on a short list for the election of a new archbishop of Perth to succeed George Appleton who had become archbishop in Jerusalem. The bishop of Bunbury had not forgotten Leonard's significant contributions to the 'priesthood' committee of the 1968 Lambeth Conference, of which both were members. Leonard took advice and agreed to let his name go forward, although he made it clear that he would find it difficult to accept the office if he were elected by a narrow majority over an Australian candidate. It was not a wholehearted agreement for he was particularly anxious about his father and was not entirely happy about the income of the see which was very much less than he was receiving as bishop of Willesden.

Leonard's father was now 86, blind and crippled with arthritis. Although he was well looked after in a nursing home run by the Church of England Pensions Board, Leonard wanted to give him the choice between going to Perth with him or staying in England. Although mentally he was in remarkably good health he needed general nursing care and had to be helped to dress, wash and bathe.

At the first meeting of the Conjoint Committee no election was made from the short list and the committee started *de novo*. At the second meeting it was deferred again and Leonard heard no more. In 1970 Leonard was on the sub-committee for the appointment of the new general secretary of the United Society for the Propagation of the Gospel (USPG) and was the person who proposed the energetic and imaginative bishop of North Queensland, Ian Wootton Allnut Shevill. In that sense he was responsible for creating a vacancy in North Queensland and received his just deserts in a letter from the officials of that diocese asking him to allow his name to go forward. They wanted a man of Leonard's known pastoral gifts who had said in an interview following his consecration as bishop that the role of the bishop in the modern world was the same essentially as it was in the early church, namely, that of caring for the clergy and the parishes. They also wanted an experienced bishop in the Queensland province who would strengthen the province itself and the national Church. The tendency for the voices of small dioceses to be ignored or lost among the cacophony of the larger dioceses had to be reversed. North Queensland reckoned that with a voice like Leonard's the Church would be militant. He was in fact elected, but decided that he could neither take his ailing father nor leave him behind, so he declined.

Changes in the London diocese were occurring at this time. The diocese had long been unmanageable episcopally, pastorally and administratively. Robert Stopford was still bishop, and in 1969 he had the help of three 'residential' suffragan bishops – Kensington, Willesden and Stepney – plus the bishop of Fulham with his responsibilities for chaplaincies in northern and central Europe. The system was being worked strictly according to the book: Stopford was diocesan, and his suffragans were that, and no more. Nobody was happy about the arrangement. Stopford's work load was colossal and he could not in any genuine way be 'the bishop' to people in Staines, Highgate and Tower Hamlets. For the laity and for the majority of clergy their bishop was the local suffragan. Although Stopford may not by temperament have been a remote figure a multitude of important commitments made him inaccessible.

It was never Stopford's style to make unilateral moves. When he saw the need for change he liked to work towards it from within the boundaries laid down by the existing system. This necessarily meant that the moves were slow but they were sure, and the smallest possible number of people

LAKELAND

Webbs of Wychbold
Worcester Road
Worcester
WR9 0DG
Tel : 01527 861 001

```
****************************************
*************** REFUND ***************
****************************************
```

24504	SOFT TOUCH T x-1	-£19.99

TOTAL	-£19.99
Cash	£0.01
Card	£19.98

Card   : VISA DEBIT
Number : ***********4453   SWIPED

Goods   :   £19.98

got hurt. Yet operating in this way of progress by stealth casts shadows and awakens suspicions. It is not the way to coordinate a mixed team.

The bishop of Kensington was Ronald Cedric Osbourne Goodchild, whom Stopford had brought from his previous diocese of Peterborough. Goodchild was warm, approachable, ambitious. Like all new suffragans he owed his purple cassock to the diocesan. He recognized his debt to Stopford and to some extent was chained by it. It is one of the many drawbacks of the method of appointing *suffragan* bishops. The Kensington area was huge (larger than quite a number of dicoeses) and Goodchild hoped that his episcopate there would be a prelude to a diocesan appointment. But he found himself ensnared by his loyalty. In terms of appointment he was the senior suffragan. Stopford was cagey to the point of being shifty about giving any indication of his own retirement date (in 1970 he was 69) and did not treat his team fairly in this regard.

The bishop of Stepney, since 1968, was Ernest Urban Trevor Huddleston, who made no secret of the fact that he had left his heart in Africa. True, he was soon saying that if he had to be anywhere in England the East End was certainly the place for him, but nonetheless Stepney was a second best. And he found the system irksome. Africa had shaped him and equipped him to be intolerant of administrative procedures which were slow and legalistic. Stopford cannot have found him an easy colleague. Huddleston was too impatient for Stopford, and Stopford too cautious for Huddleston. Apart from their common Catholic background, temperament and outlook Leonard and Huddleston were too dissimilar to have much in common or even regard for each other.

The bishop of Fulham was Alan Francis Bright Rogers. He had been a parish priest in Twickenham and Hampstead before being consecrated bishop of Mauritius in 1959. In 1966 he was brought to Fulham and when Stopford perceived that the pastoral care of the diocese would be furthered by the setting up of a fourth episcopal area, Edmonton, in 1970, Rogers moved from Fulham to Edmonton. Rogers' successor as bishop of Fulham was 45 year old John Richard Satterthwaite who, a year later in 1971, became bishop of

95

Gibraltar. Edmonton was carved out of parts of Willesden and Kensington, and Leonard wondered whether it was right to remain at a reduced Willesden or whether to ask to be translated to Edmonton. He decided to remain at Willesden.

Any estimate of Leonard's influence throughout the London diocese at this time needs to keep in mind the other bishops. In 1970 Stopford was 72 (after resigning he went on to be vicar general in Jerusalem from 1974–6, and then bishop of Bermuda); Rogers was 63 (he retired from Edmonton in 1975, was an assistant bishop of Peterborough for a further nine years before returning to London in 1985 at the age of 78 and becoming an assistant bishop); Goodchild was 60 (retired from Kensington ten years later); Huddleston was 57 but the Anglican communion had not finished with him. At the age of 65 he was elected bishop of Mauritius and then archbishop of the Indian Ocean until retirement brought him back to London (not to Mirfield) at the age of 70. And Leonard? In 1970 he was still only 49. Among his colleagues he had always been the bright boy. He did not have Huddleston's aching heart or Goodchild's growing sense of disappointment. He had climbed quickly and nobody could be in any doubt that he was still climbing. There was a feeling that there was a considerable future for him provided that he made the most of Willesden, which he did. We have seen how hard he worked and how he was both respected and loved by clergy and laity alike. He had never hidden or neutralized his Catholic position and the Evangelicals, once they had overcome an instinctive suspicion, found him sympathetic. Stopford admired and appreciated Leonard's quick and agile brain, even if at times it left him several mental paces behind. Further, Leonard's sense of humour (to an extent shared by John Gordon Eastaugh, archdeacon of Middlesex) was welcome where it was a scarce commodity, namely, at Fulham Palace staff meetings. Relations between Stopford and Leonard were unsatisfactory. How could they be otherwise with one leading the other opposing in the Anglican–Methodist controversy. Leonard owed his purple to Stopford yet he was never beholden to any man. There was always the independence of the loner in his character. Superficially Stopford and Leonard had a workmanlike arrangement but there was no trust. The manipulative twists of Stopford – and he was skilfull at them – were not for Leonard.

Throughout Leonard's episcopate at Willesden, he had ample opportunity to review, whilst an active participant, the role of the suffragan bishop. His experience under Stopford was that pastoral responsibility was delegated substantially but informally. No legal responsibility was delegated. Full staff meetings took place almost every week, but only on two occasions in the period 1964 to 1970 did the bishops meet separately, once for a residential meeting. It was in 1970 that an experimental area scheme was introduced (Kensington, Willesden, Stepney and Edmonton, with the bishop of London having episcopal care of the churches in the cities of London and Westminster). Although it had no legal backing, the degree of delegation was substantial; the diocesan bishop accepting decisions of the area bishops and endorsing them, although legally they remained his responsibility. Leonard was always clear that the position of the suffragan bishop who is no more than an episcopal curate is theologically indefensible. But there was never any danger of anyone mistaking Leonard for an episcopal curate!

An exceptionally large number of changes were taking place on the episcopal benches at this time. Leonard was not alone in regretting the kind and type of man who was being elevated to the episcopate. When someone was nominated who was unashamedly committed to our Lord and to his word in scripture Leonard rejoiced and on being asked for advice responded in this way (June 1971):

First, you must feed the flock with the word of God. The utterances of many bishops, as reported, seem to consist largely of either lamentations about the conditions of the Church or country or their thoughts about important but secondary and temporal matters. I think this is the result very often of a misguided notion that the world will take notice and think that the Church is trying to be efficient or relevant. But the Church must never try and justify itself to the world on the world's terms. Further, I believe that such an attitude seriously misjudges the world – which though it may reject the Church, still expects it to speak of God. It was significant that the local papers reported

97

those parts of my inaugural sermon to the new Willesden area which spoke unequivocally of the Gospel, whereas it was the *Church Times* which simply reported relatively trivial details of the service. You will get many opportunities to speak on secular occasions. Take them and use them to speak of our Lord. I find that if one does so, the most unlikely people will come and say, 'Thank God you spoke as a bishop' or 'as a Christian'. Many of the clergy have given up trying to teach and I believe that a bishop must show them by example, how to teach the faith and prove that people will listen and some be converted.

Secondly, the introduction of synodical government has made it imperative that a bishop should try and enable his people to see that what must control our deliberations is the mind of Christ and this is revealed to us through scripture, which cannot be disregarded or modified to suit the mind of contemporary man. I have found it essential both in my area synod and when meeting with deanery synods to begin discussions of many subjects by a time of Bible study. Otherwise, one meets either appeals to the criterion of sociology, business efficiency etc, or an unbiblical appeal to the inspiration of the Spirit that disregards what the Spirit has said in Scripture. In other words, I believe that bishops have a pressing and urgent responsibility to get synods to think in terms of what is true instead of in terms of what will work.

Thirdly, bishops must not only care but be seen to care and be known to care. . . .

How was Leonard regarded as the bishop of Willesden? He started out with a determination that his chief priority was to be a bishop, and to be seen to be such. Here was a chance of working out in practice what he had always known in theory but had not much witnessed in bishops he had known. There were contradictions and paradoxes in his personality which were evident at Willesden. Some of the strengths and weaknesses would remain constant, others would diminish and yet others flourish and increase. But it is worth recording a few haphazard reflections which come from this period. The pastoral care of the clergy was paramount. His clergy knew it was there all the time, not just when it was needed: 'I remember feeling that he was the first bishop I could relate to'; 'When I was in trouble he opened me up, examined what he saw and put me back together again but this time each part was in its right place.' If laity complained about their parish priest the priest in question knew he would have Leonard's support, and only if it was obvious the priest could not be supported would he find a harsher, but no less pastoral, bishop. Clergy widows received very special care at the time of the death of their husbands. Leonard worked himself very hard, too hard. He set himself high standards and expected high standards from his priests. When displeased, he could be very fierce.

Leonard had an intellectual grasp of problems and an analytical mind which made punctiliousness natural to him. But this meant that he could appear forbiddingly legalistic. The analytical mind was also an intuitive and impulsive one which was good in its intentions, but sometimes defective in its insights and then unfortunate in its effects. His assessment of people was erratic. He too easily accepted people on their own estimate, which led to some strange appointments. This too was deceptive for it could be the pastor at work behind the scenes giving someone a second or even a third chance. The pastoral heart throbbed for people.

Leonard's preaching varied as did its reception. It had not the freedom, directness and vivacity of conversation. 'The bishop's concern for theological truth was real and widely valued but sometimes this seemed obscurantist and over-academic'; 'The sermon brought the faith to life for me'; 'I found his preaching difficult'; 'He preached quite simply and directly about Jesus'; 'I found his semons uninspiring and unintelligible'; 'He was a great inspiration'. Strong and clear leadership was given even if it was not always followed. The issues of the time provoked him and he showed courage in the face of adverse criticism often vitriolically expressed when he believed (nay knew) himself to be right over an issue. 'Knew' was the word that riled opponents. And he was not a man who gave up easily. He would cling to an issue like a limpet. What people did not see were the doubts, hesitations and forebodings which he experienced within himself *en route* to certainty. His answers and his stances were not ready made, taken from text books. He worked them out for himself, taking counsel as desired and necessary.

There was a sense of humour and fun which was evident when he was relaxed. And there was the image and evidence of the devoted husband, father, and by now grandfather. Was there a constant picture? Yes: the priest at the altar surrounded by and leading his people in worship.

There has been much speculation about Leonard's appointment to Truro in 1973, and what was regarded as the failure to secure him for London in that year. Rather less attention has been paid to other vacant bishoprics, some of which would have been pre-eminently suitable for him and the diocese concerned. We shall see why he suddenly seemed right for Truro and not for the other bishoprics. Between 1971 and 1973 the bishopric which fell vacant by retirement, death or translation included Chelmsford, Norwich, Oxford, Guildford, Peterborough, Salisbury and Exeter in the province of Canterbury; and Durham, Blackburn, Bradford, Carlisle, Newcastle and Sheffield in the province of York. These are in addition to Truro and London.

If one discounts those in the northern province where Leonard had never served and focuses on the southern province, then why Truro, and not one of the other sees? He could be denied a see of his own so long as Stopford remained bishop of London. But if London was to be denied him when Stopford retired he would have to be placed but preferably exiled away from London. Circumstances were fortuitous. Three dioceses had had a majority of clergy who voted against the Anglican–Methodist scheme in the 1969 referendum: London: 430 for, 454 against, 13 abstentions; Peterborough: 118 for, 147 against, 9 abstentions; Truro: 108 for, 118 against, 1 abstention.

Robert Stopford announced his retirement at the conclusion of the diocesan synod on 19 November 1972, to take effect on 11 June 1973. John Maurice Key, bishop of Truro, announced his retirement to take effect on 31 August 1973.

By a Church Assembly resolution in 1965 it had been directed that there should be a 'Vacancy in See' committee in each diocese, consisting of the suffragan bishops, the dean or provost of the cathedral, the archdeacons, together with the elected proctors in convocation and the elected members of the (national) House of Laity and 'such other persons chosen so as to ensure that each archdeaconry is adequately represented and that there are an equal number of clerical and lay members', and 'that it should be for the diocesan registrar to summon this body upon notice of any diocese becoming vacant in order that it might prepare a statement of the needs of the diocese and transmit it for the consideration of the archbishops with the request that they shall forward a copy of it to the prime minister'.

In the 1965 assembly debate, an amendment to require the vacancy in see committee to discuss names was defeated, but Archbishop Coggan said that 'he wished to make it clear that he was not against the discussion of names: the motion left the door open for the mention of names where that seemed right', a view shared by the archbishop of Canterbury.

There was always a general feeling that London would go to the bishop of Chester, Gerald Alexander Ellison. Equal to that feeling was a determination on the part of many people that the right man for London was not a former bishop of Willesden (Ellison had been at Willesden from 1950–55) but the present bishop, Graham Leonard. His very considerable and wide body of supporters felt London needed a spiritual leader after Stopford. Moreover, Leonard would establish good Evangelical–Catholic working relations. Evangelical leaders such as John Stott, Peter Johnston and Norman Anderson would welcome Leonard. On the national scale he would be an antidote to the harmless nonentities who never put a foot wrong, but, equally, who hardly count for much in terms of spiritual outreach. Of course there would be risks. Leonard had never been part of the Establishment. Nor was he in the pockets of the Anglo-Catholic 'establishment', whatever some of its leaders may have thought. He had an independent strain in his personality. Leonard could not help but know that he was being actively 'promoted' by clergy and laity and some members of Parliament. Edward Heath was prime minister and probably not as interested or well informed as, say, Harold Macmillan or Margaret Thatcher. Leonard himself had to see the prime minister's appointments secretary, John Hewitt, to talk about the successor to the see of London and offer advice!

The vacancy in see committee met on 30 January 1973 at

St Andrew's Court House in the City, preceded by a celebration of the Holy Communion in St Andrew's church. Various matters were discussed. Later, in an article in the *Church Observer* (Spring 1974) one of the lay members elected by the diocesan synod, R. J. H. Edwards (now a Roman Catholic), wrote:

> Confidentiality was enjoined on members. Why? We know that confidentiality is much enjoyed by church officialdom (although rarely observed in my experience), but the authoritative debate of 1965 makes no mention of it. The meeting was attended by Mr Saumarez Smith and by Mr Carey the *provincial* registrar (apart from the London registrar as convenor). Why? Again the resolution of 1965 makes no mention of these two paid officials; nor can it be said that they sat as silent as the two church mice they had promised to be. Both intervened with advice at a point where the diocese's own elected representatives should have made up their own mind. . . . A great to-do was had on whether to discuss names (again in spite of the authoritative rulings in 1965): our visitors from outer space were not enthusiastic that we should. However, a majority vote agreed to do so, and it is interesting that virtually all members of the committee who had been (or thought they were going to be) separately consulted by an official whose office is not one hundred miles from Whitehall voted against names. By such means are attempts made to gag the elected committee in which the archbishops reposed such confidence in 1965.

A draft statement of the needs of the diocese was prepared, considered and completed at the second meeting of the committee on 5 February 1973. Leonard was asked not to come to this. In view of the subsequent appointment to the see, this statement is of some interest. The diocese at the time contained about 550 parishes and approximately 1000 clergy. The population was about six million people and in topograhy it was almost entirely urban. It was considered essential that the experiment of a diocese divided into episcopal *areas* since 1970 should be carried forward and brought to fruition under the next bishop. 'It is generally desired that a new bishop should seek to create a quasi-provincial structure, perhaps consisting of autonomous dioceses along the general lines of the episcopal areas, but being serviced by central agencies. It would seem, therefore, that a new bishop will have to consider the creation of a structure hitherto unknown in the Church of England.' What kind of bishop did the diocese desire?

(a) *Qualities needed*. Whilst it is desirable that he should be a good administrator, above all it is essential that he should be a spiritual leader with pastoral gifts in relationship to others. In particular, he will need to be deeply conscious of his role as the senior pastor in a college of bishops. It will also be necessary that he should be a man of vision and flexibility, open to new ideas and with an ability to speak with a prophetic voice and make the best use of contemporary means of communication.

(b) *Capabilities*. He must be a man capable of seeing that the task to which the new bishop of London is appointed is one different from that to which any previous bishop of London has been called. It will be for him to lead the diocese in the creation of new structures and the extension of the existing experiment with all the tensions and differing opinions which this is bound to involve. He must also have the ability to delegate.

Although he need not necessarily be an academic theologian, he should have an ability to show people how to expound the faith. This is especially needed in the large urban areas where the Church is at present losing ground to the claims of a materialistic society, and also in those circles where there is a desire for a spirituality relevant to contemporary life.

Whilst a bishop of London is bound to have a position of considerable national significance, he should primarily be chosen as the chief pastor of the diocese.

(c) *Age*. If the committee's assessment of the work of a new bishop of London is correct, then clearly a man should be appointed capable of giving at least ten years of creative and vigorous service to the diocese. Preferably he should be in his early 50s.

(d) *Churchmanship*. In a diocese as diverse as the present diocese of London, there are many shades of churchmanship but recent indications have revealed that the diocese has not inclined towards a radical theological outlook. It is essential, therefore, that the new bishop, whilst he would be expected to have positive theological views of his own, should be a man who can work with sympathy and understanding in a variety of traditions.

(e) *Experience.* Because the task confronting anyone appointed to the diocese of London demands a background of wide experience it is desirable that he should have considerable knowledge of parish work. Whilst it is appreciated that the bishop of London is normally chosen from among the existing diocesan bishops it is not thought essential that this should be so.

Leonard's mitre was a perfect fit for most of these needs while some of them seemed to deny the possibility of Gerald Ellison being considered. As has often been the way with Leonard, his greatest support came from parish clergy and laity. The diocesan hierarchy were almost uniformly against him.

Inside the vacancy in see committee (clergy and laity) and outside in the diocese, there was a groundswell of support for Leonard as the next bishop. Pressure on the prime minister and his appointments secretary was consistent and insistent. But in the established hierarchy of the Church of England Leonard was not popular. The question was, could he be ignored? It was generally felt that Gerald Ellison would at last move from Chester but how could a 62-year-old go to London when the vacancy in see committee was clear that a younger man was required with qualities and capabilities very different (not necessarily better) from Ellison's? The real scandal was that Ellison, a very able bishop, had been left at Chester for 18 years. Ellison had absorbed the ideas of a former bishop of London, Charles James Blomfield; and one of the most influential archbishops of York, Cyril Forster Garbett (to whom Ellison had been chaplain), remained his exemplar. Although Ellison has always looked the Establishment man *par excellence* he had many independent views and was prepared to voice them on some reforms being pushed through the Church Assembly. His interventions in radical causes were the more effective because of his innate conservatism. He was not easily labelled.

Leonard could not help but know what was happening on his behalf, but he neither countenanced nor encouraged it. Of course, he would have liked London but he accepted the probability that his views would preclude a move. At the same time it was recognized that it would be difficult for a new bishop of London to have Leonard as an 'area bishop' of Willesden. In April 1973 the future was known. Leonard heard that Ellison would be going to London and he would be offered the bishopric of Truro. Once decided, action was quick. The formal letter from the prime minister (Edward Heath) was dated 15 April 1973 and couched in the usual phrases: 'I have come to the conclusion that I could not do better than to submit your name to Her Majesty for this important appointment.' Truro is more interesting than important. Leonard ascertained that the appointment had the good will of the archbishop of Canterbury (Michael Ramsey) and replied to the prime minister the following day (26 April) accepting the offer. 'My prayer will be that I may be a faithful pastor to the diocese and be enabled to further the cause of true religion.'

If the authorities thought they would satisfy all parties by announcing the appointment of Ellison to London and Leonard to Truro on the same day, 15 May, they were mistaken. *The Times* headline, 'Selection of new Bishop of London seen as an affront to diocesan hopes', was a mild way of expressing the anger of many people in the diocese. One of the lay members of the General Synod, who was on the vacancy in see committee, C. Peter Dixon, committed the Establishment sin of breaking ranks and secrecy by writing a letter to *The Times* (21 May) wondering why the diocese was asked its views when they appeared to have been ignored. There was a fuss and much correspondence, which tended to be personal rather than principled. On the whole it had the effect of producing a surprising number of unsought testimonies for Ellison. Yet when the greater chapter of St Paul's Cathedral met on 25 June, eight members refused to vote formally in favour of the Crown's choice of their next bishop. There were Prebendaries Harold Riley of St Augustine, Kilburn, George Oakley of Willesden, Henry Cooper of St George's, Bloomsbury, John Pearce of St Paul, Homerton, G. A. Lewis Lloyd of Chiswick, Ronald Arthur of St Clement,

Finsbury, R. Peter Johnston of Islington, and S. J. S. Beebee of Cranford. Five of these priests had been members of the vacancy in see committee.

The London controversy set light to a larger issue: how much longer could the State's control over the selection of the Church's leaders be maintained? We know the answer for the moment: a long time. But it was seriously under question as it was again in 1974 when the archbishop of Canterbury retired. In organizational terms the Church seemed to be in a mess. Why was there no one, or even a trio of obvious candidates, for the succession? The people who were mentioned were still ripening, or had no wide support or recognized gifts of leadership. Accordingly, the mantle fell on Frederick Donald Coggan, archbishop of York, who was regarded as a 'caretaker' archbishop! For whom? Leonard was not disappointed at Canterbury being in the hands of someone who had the mission of the Church for evangelism so much at heart, though if a caretaker had to be appointed he would have preferred Ronald Williams of Leicester.

With Coggan at Canterbury Leonard hoped that there would be a balance of churchmanship between Canterbury and a new man at York. He was hoping for someone at York whose approach would be that of Catholic orthodoxy. What he meant by that phrase is both arresting and revealing. If the balance was to be kept it was not so much a matter of 'High' as compared with 'Low' as of balancing a liberal approach with an orthodox one. Coggan was no radical but neither was he a conservative in the way that Leonard may be regarded. In many matters, Coggan represented the liberal Evangelical tradition on such issues as marriage and divorce and the ordination of women, on which Evangelicals were divided. It was possible then, and is prevalent now, for a man to be quite happy with High Church ways and at the same time hold radical views which are not characteristic of the Anglican position and which are quite different from the true radicalism which follows if orthodoxy is implemented fearlessly.

In Leonard's judgement Coggan and the Church needed someone at York who would have the confidence of the Catholic element in the Church of England and who would have it because he was willing to learn from the wisdom of the

Church in the past and did not imagine that the answer was always to be found in something new. In short, Coggan's approach needed to be complemented by an orthodox approach rather than by a radical one, however 'High'. Coggan's concern for the moral life of the Church was laudable but if it was to bear fruit he needed to be supported by someone who would emphasize that belief is prior to behaviour and that the reaffirmation of orthodox doctrine in a way which is understood was one of the greatest needs of the Church. That is pure Leonard. In a different way it was also Ronald Williams of Leicester. But it was Stuart Yarworth Blanch who was translated from Liverpool to York. Leonard had already gone to Truro.

9

Bishop Benson's Legatee

History, adventure and romance fill that land we now call Cornwall. This is where Leonard was going as bishop of Truro, and for all he knew it was likely he would retire from that place. He has a feel for place, a sense of history and the romantic. He is emotional, even if he keeps his emotions mostly, but not always, under control. What mingled associations would greet him! St David, St Mewan, St Teilo and St Essey carried the message of the Gospel from Wales. Irish missionaries such as St Piran and St Buriena had made and left their marks there. From Brittany and other places across the water had come St Breock, St Mylor and St Budock. The early effect of Christianity in Cornwall was haphazard and local. As in Ireland and Scotland, bishops had no fixed sees. They visited rather than ruled districts occupied by particular clans. Not until 833 did any bishop in Cornwall make a profession of obedience to an archbishop of Canterbury, and then to Ceolnoth of Canterbury. It was more than 100 years later that Conan, bishop of Cornwall, became, as it were, an English diocesan bishop.

All over Cornwall the rich legacy of its independent past is contained in its place names. More villages carry the name of the local saint, the bishop who brought the Christian faith to that place or made it live for ever, than in any other part of England. Down the ages Cornwall gradually lost its own bishop, but never its independence. By 1027 the bishop was bishop of Crediton and Cornwall but a few years later, in 1050, it was transferred to Exeter. Until Henry Phillpotts was bishop of Exeter (1831–69) the Cornish portion of the Exeter diocese was neglected or ignored. Phillpotts reversed the trend and saw the need for an independent bishropric. In 1847 a bill was introduced into Parliament for the founding of four new bishoprics including one for Cornwall with the cathedral in Bodmin. The bill failed. It was left to Frederick Temple, bishop of Exeter (1869–85), to revive the issue and to raise the endowment which led to the passing of the Truro Bishopric Act in 1876. Who would breathe life into a new diocese? Who would be capable of understanding and appreciating the idiosyncracies of Cornish history and the individuality of the Cornish race? More recently there had been the strong influence of John Wesley, and dissent was stronger than the Established Church in many places. Who could counter this and give a strong lead in sound churchmanship? A priest of vigour, ability and certainty was required.

Into the new see of Truro, 1877, swept Edward White Benson from Lincoln, where he had been chancellor and canon residentiary. He had everything that was required, and more. Aged 47, he had energy and vision. There was scholarship too; his *magnum opus* was *Cyprian, his Life, his Times, his Works* (1892). His approach to everything he tackled was a religious one. He sought a principle to give coherence to a policy. Fostering the growth of spiritual vitality was always to the fore. It was sensible to appoint a Tractarian in reaction to the strong and politically-minded Methodism then prevalent. Benson loved historical parallels and knew how to use them in tandem. Hence he was able to inspire the building of a new cathedral worthy of the great mediaeval ones, yet in a proportion right for Truro.

Benson is mentioned here because it has often been said that Leonard was heir to Walter Howard Frere, bishop of Truro (1923–35); that is, however, a superficial assessment. They were both Anglo-Catholics, though their expression of it differed. Frere was a member of the Community of the Resurrection. He was a monk *tout court*. An aristocrat to his finger tips, he had distinction in his bearing and charm in his manners. He was attuned to the Celtic atmosphere and was ready to foster Cornish studies. Frere's great gift to the Church was his liturgical scholarship for which he had a European reputation. He was also an accomplished musician. Frere had the advantage of following Frederic Sumpter Guy Warman (1919–23), an Evangelical with a liberal slant. He had been the wrong bishop for Truro and moved to Chelmsford in 1923 and to Manchester in 1929.

Leonard, Benson's legatee, succeeded John Maurice Key
who had been bishop of Truro since 1960. Key was used to
country life as a parish priest and as suffragan bishop of
Sherborne (Salisbury) before moving to Truro. He was
middle of the road in most things, seeking to hold the balance
between all extremes. There was a touch of 'county' about
him too, in a county that had a few influential families and
titled people. What Leonard would have thought of Key had
he seen him presiding at his last synod wearing baggy trousers
and a shabby alpaca coat is best left to the imagination.

The dean of Truro since 1960 was Henry Morgan Lloyd.
An ex-naval chaplain, awarded a DSO and ten years as dean
of Gibraltar before moving to Truro, he had good relations
with Bishop Key. Prior to Lloyd's appointment the office of
dean had been held by the diocesan bishop, the day to day
work being exercised by the sub-dean. Henry Lloyd had firm
views about the place of the cathedral in the life of the diocese
and his place in the cathedral. His bishop was not one to
interfere. The bishop may appoint the canons, but the Crown
appoints the dean! That was Maurice Key. Then came
Graham Leonard. Henry Lloyd writes:

> When all the various consultations required had taken
> place, in a final talk between the dean and chapter and the
> prime minister's appointments secretary, the name of the
> suffragan bishop of Willesden was mentioned as a possible
> candidate. Perhaps due to the fervent churchmanship of
> the founding bishops and the Cornish Celtic sense of the
> numinous the diocese generally had an inherent awareness
> of its Catholic heritage. So although Graham Leonard was
> well known to be an Anglo-Catholic with some very
> strongly held views, it aroused no disagreement on account
> of his reputation as a dedicated spiritual and pastoral
> leader. His name had already received some discussion in
> general terms and it seemed that his election by the general
> chapter would not arouse any controversy. Eventually some
> anxiety was expressed lest his appointment might mean a
> possibly extreme swing of the pendulum.

And so to Cornwall with Bishop Graham Truron:

> The railway line from Paddington to Penzance is to my

mind the most beautiful and striking in the country. From it can be seen prehistoric monuments in the Vale of Pewsey, five castles, the mysterious Tor at Glastonbury, two white horses cut in the chalk. You cross Sedgemoor full of historical associations, travel along the dramatic stretch by the sea at Dawlish and brush through the rhodedendrons along the Glynn Valley. Yet for me the most spendid and dramatic moment of which I never tire, is when you come along the viaduct into Truro and see the cathedral springing up from the city with its three spires pointing heavenwards.

This was to be the theme of his enthronement sermon and of his episcopate.

The enthronement took place within the setting of the Eucharist in the cathedral church of the Blessed Virgin Mary in Truro on the feast of St Michael and All Angels, 29 September 1973. For his sermon he used the illustration of John Baptist Vianney, more familiarly known as the Curé d'Ars, to telling effect. Vianney arrived in his parish with his goods in an ox-cart and when a shepherd boy gave him directions he replied, 'You have shown me the way to Ars; I will show you the way to Heaven'. Leonard recognized that he would have to ask his way in Cornwall, and would not be ashamed to do so. If they showed him the way, he would try to show them the way to heaven.

Perhaps that sounds to you rather old-fashioned, even a little arrogant. Old-fashioned it may be, but none the worse for that at a time when the Church is so earthbound and seems to have lost the vision of eternity. Arrogant? No, unless we have fallen into the modern error of supposing that we can only preach what we imagine we have fully understood. We, bishops, priests and people are commanded to proclaim the everlasting Gospel which has been revealed by God. We have to commend the faith which was delivered to the saints and which we have received. We do so joyfully yet with awe for we are handling the burning coals of the Love of God. . . . So, I ask you to show me the way to your hearts that I may know you and love you in Christ and show you the way to Heaven – that is to eternal happiness.

He did not say that people would float to Heaven on a cloud of bliss. The Christian is called 'to suffer with Christ if we are to be glorified with him'. Suffering was never far from Leonard's thoughts. He was emotionally affected by the news of the assassination of Janani Luwum, archbishop of Uganda. He had met the archbishop and made no secret of his own concern lest he might fail in the event of persecution and torture.

Leonard's challenge was also a command: 'to live to the glory of God and to proclaim his Gospel. We shall only do so if we are ourselves responding to this Love, acting on his promises with a clear vision of our eternal destiny and of our vocation to suffer. Then, and only then, shall we love others into the Kingdom. There is no other way. You cannot order, scold, bribe or frighten people into the Kingdom, you can only love them into it with a love which is of God, and therefore tender yet at times stern.' People left the enthronement service with different emotions and thoughts. It had been a dramatically inspiring occasion. Leonard knows how to walk in church: 'glide' is probably a better word. There was something special about his bearing which 'every inch a bishop' does not quite describe. It seemed natural, if astonishing to some, for clergy to genuflect to receive his blessing. What a contrast to Maurice Key. There would be no more baggy trousers in the diocese. Few people saw him in anything but cassock outside church. The sermon too was so different from anything that had been expected: delivered a little too slowly and portentously, it nonetheless prompted thought and reflection. They knew where they were being taken, but how? They would find out over the next few years.

Leonard was quick to decide on goals for his episcopate. He wanted to give the diocese some vision; he aimed to link isolated and apathetic Truro to the Church at large, and make the diocese face the question of finance. Truro Diocese covers the county of Cornwall, the isles of Scilly and one parish in Devon. Travel was not easy along country roads so relatively short distances took a great deal of time to cover.

If Leonard was going to be a Father in God he must have staff to assist him. His resident chaplain from Willesden came with him. The bishop's house, called Lis Escop, was not the greatest of joys. Its natural setting was one of beauty and

Priscilla slowly turned the garden into what was in the best tradition of Cornish gardening. The building itself was idiosyncratic, looking more like a cottage hospital than a family home, and approachable by car only. This had the unsuitable effect that the clergy did not drop in at the bishop's house as much as they might have done, and as Leonard would have liked them to have done. Yet he did know them very well and was very close to them. Not only was he close to the Catholics, but he had very fruitful friendships with some of the liberal and Evangelical priests.

Leonard needed diocesan as well as domestic assistance. His predecessor had the help of William Quinlan Lash, a former bishop of Bombay, as assistant bishop of Truro (1962–73). When Leonard arrived in Truro Cyril Edgar Stuart, a former assistant bishop of Uganda (and afterwards assistant bishop of Worcester) then living in St Austell offered his services. He was too old, having been priested in the year of Leonard's birth. A full-time bishop was needed and history and romance joined hands at this juncture. Was not St Germans one of the places named in the suffragan bishops' act of 1534? Had there not been bishops of Cornwall and St Germans in the distant past? In the recent past there had been a brief resuscitation of the bishopric when John Rundle Cornish was suffragan bishop of St Germans (1905–18).

Leonard decided to petition the Crown for the complete revival of this bishopric and his efforts were met with approval and success. Who should be the bishop of St Germans? To say that Leonard acted on impulse is only half the truth. It is a marked characteristic of the man. But he really believes that he is guided by God and so acts on his intuitions with enthusiasm. Where other people are involved, as often they are, it can be rather disconcerting, even alarming! Making appointments and decisions with clarity and directness are the actions of the essentially innocent. It is little wonder that there are many coincidences in his life, and they are of God. In October 1973 Cecil Richard Rutt, the talented bishop of Taejon, was well ahead with his plans for dividing his Korean diocese and having two Korean bishops selected. He wrote to two bishops in England saying that he would be looking for a job in England the following summer. One of these bishops was Leonard who, on the same day, had written to

Richard Rutt saying he understood he might be returning to England and enquiring of his interest in St Germans if the Crown approved the revival of the suffragan bishopric. Richard Rutt comments on the coincidence: 'Later this seemed par for the Cornish course. In Cornwall coincidences multiply and one gets used to the unusual. That was one reason why both Graham and I were so happy there.'

It was an inspired appointment. Richard Rutt was a Japanese interpreter with the Royal Navy and had read Modern Languages at Pembroke College, Cambridge. Trained for the priesthood at Kelham (the Society of the Sacred Mission) he soon answered a call to be a missionary priest in Korea where he identified himself completely with the people of Korea. He had become an authority on Korean literature and in 1964 he was awarded the Tasan Cultural Award for his writings on Korea. He was quite soon at Leonard's side and invested as bishop of St Germans on 23 May 1974. These two men had all the essentials of the faith in common, but otherwise they complemented one another. Richard Rutt's linguistic skills were not lost on his return to England for he recalls:

> Graham delighted in the work of the Cornish bards and the Cornish language enthusiasts. He hadn't time to get involved with either of these things and had not really the inclination to work hard enough at the language to do very much with it. He could however give the blessing in it and he and I together evolved an advisory board for services in the Cornish language which both guided the somewhat untidy and limited practice of public worship in Cornish, and also greatly encouraged those bards who had been looking for some kind of episcopal oversight. This was done with the cooperation of Methodist bards from the beginning. It culminated I suppose in the celebration of the first Eucharist in the Cornish language on St Piran's Day 1977. I was the celebrant.

Richard Rutt had become as fluent in Cornish as in Korean.

On 31 October 1978 the announcement came that Richard Rutt was to be the new bishop of Leicester. Again, Leonard's choice of a successor for Rutt was intuitive, impulsive and inspired – a surprise to those involved. This time it was a

Franciscan, well known throughout the Church of England as Brother Michael SSF (Reginald Lindsay Fisher). He was consecrated in St Paul's Cathedral, London, on St Mark's Day 1979. In both Richard Rutt and Brother Michael SSF Leonard had gathered to his side men of distinctive personality and gifts different from his own. Within the diocese it was said that the bishop of St Germans was soft on the outside and hard on the inside but that the opposite applied to the bishop of Truro. Indeed, with his eyes glinting behind gold-rimmed spectacles, a pectoral cross suspended on a gold chain, and the scarlet piping on his soutane, Leonard could indeed appear formidable. His public statements on moral issues seemed harsh, but his private care of particular men and women revealed a deep and generous understanding of human weakness, as well as a readiness to share in all the ways of reconciliation.

'Pastoral care' can so easily become a phrase devoid of meaning. It has to be given and it has to be felt. One incumbent was dying from asbestosis. As he became progressively worse, and his death was not too far distant, Leonard visited him two or three times a week and greatly assisted him in his departure from this life and preparation for the next. Another example concerned a priest who had deserted his wife and gone off with a woman in the parish. Leonard felt this acutely and tried very hard to effect a reconciliation. When that failed he went to great lengths to ensure that the deserted wife was financially sound and had somewhere to live. In another unfortunate incident a clergy wife had deserted her husband. Leonard left immediately to support the priest and then talked to the parochial church council stressing the importance of supporting their parish priest and thereby minimizing the damage in the parish. He has always been deeply concerned for the personal lives of his clergy and their families. The most powerfully consistent thing in his own personal life is his wife Priscilla, who so remarkably complements him. There is deep and manifest love and trust between them.

Canon Philip L. Maddock, treasurer of Truro Cathedral, adds an observation:

[Leonard] expected high standards from his clergy as

regards diligence, loyalty and pastoral zeal, and he was proud of those, the great majority, who fulfilled his expectations, the more so as he came to know the special pressures many of them bore in ministering, often single-handed, to scattered flocks, and often living on remote farms virtually inaccessible by public or private transport. If he was concerned with their quality as priests, so too he was always concerned about the quality of their living and working conditions. Above all, he was appreciated for the selfless way he ministered to his clergy and their families in times of personal difficulty, financial hardship, sickness or bereavement. It was commonplace for him to visit them at home and in hospital as occasion required, not infrequently at 'unacceptable' hours, often before his own long working day began, or well after it should normally have ended. Those who experienced this part of his ministry cannot speak too highly of the loving and sensitive way in which he supported them at such times. On at least one occasion, he was unashamedly weeping with the mourners at a Requiem Mass for a priest, who had died at an unusually early age.

It was this willingness to identify himself with people on all manner of occasions, joyful and tragic alike, that endeared him to people of all sorts of churchmanship and none. He has a great sense of fun and I can remember how frequently during special services in the cathedral, evidence of episcopal mirth would emanate from the throne.

Not every priest witnessed the fun and the humour, but most of them knew of the music. It was obligatory for visitors to Lis Escop to enjoy the music that Leonard enjoyed! The range was wide, but featured Elgar particularly and medieval music. He possessed a full range of recorders from sopranino to bass, which he played very attractively. This was one of his most important forms of relaxation and his joy in it was unfeigned. Many were the incumbents who looked forward to a visit from the bishop when this gave an opportunity to play recorders. On one occasion, when he discovered that a vicar, his wife and his daughters all played recorders his pastoral visit was delayed at the vicarage and he was late for all the carefully planned engagements which followed.

Leonard has always had a well-stocked workroom too. He has a good eye for a tool for metalwork or woodwork. In rare leisure moments he is happily occupied renovating old pieces of furniture or mending broken appliances. Richard Rutt comments that

It is hard to think of him without Priscilla. It is nearly as hard to describe the effect they had together. As hosts they were impeccable and whether one went by invitation or merely dropped in, the welcome was the same. He is in fact very much a family man, devoted to his sons and even more to his grandchildren. We all liked to see them coming because we knew there was a possibility he might get the rubber dinghy out and have the best part of a day on the Fal with them. It was one of the ways in which one could be sure that he would not overwork. His patriarchal blessing of each little child at bedtime, modestly done, was typical.

The parish visits, which had started at Willesden, became episcopal policy at Truro. The twice weekly visits were the most important and best-remembered features of Leonard's work there. Canon Richard Maynard, team rector of Saltash, writes:

Graham would go from cottage to farm, from elderly widows to classrooms full of mixed infants, with enthusiasm and interest in the lives and work of everyone he met. Old ladies were reluctant to let him go, and small children found him fascinating. He was at home talking to a housebound widow in her cottage, a nobleman in his mansion, or singing 'Pooh songs' with small children.

On his last pastoral visit to St Germans he visited Ernie Price. Ernie had had both his legs amputated and greeted the bishop from his bed. They swapped wartime experiences. Ernie told the bishop about waiting to be evacuated from Dunkirk. A few days later Graham's appointment to London was announced. 'I cannot believe that that man could find time to visit me, and stop and chat and drink tea in my home, when he must have known how much work he would have to do when he took up his new responsibilities'. That was Ernie's reaction when I went in to see him again the following week.

Leonard's progress in the parishes revealed a phenomenal memory for names. People remembered him and more to the point he remembered them and the occasion. Whilst witnessing the queen's birthday salute in Hyde Park in 1988 during another parish visit, a lady from the crowd introduced herself to Leonard. She knew him from a Truro parish visit. He remembered the occasion.

Leonard's experience in Truro strengthened his conviction that the parochial system should not be dismantled but re-established. Here in a rural diocese the parish priest had the realizable privilege of having the pastoral care of the whole community. In a paper written for a combined conference of the Parochial Clergy Assocation, the Anglican Association and the Prayer Book Society, and delivered in his absence in September 1976, Leonard said:

> At the same time he is also concerned with the building up of the body of Christ, leading it in worship, teaching the faithful. He is also the bearer of the Gospel and the enabler of the community within which the Gospel can be lived. This concept of pastoral care is one of the greater glories of the Church of England, which has survived the efforts of Erastians and Puritans to reduce it to one aspect or the other. The traditional role of the Anglican parson is to be distinguished from that of the French *curé*, who, while concerned with the parish is seen as primarily concerned with spiritual matters, and from that of the Reformed minister whose prime concern is with his own flock. It is a role which makes heavy demands upon those who are called to exercise it. It is a role which in my judgment reflects the true relationship between Church and society.

Leonard criticised any proposals that would undermine the confidence of the parochial clergy or unsettle the laity. His ideal was one priest for one parish. The gathering momentum for uniting benefices elsewhere in the country was anathema, a policy of defeat, in Truro. Whenever possible he challenged the assumption that (1) the 'gathered church' principle was the right one for a pluralist society, and (2) that it was a waste of money to spend it on rural parishes and that the Church's resources should be devoted substantially to the urban areas. It was faithless not to believe in a growing

Church. In Cornwall the population was rising. In the diocese the number of communicants, of confirmation candidates, and of those on the electoral rolls, was rising.

There began to be perceived and experienced a sense of renewal in the diocese. Leonard was everywhere, enjoyed mastering the geography of Cornwall and clocked up a high annual mileage as he developed knowledge of and affection for the countryside and coastline. There are many memorable pictures of him: reading a paperback translation of Thomas Aquinas while sitting on his suitcase waiting late at night at Paddington for a train to take him back to Truro; in his cassock leaning against a five-barred farm gate; with some Orthodox prelates visiting remote sea-girt shrines of Cornish saints; enjoying himself at the dinner of a theological club making merry about academic attempts to discover the origins of the 'other' bullock in *Judges* vi; giving a speech in which he emphasized his witticisms with much eyebrow play and a twinkling glance around the company to ensure the joke had been taken; recounting a funny anecdote, doubling up with laughter and slapping his thighs in an unforgettable gesture; consecrating far too much wine in an Evangelical parish and reacting with amusement to the vicar's comment that it was the first time the sacrament had been 'reserved' in that Evangelical church; insisting at an annual meeting of the Confraternity of the Blessed Sacrament, of which Leonard was episcopal patron, that the Angelus be sung rather than said (as the organizers had planned), and himself conducting an unofficial rehearsal of the congregation before the Mass with characteristic gusto; and making excellent elephants out of plasticine in an infant's school. The pictures could be multiplied many times. For the moment, just one more. While celebrating Mass and confirming at St Ives in 1979 on the Feast of Corpus Christi (a favourite feast), Leonard began to preach about the various feasts of the Church's year and of the particular importance and feeling of each. When he came to Corpus Christi he broke down completely, overcome by his thoughts. Afterwards he said that he thought he had made a fool of himself. He hadn't for it had given the congregation a special and privileged insight into his own devotion to the Blessed Sacrament.

Colour, ceremony and symbolism mean much to him;

pomp means nothing to him. He did not relish even the minor degree of pomp which was involved in the visit of the queen during her jubilee year although he richly enjoyed her visit and he has great admiration for her. Leonard would walk in procession smiling at those in the congregation who knew him, as he scattered blessings on them. He was never so happy as when a stray goat or other animal intruded upon his episcopal progress.

Before looking at diocesan progress and the chief events of his years at Truro it is important to refer once again to people's expectations and experiences of him. Leonard was and still is quite unlike the rigorous moralist that he is made out to be. The public face of an apparently hard and dogmatic disciplinarian and upholder of the letter of the law contrast sharply with the personal and private man who is a compassionate bishop and greatly caring pastor of clergy whom he believed God requires him to love and protect. That concern could, and frequently does, include loving them to the assurance of forgiveness and a new dignity of their humanity. But in it all, he has a very professional approach to priesthood and his episcopate. That is why he is concerned with correct ceremonial, and wearing the 'right' vestments. It is part of an almost fussy perfectionism, but at its best it is a facet of Leonard's professionalism. He never stops being a bishop, consciously, almost self-consciously, night and day. His clothes, when he is not in a cassock, are very relaxed but his cassocks are many and immaculate, reflecting his attitude to his vocation; after all, he is really always on the 'job' and dresses accordingly. At home he usually wears a plain black priest's cassock. Understanding all this as part of his vocation is important. He enjoys being a bishop because he wants to show a bishop's love for the flock. In his vesture and gesture there is a simplicity that is engaging. He enjoys it. He does not flaunt it and never uses it to emphasize rank.

Now we turn to diocesan progress and the chief events of his episcopate. Here we see Benson's legatee in glory. Benson's view of the Church, his care for the good order of the diocese, his pastoral concern for priests and his romantic response to Cornish tradition were all echoed in Leonard.

On his appointment to Truro there was some tart comment about his going to a county where Methodism was strong

This showed a double misunderstanding. The diocese of Truro had voted against the Anglican–Methodist scheme and the Methodist Church there was unique. It came in a variety of shades ranging from the Bible Christians, who were really independent revivalists, to Wesleyans, who regarded them-selves almost as a society within the Church, in accordance with the original ideas of John Wesley. Dual membership was common, that is, Communion was received at the parish church in the morning and evening service was attended in the local chapel. There was an established flavour about Methodism in Cornwall, for example, Leonard led the prayers for the county council alternately with the Methodist chairman. At the same time Leonard was regarded as 'our bishop' and referred to as such. Ecumenically there was a desire for the closest and happiest relations, without the blur-ring of identities. Leonard was careful not to make the mistake of his predecessor, Maurice Key, who, on his way home one night stopped for fish and chips in a small town. But he bought them from the wrong (chapel) shop – the Church of England chipshop was on the other side of the road!

The Roman Catholic priest in Truro (1976–83), Fr. Anthony Maggs, CRL, has this memory:

I invited him to preach in our church, our Lady of the Portal, for the feast of the Immaculate Conception. He came and gave a thoroughly orthodox address. As a souvenir of his visit he gave me a copy of *XV Devotions of Our Lady from Anglican Writers of the XVII Century*, with this inscription:

My Soul the Lord doth thank for on the Day
Men praise the Holy Virgin as the Way
Made sinless and the Highest of our Race.
Heaven's Portal call'd to be and full of Grace,
To Truro's shrine I went at Rome's behest
With ready Will not needing to be pressed
There Friendship I did gain without alloy
And this I give as Payment for my Joy.

Synodical government was hardly out of its nappies. Truro had a tradition of independence (and so had its bishop) and so was not much enamoured of this new, squalling infant. As it developed, Leonard was more content with its function and effectiveness within the diocese than at national level. Some of the most contentious issues confronting the Church were now before the diocesan synods. One of the first, on 26 October 1974, was the motion: 'That this synod considers that there are no fundamental objections to the ordination of women to the priesthood'. The voting was as follows: clergy: 24 for, 65 against; laity: 40 for, 51 against, 1 abstention; the bishop voted against the motion.

We leave this particular issue until a later chapter. On this and other controversial issues when Leonard's position was known and clear, how did he behave as a bishop in synod? The requirements of synodical government promised that theological matters must be debated by the whole Church, bishops, priests and laity. Moreover, as Leonard reminded his own diocesan synod, 'though the bishop can express his own judgment and take part in the debate, his own vote in the House of Bishops, does not count in the expression of the decision of his diocese. The votes of the houses of clergy and of Laity only are taken into account'. Canon Philip Maddock commented that 'Graham's handling of the diocesan synod was impressive, not least when comparatively unpopular or controversial matters were on the agenda, as for example when he first introduced to synod his proposal for a substantial increase in clerical stipends. Himself an able and forceful debater, it must have cost him a good deal to refrain from playing a more active part in debates; however, where so often he came into his own was in the closing stages of a debate, in the forming of motions, where the choice of words was critical.'

We are back to the critical confusion of a Church that is episcopally led and synodically governed. In an age of instant remedies history is likely to show that synodical government was rushed through without taking into account the strengths and blunders of such 'government' in other provinces of the Anglican communion. Nothing substantial or significant changed at the bureaucratic centre in Westminster.

However, Leonard had to make it work in Truro. There were those who wanted an inspiring lead, that is, a bishop who would confirm them in their convictions or prejudices. How surprised they were when their 'hero' bishop confronted them with issues which they must face, rather than answers they must accept and directions they must heed. In a paper on 'Bishops and Synodical Government' Leonard gives a thoughtful explanation of his position, which has not changed. What he says helps us to understand his actions.

(1) *Apostolic mission and authority*. It is the function of the bishop to point to our Lord as the source and head of the Church. This he will do not merely by teaching, but but the emphasis which he gives, not least in his own spiritual life, to worship, the sacrament, prayer and meditation.

(2) *Guarding against erroneous doctrine*. As is well known, the ecumenical statements of the faith in the first five centuries, to which the Church of England in its formularies gives special weight, were hammered out in the face of heresies and to a large extent occasioned by them. The same process should motivate the bishops and the Church in the necessary re-expression of those statements in contemporary terms at successive periods in the life of the Church. It is the function of the bishop to discern and expose those attitudes and ideas in the thought of his age which are compatible with Christian truth and those which are not, and so be able to give guidance on the application of Christian truth to contemporary problems. To speak only of guarding against error can give the impression that the bishop has to exercise a purely preservative and uncreative function, whereas seen in its fulness it is a highly demanding and creative activity.

(3) *Representing the unity and universality of the Church*. In this respect the bishop should have regard to both unity and universality in time as well as in space. Regard for the former is especially necessary in an age which puts novelty at a premium and assumes that the Church in the 20th century has received singular gifts of the Holy Ghost. The witness of history as well as the wisdom of the Fathers and other great Christian thinkers must be allowed to contribute to the bishop's mind.

(4) *Pastoral care*. The purpose of pastoral care is often described in the words of *Ephesians* as equipping the saints for service but it is not so often remembered that the purpose for which they are to be equipped is for the

building up of the body of Christ until 'we all reach unity in the faith and in the knowledge of the Son of God and become mature, attaining the full measure of perfection found in Christ'. In other words, the purpose of pastoral care is the same as that of synodical government. It is for this reason that the quality of pastoral care exercised by those involved in such government has a direct effect upon its healthy operation. It is significant that in the tenth chapter of St John the points which are stressed about our Lord as the Good Shepherd are first his authority, and second his knowledge of the sheep and their response to him.

(5) *Ordination and appointments*. The direct effect of these functions upon synodical government is not so great though it must be noted that in the earliest times the bishop was given a distinctive responsibility in these spheres which he exercised after consultation with what would now be regarded as the synodical body.

Leonard's theological understanding of synodical government would have led him quite naturally to use his *cathedra* as a place for teaching. The relationship between bishop and dean was traditional inasmuch as it lacked personal warmth. Leonard loved the cathedral and his fertile liturgical mind constantly thought of improvements and furnishings but he knew that his suggestions were among the least welcome. If he could not have the dean of his choice he could appoint a new canon residentiary and chancellor when Harold Arthur Blair retired in 1975. In his place he brought Martin Stuart Farrin Thornton who died in 1986. Martin Thornton was already well known for his writings on pastoralia and spirituality. In a foreword to Thornton's last book (*A Joyful Heart*) published posthumously in 1987, Leonard writes:

I think his greatest quality as a priest and teacher lay in his ability to give to people the desire to love God. To hear him or read his books was to experience a quickening of the spirit and to want to grow in holiness. This he achieved without using any of the cheap ways which some use to try and make religion easy, when all we remember is the illustration and little of the truth which it was intended to convey.

Another appointment Leonard made was that of his friend Eric Mascall, who was made an honorary canon of Truro and theological adviser to the diocese. Although a visiting, not a residential, appointment it provided opportunities for lectures and consultations in the diocese and for Leonard to have access to a priest and thinker for whom he had great respect. Mascall's appointment as canon theologian was a revival of a tradition initiated by Benson; former holders include Henry Scott Holland and Max Warren.

In 1977 the diocese celebrated its centenary. In March Leonard made his Primary Visitation. The clergy were summoned to attend 'on your canonical obedience . . . habited in canonical dress (cassock and gown, if you have one)' at one of five centres. There were festivities throughout the year and the chief one was the Eucharist in the priory grounds at Bodmin on 8 May at which Archbishop Donald Coggan preached. Thousands of people attending the Eucharist and other centenary events were witnesses to a new spirit in the diocese. The chairman of the House of Laity, J. N. Dowling, remembers that 'When Bishop Graham came to the diocese the diocesan bishop was a remote figure, but the new bishop with his pastoral visitations, which staggered his brother bishops, had changed the image. He has been a people's bishop, a Father in God.' Every opportunity was taken to gather the diocese around its bishop. During the cathedral's own centenary year there was what was called a bishop's day in July 1980. All the parish clergy were invited to the cathedral at half hour intervals during the day with representative laity from all parishes to meet their bishop and to celebrate the Eucharist at one of the cathedral's altars or, in at least one case, say Evensong. Leonard met each party on arrival and gave them a brief talk, and later there was an informal get together in the chapter house. Leonard's idea was to reproduce on one day in the cathedral what happened every Sunday throughout the diocese and so help the people to be aware of their unity in worship, however isolated they might feel.

The parishes were always central to his thinking. In 1974 the House of Bishops approved the 'Sheffield Scheme' (known as such after its chairman, Bishop Gordon Fallows of Sheffield) which worked out a basis for establishing 'fair shares' of clergy for each diocese. Full-time clergy would be placed in areas of greatest need. When the working group was established Leonard was not a member of General Synod. If he had been, he would have objected to the phrase 'fairer distribution' and pressed for some such phrase as 'a distribution which more truly reflects the nature of the Church and the principles of the Kingdom'. In some comments he wrote: 'The report assumes that 'fairer distribution' means fair shares on a pro rata basis. The evidence of the New Testament does not lead me to suppose that distribution on such a basis expresses and embodies a principle of the Kingdom (see, for example, the parable of the labourers in the vineyard and the parable of the talents).'

Once again Leonard was needling the reformers and some of his fellow bishops by questioning the basis on which the report was built. It was not spiritually sound and there was virtually no discussion of the quality of pastoral care. His critics were even more annoyed, even exasperated, when he accused them of being insufficiently radical.

> The report assumes that the parochial basis of the Church of England must remain unchanged, without considering whether certain areas should not be designated 'missionary areas' to be treated differently with regard to staffing. It seems to me to overlook the fact, well recognized in other spheres, of pastoral contact with a limited number of people and that the reduction of the population of a parish from say 20 000 to 10 000 does not necessarily relieve the tensions of the pastor or improve the quality of his pastoral care.

A completely new approach was needed. Withdrawing clergy from country parishes was no way forward either. The effects of pastoral reorganization were beginning to show the law of diminishing returns both spiritually and financially, resulting in many parishes being without a resident pastor. Grouping parishes was no answer when it took no account of the diverse nature of rural parishes and the profound effect of history on rural communities.

In his first year, Leonard had visited 130 parishes. The purple-cassocked bishop was seen throughout Cornwall. By his pastoral presence Leonard was encouraging the Church

126

to lift up its head and be the Church. Within a relatively short time the number of ordinands increased, the giving increased, the sense of fellowship and depth of discipleship grew. The diocese was not allowed to indulge in the luxury of contentment. The major issues before the Church and society came before the diocesan synod and the parishes. All this may suggest that Leonard never left the diocese. Yet he probably travelled more miles than any other English bishop. There was an occasional murmur, 'He's away again'. Away might mean London, Oxford, Ripon, Northampton; it might also mean the USA, Nairobi, Crete, Moscow, South Africa, Athens or Australia. With customary enthusiasm and incredible energy he threw himself into everything conceivable.

He tried to put too much into every day and was often disappointed because his taste for conversation and his willing gift of time to anybody who came along usually meant that by the end of the day he had not done all that he hoped for. Tiredness occasionally overcame him, to the point when he was practically inarticulate. He was saved by rigorous adherence to holidays, one month 'away from it all' in the summer. For the rest of the year he was speaking in two or three places in the course of a week, working at his committees of General Synod and also getting in a full week in the diocese. He was the most regular British Rail customer for the overnight sleeper. What were his other major preoccupations?

10

Wider Responsibilities

'Congratulations – as you enter the front row of the scrum' had been the typically appropriate form of words used by Ronald Williams, bishop of Leicester, to greet Leonard on his appointment to Truro. A bishop of ability and distinction is pounced upon to chair this commission and to join that committee. Despite the tensions between archbishop and bishop (Ramsey and Leonard) over the Anglican–Methodist scheme, Leonard could not be ignored. On 23 November 1973 Ramsey invited Leonard to fill a vacancy on the Anglican–Orthodox International Doctrinal Commission following the retirement of the bishop of Winchester, Falkner Allison. He also became one of the archbishop's counsellors on foreign relations. The Anglican chairman was the bishop of St Albans (Robert Kennedy Alexander Runcie) and the Orthodox chairman was the Greek Orthodox archbishop of Australia (Stylianos).

Leonard had already attended the 16th centenary celebrations of the death of St Athanasius in Cairo. He attended five major meetings of the commission other than the London-based ones of the archbishop's counsellors. The meetings were: 1974, Crete; 1975, Truro; 1976, Moscow; 1977, Cambridge; 1978, Athens. The full commission met in Moscow. Sub-commissions met on other occasions and Leonard was joint-chairman with Archbishop Stylianos of one of these commissions. Other Anglican members were Bishop Richard Hanson, the Revd Roger Beckwith (warden of Latimer House, Oxford) and Colin Davey, vicar of St Paul, South Harrow. It was said that Leonard was there to keep Richard Hanson in order, although the Orthodox appeared to have confidence in Hanson. The sub-commission discussed such subjects as 'Inspiration and Revelation in the Holy

128

Scriptures' (Crete); 'Scripture and Tradition in the Life of the Church' (Truro); and 'The Church and the Churches' (Cambridge).

Leonard found the work of the commission frustrating. How often it seemed as if people from two different worlds with different thought patterns were meeting. The Orthodox Church had little apprehension of how the Anglican communion works and thinks. The reverse was equally true. However, Leonard's understanding of worship coheres with the Orthodox view. In sermons he will stress that the communion of saints is no empty phrase. They represent the largest portion of any congregation here and now: a vision that Anglicans find hard to conceive.

Discussions *were* difficult because the Orthodox regarded everything as settled. What therefore was there to discuss? The Greeks were the pacemakers with the influence and they did not have much interest in Anglicanism. The Eastern Europeans, including the Russians, had more understanding of the Anglican Church but they were hampered by Anglican disunity. How could the Orthodox be expected to understand a Church that claimed to be Catholic and worldwide when several parts of it reached diametrically opposing decisions? How could the Orthodox have much interest in a Church that appeared to think worship was for the sake of the worshippers? After the sub-commission meeting in Truro Leonard wrote that 'For the Orthodox, worship is something offered to God in thankfulness for his goodness, with that loving obedience that is willing to accept the cost of serving him'. For the Orthodox worship is timeless; for the Anglican it takes an hour.

Athenagoras, the Greek Orthodox archbishop of Thyateira and Great Britain, gave some Anglican members a difficult time. He was pressed by theologians in Greece and Russia to break off the theological conversations with Anglicans who had moved away from their classical formulations, considering the ordination of women to the priesthood, and in parts of the world proceeding with such ordinations. Locally in England the denigration of the Incarnation by people like Professor Maurice Wiles angered him. Archbishop Athenagoras wrote a strident letter in the *Orthodox Herald* (May–June 1976) on the problem of the ordination of women to the priesthood. Bishop Richard Hanson responded sturdily defending this Anglican innovation, which in turn provoked a written response from Leonard, arriving at the opposite conclusion. There were those on the Orthodox–Anglican joint doctrinal discussions who thought this issue could somehow be made palatable for the Orthodox. It wasn't and it cannot.

Leonard felt the discussions were never in danger of reaching even modest conclusions. He liked to push groups towards goals. The Orthodox could not be pushed, persuaded or cajoled. Even when there seemed to be a little progress, as with the Truro sub-commission, the 'findings' were negligible. It is surprising that Leonard persevered in this sphere. Almost his only encouragement came from Orthodox leaders, people like Archbishop Bessak Toumayan (Armenian) who, as a representative 'of the ancient churches' regarded Leonard as 'a champion of the true faith and upholder of the traditions of the Church'. In 1976 Leonard was about to take over and start a dialogue with the Oriental Orthodox Churches, but a letter from Archbishop Coggan put an end to that. In retrospect it is as well that Leonard was rescued from a further commitment in this direction. He would have achieved little and he knew it.

Another letter from the archbishop of Canterbury came at the beginning of March 1976, asking if Leonard would accept the chairmanship of the Board for Social Responsibility in succession to Bishop Ronald Williams of Leicester. Both archbishops were concerned to find the right chairman for a board that would be looking at major ethical and moral issues coming before the Church. They wanted a chairman who could keep a guiding hand on a difficult board and its radical secretary, Giles Ecclestone. They were also seeking a bishop who was, or would be soon, a member, and thus spokesman in the House of Lords. They wanted Leonard. It would mean dropping some other commitments such as the Anglican-Orthodox dialogue, as it would demand time, effort and travelling to and from London. Leonard was easily persuaded, accepting by return of post. The appointment, which had to be approved by the standing committee of General Synod, was not universally welcomed. Would Leonard be an impartial chairman? The reason for appointing him suggested that he would be a chairman with a point of view and one that would be expressed.

The board was essentially an advisory body, responsible for formulating advice on matters of concern in society and transmitting it to those who needed it. There was a feeling that this board was getting too big for its boots and that the bureaucrats were deciding what should be studied. Moreover, the subjects seemed ever more numerous and all-embracing of any and every issue in Church and State. Were there too many statements? Were they shaped by a Christian perception? Was the theological base sufficiently strong and deep?

Space does not permit the discussion of all the matters which came before the board during Leonard's chairmanship, but the major published reports are listed below. A number were in progress before Leonard's chairmanship but came to fruition during it, namely between 1976 and 1983 (dates given are those of the synodical debate): *On Dying Well* (Feb 1976); *Human Rights: our Understanding and our Responsibilities* (Feb 1977); *Britain in a Multi-Racial and Multi-Cultural Society* (July 1977); *The Irish Problem and Ourselves* (Nov 1977); *Humanity and Sexuality* (July 1978); *A Church of England Special Fund for Race Relations (Second Report)* (July 1978); *Prisons and Prisoners in England Today* (February 1979); *Political Change in South Africa* (November 1979); *Pluralism and Community* (July 1980); *The Church of England and Politics* (November 1980); *Homosexual Relationships: a Report*, also a memorandum by the chairman, and *Homosexual Relationships: a contribution to discussion* (Feb 1981); *Facing the Facts: The United Kingdom and South Africa* (July 1982). There was also a flow of reports and papers from the social and industrial committees, such as *Work and the Future* (1979), *Nuclear Choice* (1977), *Housing and Homelessness* (1982).

Before turning to a few issues on which Leonard had himself something to say, as distinct from having to say something on behalf of the board, it is worth mentioning the Church of England's difficulty in producing moral statements. Ian Ramsey's aphorism – 'Sure on religion but tentative in theology' – had become a guide. In its research and pronouncements there was little attempt to found an appeal or argument on authority or to foreclose further discussion by reference to scripture or the tradition of the Church.

Solutions to moral questions were sought in the context of a revaluation of the Christian tradition in its bearing on the issue as it newly presented itself. Statements, reports and advice flowed from many sources, not even as tributaries from a single source – Lambeth conferences, convocations, the Anglican Consultative Council, ad hoc archbishops' commissions, the Board for Social Responsibility.

Leonard was uneasy about this dispersal without a centre of authority. What did he think was the Church's greatest need? In three words – a doctrine of creation. In the mid-1970s, *and* today, this doctrine is the most neglected and the most needed, particularly in view of the influence of existentialism. Leonard does not think that Christology, or sociology, as examples, can be adequately considered except against a background discussion of the fact that Christians believe that the God who is in Christ is the God who creates. It is also essential for adequate presentation or discussion of the sacraments and morality.

Towards pressing issues of the day Leonard's approach is thought to be oblique. And it is, if analysis and comment is expected on the world's terms, in secular phraseology. Fellow bishops find Leonard's approach difficult, occasionally obtuse. They should not, for everything derives from his theological perception. An example comes from his first contribution to the General Synod as chairman of the BSR. The occasion (26 February 1976) was to receive the report *On Dying Well: an Anglican contribution to the debate on euthanasia* (1975). The working party had been chaired by the Lord Amulree, consulting physician of University College Hospital and former president of the British Geriatric Society. The debate was one of importance as the Voluntary Euthanasia Society had published a widely noticed pamphlet *Death with Dignity*. In the course of his speech Leonard said:

Yesterday I asked the archbishop of York [Stuart Blanch] if the passage of scripture which he was going to expound today was going to bear any relationship to the report *On Dying Well*, and he told me that it was not; but in fact I would have thought that the whole exposition was a most magnificent introduction to our debate, for the simple reason that it proclaimed that liberty comes through obedience. He spoke of the glory and splendour of the law fulfilled in the spirit. That, I believe, speaks to us immediately and deeply in our debate now.

That is a good example of Leonard's position, further underlined when he quoted a sentence from the report: 'Freedom is set within a context of obedience, responsiblity within a context of divine invitation and grace.'

On the particular subject of euthanasia Leonard took the general view that the 'divide between permitting those who say that they wish to die to be put to death, and the removal of those who are a burden on family or State is, I believe, a narrow one'. Leonard's emphasis was on better and deeper care for the dying. His spiritual care for the dying has always been important to him – and even if he could not always be there at their end and their beginning.

Canon Deryck Davey of Liskeard, an Evangelical, writes:

One thing I noted of particular value was his personal ministry. He was assiduous in visiting my first wife when she was dying of cancer and she was surprised and relieved to find him a mountain of spiritual strength to her. It was symbolic of his over-stretch that, when she was at her last, Graham was busy going to and being in America. So he missed her going, and she sadly missed his ministry. For his kind of ministry then I shall always be most grateful.

His second speech to the General Synod as chairman of the board is reckoned to be one of his best. In it he said everything that needed to be said, had the whole of synod with him, was greeted with prolonged applause, further debate or discussion was not necessary and the motion was carried *nem con*. The motion concerned the proposed making or screening of a film by a Mr Thorsen purporting to present the sex life of Jesus Christ and shared 'the widespread revulsion already expressed at the prospect of a pornographic film'.

Leonard did not join then, and would not join now, the unthinking populists who moralize with their mouths but not with their brains, and have hatred in their hearts and anger in their souls. They condemn without ceasing and have a lynching mentality. Leonard began his synod speech on the Thorsen film with some words of T. S. Eliot from *Murder in the Cathedral.* After enduring the assaults of the four tempters, Thomas à Becket says: 'The last temptation is the greatest treason: to do the right thing for the wrong reason.' The General Synod must not do that. Leonard had read the script of Thorsen's proposed film and knew it to be pornographic and a terrible debasement of Jesus Christ. The resolution must be passed, but for the right reasons, of which Leonard selected two: 'The script represents the perverted use of the divine gift of imagination.' He was able to quote Dorothy L. Sayers' *Man Born to be King* and Stuart Jackman's *The Davidson Affair* as examples of imaginative writers who drew out the significance and richness of the Gospel record. Secondly, 'Christians believe that our Lord is both truly man and truly God and will therefore regard the script as blasphemous. Many, however, who would not call themselves Christians, venerate him as a man of utter goodness, holiness and integrity.' Leonard had non-Christian allies. The Moslem community, who regard Christ as a major prophet, were outraged by the prospect of such a film. 'I believe that we should pass this resolution because there is a valid and proper distinction between freedom of expression and licence, a distinction which has become hopelessly blurred in the case of sexual morality. Freedom of expression becomes licence when it is used to do violence to others, whether it be the use of freedom to oppress others unjustly, to indulge in racial discrimination or to corrupt men's minds, imaginations and wills.'

In proposing the motion Leonard reminded the synod of a way in which Christians had failed: 'We have presented chastity as a barren, negative and loveless virtue. We must present it in its true nature – shining, beautiful, sinewy and strong – that quality which unites true love and passion and by directing the force of the natural instincts implanted by God, enables us to share in the glorious creative activity of God in every aspect of our lives.' Leonard returned to this theme at greater length when he addressed the national convention of the National Viewers and Listeners Association in April 1987. His title was 'The Splendour of Chastity' and he offered his audience theological fare which some would find unpalatable or indigestible. Leonard provides true food, which is quite different from half-cooked simplicities and burnt certainties.

1 The Revd Douglas Leonard.   2 Graham Leonard, aged 3.

3 Graham Leonard with his wife Priscilla and sons James *(left)* and Mark, 1953.

4   A pastoral visit to a parish: Leonard and Prebendary George Oakley, Vicar of
Willesden Parish Church, with the children of the Church School.

5   After the enthronement in Truro, 1973. *(Robert Roskcrow Photography)*

The Leonards after the announcement of his appointment as Bishop of London. (© *Times Newspapers Ltd*)

During the enthronement as Bishop of London in 1981 with *(left)* Alan Webster, Dean of St Paul's Cathedral. (© *F. & J. Hare Ltd (Harrow) 1981*)

8 Foreign travels: visiting the Coptic Pope Shenouda III when he was exiled to the monastery Anba Bishoi at Wadi Naturn.

9 The 'Tulsa Affair': during the controversial confirmation with *(left)* the Revd John Pas and *(right)* Leonard's chaplain, the Revd John Shepherd.

The most explosive issue which faced Leonard during his chairmanship was that which issued in the 1979 report *Homosexual Relationships: a contribution to discussion*; a report which almost never breathed synodical air. This was an occasion of the Church reacting to a change in legislation – not a change in people's attitudes. In 1957 the report on *Homosexual Offences and Prostitution* was published by the Government. A major recommendation was that homosexual behaviour between consenting adults in private should no longer be a criminal offence. The committee, known as the Wolfenden Committee (after its chairman John Wolfenden), was quite clear that the criminal law was quite separate from personal morality. This was a view with which the Church of England concurred. An earlier report of the Church of England Moral Welfare Council, *Sexual Offenders and Social Punishment* had concluded: 'We would submit however, that it is not the function of the State and Law to constitute themselves guardians of *private* morality, and that to deal with *sin as such* belongs to the province of the Church.' Indeed, this report had been the Church's evidence to the Wolfenden Committee and formed the main plank of the Wolfenden Report. In 1967 the Sexual Offences Act removed criminal sanctions from the conduct known as buggery and gross indecency when (with certain exceptions) this took place between consenting adult males in private. This act received strong support from Archbishop Ramsey and some bishops during its passage through Parliament.

In 1974, four years after a previous, unpublished report, the Board for Social Responsibility set up another working party to study the theological, social, pastoral and legal aspects of homosexuality. The bishop of Gloucester (John Yates), who himself became chairman of the Board for Social Responsiblity in 1987, was its chairman. In March 1978, after 27 meetings (including three residential ones), the draft report was sent to the board. The report was unanimous. Among its findings was a declaration that there are circumstances in which some people may justifiably choose a homosexual relationship with the hope of enjoying companionship and sexual love similar to that in marriage. Thus physical or genital expression was recognized. Nonetheless, it rejected casual and promiscuous alliances and found that the concept of homosexual marriage could not be validated. Being a homosexual should not hinder membership of the Church of England nor receiving Communion. Responsible homosexual unions, if not scandalous, should not be criticized. The working party also proposed that the age of homosexual consent should be lowered from 21 to 18.

The original initiative for the study had come from the conference of principals of theological colleges. Homosexuality was a problem in some colleges and promiscuous activity was a scandal in more than one college. The working party proposed that a priest who was a practising homosexual should offer his resignation to his bishop, who would then decide whether it should be accepted or not. As for ordinands,

> We do not think that a bishop is justified in refusing to ordain an otherwise acceptable ordinand merely on the ground that he is (or is believed to be) homosexually orientated. But an ordinand would be wrong to conceal deliberately from his ordaining bishop an intention existing in his own mind to live openly in a homosexual union after ordination or to campaign on behalf of a homophile organization.

The report arrived like a bombshell on the board that had commissioned it. The working party met selected board members on 20 April 1978 when criticisms were aired and the working party were asked if they would effect some revisions in the light of board members' comments. Leonard was always clear that the integrity of the working party must be respected. The report was theirs.

Leonard's initial reaction, which was not much modified by debate, was consistent with his theological bearing. Here are some points from his notes:

> Part of the problem which extends to other areas of moral concern lies in the identification of what is morally possible in the given situation with the morally good. This I think arises from (a) a misunderstanding or false conclusion drawn from situation ethics; (b) the removal of criminal status from certain sins; (c) the attitude that suffering is the worst evil and that anything is justified that alleviates it; (d) (particularly for Christians) the effect of biblical

criticism on the authority of scripture as providing moral standards. These points all bear on the problem of making moral judgments in the field of homosexuality whether by a body like the working party or the board, by homosexuals or by the general public.

Homosexuality: the biblical evidence. It is this chapter which gives me real concern. The preface says that 'the working party was convinced that it must take into account a Christian appraisal of sexuality in general and of its genital expression in particular' which is right. This chapter, however, plunges straight into homosexuality and gives the impression that the purpose of the appeal to scripture is to discover statements.

It is essential, I believe, that there should be a chapter on sexuality and the Christian Gospel before the specific question of homosexuality is discussed. This would involve a much more fundamental consideration of the theology of creation and of the way in which the Old Testament is fulfilled in the New. On the second point the chapter is particularly weak both with regard to homosexuality and to love. Does the fact, for example, that 'The new people of God are not bound by blood relationship' mean a totally new concept of love unrelated to the adumbration of love found in the Old Testament? The sudden introduction of the concept of unconditional love without reference to the Cross is misleading. In one way the unconditional love of our Lord was conditioned, conditioned by the moral and holy will of the Father with the result that the love of Jesus was expressed in suffering and death. I think perhaps that what is needed above all else is a consideration of what the Christian Gospel means by the word 'love' and its relations to the natural instincts of man however they may be subsequently defined. To dismiss the Old Testament as is virtually done and appeal to the Christian Gospel of love without defining it, does not I believe do justice to the Gospel, not least in the consideration of the affect of grace on our ability to meet the moral demands of God.

Theological and ethical considerations. The weakness in the handling of scripture is I believe also evident in this chapter. The impression is given that the personalist view stands in contrast to the view derived from scripture or

137

natural law and springs from a criterion to be found in neither. I believe that it needs to be presented as a view grounded in both, and needing both to provide the criteria for its effective application. The weakness of the personalist view in isolation is that it provides no criteria for the definition of the 'quality of personal relationship'. It is at this point that the consideration of what a Christian means by love is so urgently needed.

The board was more representatively Anglican than the working party. The latter did not have a parish priest on it, nor anyone representing the distinctively Evangelical tradition. It may be added that neither did it have a known homosexual on it. The board was immediately and intransigently divided on the report. It was clear from the outset that there was no way in which the board would be able to endorse the conclusions of the 'Gloucester Report' as it was known. An earlier report had not been published. Was this one too to be shelved?

A major difficulty with the style of the report was that it came from many hands. The earlier chapters had been penned by individual members of the working party. They were not the products of consensus as were the later chapters. The report carried a 'clinical' unanimity which did not reflect the emotional and intellectual tussles of the working party. There was evidence of research, but did the conclusions lead this research in parts of the report? The observations of board members were noted and Professor Gordon Dunstan was asked to prepare a paper collating these. He produced a masterly set of observations, expressed with sharpness and asperity, which might with merit and justice have appeared unamended in the published report. However, Dunstan was fortunately not a person to allow too much dilution to the 'observations'.

While the board was discussing the report, the Church which knew that Gloucester had reported was getting restless. The subject was emotive. What had the Church to say? In guiding the board, Leonard was justifiably anxious to obtain consensus. After a great deal of wrangling and careful handling by Leonard it was decided that the Gloucester Report would be published as 'a contribution to discussion' with a foreword by Leonard and would include 'critical observations' from the board. (The board had taken advantage of Leonard's absence from one meeting to give him sole responsiblity for writing the foreword.) The report was published on 19 October 1979. Leonard's foreword included the all-revealing statement: 'The question of homosexuality raises questions to do with the authority of scripture and the Church's tradition. Because of this, we do not think that the Church of England is yet ready to declare its mind on the subject of homosexuality.'

Inevitably, the report received a lashing from homosexual organizations such as the Gay Christian Movement and the Campaign for Homosexual Equality. They were strident in their condemnation as was a radical element in the Church. 'Where was the Church as a forgiving body?' they asked. Such people confuse forgiveness with condoning, ignoring the fact that in the Gospel the divine forgiveness is accompanied by grace. Penitence only springs from a bad conscience. Repentance involves both an acknowledgment of sin and the willingness to live in a new relationship to God through Christ in which one chooses deliberately to live as one who accepts his sovereignty. To live as a forgiven person is not merely to be someone whose specific acts are forgiven but to live in a creative healing and reconciling relationship in which the awareness of the glory and desirability of holiness is developed side by side with a deepening and joyful realization of the meaning of being forgiven. What is not possible spiritually is to take advantage of the divine forgiveness for specific acts while remaining committed to the world, accepting its disorder. Being forgiven and living in the new relationship are inseparable.

But many sensitive homosexual clergy and laity of the Church felt a stigma was attached to them on account of their sexual orientation. Other practising homosexual couples witnessed to the joy, the beauty, the goodness and the wholeness of their stable relationships. Each wanted the stigma removing and, *ipso facto*, a pronouncement by the Church that homosexual behaviour was not sinful. Among some homosexual Christians (and Leonard preferred the word to be used as an adjective rather than as a noun) there was not only a demand to be released from celibacy, but an apparent demand that they should have the right to be promiscuous.

The report was almost silent about the central fact of Christian theology and the characteristic feature of Christian ethics, namely, forgiveness. Was this because the authors had excluded all notions of culpability, of sin? In the final published observation of the board Leonard's mind can be seen. It concerns his conviction that in moral theology conscience is always to be followed. And conscience is always in need of education and correction. Thus if a homosexual priest who has 'come out' and openly acknowledged that he is living in a sexual union with another man, and believes that a decision so to live can be justifiably made in good conscience, he must also realise that he is not exempt from the pastoral disciplines of the Church. 'If the Church believes that a practising homosexual priest should not continue in office it must take the responsibility for removing him and for doing so in a way which is legally and morally defensible, and must be prepared to spell out its reasons.'

Much of this highlighted a dubious trend in contemporary Church affairs. Does the Church change the standard in order to accommodate individual propensities? In order to love the sinner, is it necessary or desirable to deny the sin as sinful? Was the divide between sinful man and the demands of the Creator God becoming blurred?

Leonard was never in danger of falling into the trap of confusing compassion with amoral sentimentality. Under his chairmanship the board had worked hard for 18 months between reception and publication of the report, and it was to be another 16 months before it was debated by the General Synod on 27 February 1981. There were times when a decision 'not to publish' would have been the easiest course to take. As a person who was used to being in a minority he knew well how important it was to accept opposing points of view. At the same time he struggled and achieved consensus, if 'only just'!

As the General Synod debate approached expectations were aroused about its outcome. Should the Church change its mind, and its disciplines, regarding homosexual practices? This was unlikely because the synod was not being asked to 'do' anything. Leonard had made it clear that it was not ready to declare its mind. Pressures to do so would be resisted. Leonard knew this would not satisfy those who claimed that the Bible reflected an unambiguous divine condemnation of homosexual relationships. Neither would homosexual clergy and laity be whooping with delight. In the event, the synod debate was at a consistent and calm level; the report was merely received. The secular climate was for change and the issues were to resurface in a more strident form when Leonard was bishop of London.

Any chairman of the Board for Social Responsibility is deluged with paper and reports. He can only read a small proportion of what he receives and decide which can have a major claim on his time and attention. Occasionally he will be asked for a statement on some fleeting issue. In this respect Leonard was fortunate to live in Truro. The journalist's pencil and interviewer's microphone did not often stray too far from London. However, in 1978 there was criticism of Princess Margaret's relationship with Roddy Llewellyn and of a recent holiday on the Isle of Mustique. Some members of Parliament were vocal in attacking the princess, others in defending her. Leonard, as chairman of the board, was asked for his comments. He said, 'I would have thought that the thing that had to be resolved now was in fact how far she can go on being a public person. If you accept the public life, you must accept a severe restriction on your personal conduct.' The princess could withdraw from public life as 'a possible way of enabling her to sort out her own affairs'. Going to Mustique with Llewellyn was 'very foolish . . . It's asking for people to draw conclusions, whether they're right or wrong. If this were happening to someone in my own family I would simple advise them not to do things which could be misunderstood'.

Tabloid headlines are made of such statements, and Leonard found himself front page news, with a consequently heavy post bag. What was not reported was his answer to further questions: that he was praying for Princess Margaret, 'that she should be given the strength to make the right judgement'.

In considering political issues Leonard endeavoured to keep to principles and to avoid personalities. There were still too many reports flowing from the board. It was as if the Church should not only have a view about everything, but that there should be a working party to support it! Some of these parties reported, the reports were debated and received, and then returned to the oblivion whence they came.

The clamour for Leonard to pronounce was loud and clear, but it was directed to the wrong person in the wrong position. It was not the function of the board to advocate specific measures to deal with problems confronting the nation. Leonard saw it as his duty to try to bring a Christian judgement to bear upon them and to expose the underlying causes which must be faced and dealt with if measures taken were to be effective. In January 1979 he issued a statement selecting three underlying causes

> all of which concern human attitudes, for it is ultimately our beliefs and attitudes which determine the health of our society, not impersonal factors beyond our control.
>
> The first is the assumption that there are no absolute standards of right and wrong and that every man, woman or section of society can do what is right in their own eyes. . . . The second underlying cause is the assumption that man is intrinsically good, will always behave sensibly and bear the needs of others in mind. . . . The third cause is the assumption that welfare, measured solely by material standards, will produce happiness and security.
>
> These assumptions must be challenged by every member of society, by employer, employed or consumer alike, of whatever creed, or of none, for this strikes at the heart of our common life. Only if they are challenged is there any hope of a society in which freedom and responsibility will flourish and the specific measures which must be taken be effective.

Leonard's approach was disappointing to those who wanted concrete proposals to rid society of the ills which beset it. It was much more difficult to stand one's ground on principle. Equally it was not always easy to sustain such a position in the board. Some radical members of the board were exasperated with his intransigent views, though charmed by his personal manner and filled with admiration for his chairmanship. The one criticism was that he tended to talk too much, even though it was acknowledged that he was amazingly well informed.

In 1975 (23 November–10 December) Leonard was one of

the elected Church of England delegates to the fifth assembly of the World Council of Churches in Nairobi; 676 delegates attended from almost every country in the world. This is not the kind of gathering out of which Leonard expects bounty or wisdom. He was not disappointed. The World Council of Churches has a jargon all of its own, and its papers and reports are sometimes quite unintelligible.

Leonard was a member of the 'Hearing on Education'. The purpose of the hearings was to enable the staff of the various divisions of the secretariat of the WCC to report on their programmes which the delegates could then discuss. In the early sessions of the hearing on education the bishop and others felt that they were being subjected, without any opportunity even to question manipulation and indoctrination, to accept a highly critical attitude of education as commonly understood in the West. They were told that the purpose of education was to produce conflict and confrontation. Ironically, although western education was being criticized for indoctrination and manipulation, Leonard felt that the methods being adopted by the staff administered the use of such methods to a far greater degree than he had ever experienced in the West. After attempts to secure at least one opportunity to ask questions, Leonard, Canon Elliott from Northern Ireland, and some nine other delegates said they must leave to enable them to discuss the programme. They eventually returned with a document, much of which was incorporated in the final report of the hearing. Their action was welcomed on their return by delegates from the Third World, including Indonesia and the Philippines.

Leonard advocated a return to the teaching of William Temple, with his insistence that the realms of Law and Gospel must be distinguished. There was a utopianism about Nairobi that was unhealthy because it was not specifically Christian. The coming of the Kingdom is in the hands of God. Leonard was struck by a remark by Canon Eric Elliott (Church of Ireland), who said there were two ways of killing a man, 'One is to give him no hope and the other is to give him a false hope'. Similar sentiments were expressed when Leonard introduced the report *The Church of England and Politics* to General Synod on 14 November 1980: 'The Church must be prepared to accept the responsibility, and, if need be the

GRAHAM LEONARD

odium, of assessing all party political programmes and trying
to bring them under the judgement of the Word of God.' Woe
betide the person who pins a political label on Leonard only
to find that he does not see things from the same vantage
point as the party politician. His chairmanship of the board
meant that he had a number of set pieces to perform in the
General Synod, namely when introducing reports. He spoke
on other issues too but General Synod has never been a
favourite of Leonard's, and we shall see why in a subsequent
chapter.

By this time Leonard was recognized as the leader of the
Catholic movement in the Church of England. He had to
ration his acceptances to lecture, speak and preach in this
country as he was much in demand overseas. He visited the
United States in 1974, '75, '77 and '79. There was an
exhausting schedule for him in 1976 when he made a month's
visit to South Africa, taking in Johannesburg, Durban, Natal,
Pretoria, Bloemfontein, Cape Town, Port Elizabeth,
Grahamstown and St John's Diocese. A similar gruelling
month was spent in Australia in 1980 visiting Adelaide,
Melbourne, Sydney, Ballarat, Wangaratta and Newcastle.
Leonard's lectures and sermons were always concerned with
the growth of the spiritual life and the proclamation of the
Catholic faith. He was seen as a rock which no storm or
tempest could move. He communicated strength yet pointed
away from himself to God. He was still wary of the applause
of the crowd, while he appreciated being appreciated. Nevertheless, there was no toning down of the message he had to
proclaim. As a teacher he had to be listened to with care, for
he dealt with substance, not with packaged answers. The
substance took some digesting.

Teaching and encouraging Catholics overseas was one
thing; in England it was something else. The Catholic movement had lost its direction. In the Church of the 1970s many
parishes which would have called themselves Anglo–Catholic
had turned in upon themselves, becoming shrines to a fading
vision, which few people visited. A coordinated effort was
needed to put the Catholic movement back on the map. The
result was Catholic renewal: 'The time has come for us to
return to our roots: for a Catholic renewal in the Church of
England.' This was spearheaded by the Church Union under

the presidency of the bishop of Chichester, Eric Kemp. From the outset the renewal included all those elements which Leonard had been insisting upon for years. First, renewal of faith in God Creator and Sustainer of the universe, in Jesus Christ and in the Holy Spirit. Then and only then comes renewal of faith in the Church, in the holy sacraments, in God's gift of the apostolic ministry. And there must be renewal of hope. In an early statement the emphasis was on the recovery of wholeness: 'Catholic means whole, integral, complete: its opposite is partial, unbalanced, sectarian. Today, as we see the decay of narrow and inadequate forms of Christianity, and the revival of pietistic and harmful byways of belief, the renewal of Catholic truth and life will not occur without a struggle. But it is essential if the true God is to be preached.'

One of Leonard's chief contributions to Catholic renewal, other than the importance and influence of his own person, was his endeavour to shift the thrust of Catholic devotion and enthusiasm from devotion to a cause to devotion to our Lord. Catholic renewal had a conference at Loughborough University in 1978 attended by over 1000 people. It succeeded in firing people's imagination. The atmosphere was a little like a mission, and none the worse for that. Teaching and worship, not intellectual debate, were to the forefront. There were manifold opportunities for Leonard to engage in intellectual and theological debate as the Church began to consider the most contentious issues before it, but who would lead the Church through the turbulence?

11

'Exultet Londinium: miserere mei Truron'

On 5 June 1979 Frederick Donald Coggan, archbishop of Canterbury, announced that he would resign the archbishopric on 26 January 1980. Although only 69, the announcement came with dramatic unexpectedness for which the Church, like the Press, was unprepared. Nevertheless within hours the Press, radio and television were lining up candidates for St Augustine's chair. The Church's corridors of persuasion were likewise humming with rumour and plot and throughout the country interest was awakened in who the new archbishop might be.

The procedure for nominating a person was clear. For the first time the archbishop of Canterbury would be appointed on a recommendation to the prime minister and the queen by a Crown appointments commission of 16 people. The basis of the new system for appointing archbishops and diocesan bishops was worked out between representatives of Church and State in 1975 and 1976 in the light of the Chadwick Report, *Church and State* (1970), and approved by General Synod in 1976. Although there were a number of new features, it remained, like the preceding system, selective and not elective. The Church was given a decisive voice in the appointment of its chief pastors, with the prime minister remaining, constitutionally, the queen's final adviser, but undertaking to consider only those names put forward for a particular vacancy by the Church's own elected commission. Instead of the former convention under which the archbishop was selected from three suggested names, it was agreed that there should be two names only, to be given in the order decided by the commission. In giving final advice to the queen, the prime minister retained a real element of choice. This was made clear by Prime Minister James Callaghan in a statement

146

made on 8 June 1976: 'The prime minister would retain the right to recommend the second name, or to ask the committee for a further name or names.'

A special procedure was adopted for considering the primacy and see of Canterbury. The prime minister chose Richard O'Brien, chairman of the Manpower Services Commission, to be chairman of the nominating commission. The commission worked almost too quickly for the widest of soundings and consultations to take place. The standing committee of the General Synod met the prime minister's and archbishops' appointments secretaries on 22 June 1979. Perhaps the most negative reaction to Leonard's name came at this meeting. Partisanship was held against Leonard. What were the members of the influential (and too important) standing committee suggesting? Some of the contending bishops could not be said to be partisan. Indeed, they could not be labelled at all for it was difficult to know for what they stood. Was Leonard to be excluded from Canterbury because he knew what he believed in favour of someone who would not even believe that they knew? Was it Anglo-Catholicism? Again it was (or should have been) known that he was not universally liked in that constituency. Some were disaffected when he voted for the 10 Propositions and then joined the Council for Covenanting. He was too firmly a biblicist for some of the ritualists. Was his highly-praised work as chairman of the Board for Social Responsibility forgotten? He had guided the Church through a number of rapids. At the 1978 General Synod he had spoken forcefully against the ordination of women. But who had invited him to do so? – the standing committee of the General Synod. Of course, despite his close involvement with the General Synod, Leonard was not natural in the system. Was that the reason for the partisan tag? Or were the objections more personal, connected with the man?

Whatever the reasons (and it is not to say that Leonard would have been the right choice for Canterbury), the standing committee considered his name too abruptly, to move on to a more congenial character. The commission met from 9 to 11 July at Launde Abbey. Two names were put to Richard O'Brien and Bishop David Say of Rochester, one of the two bishops elected onto the commission, who took the names to the prime minister two days later. For various reasons the appointment was not made until 7 September.

Many names were mentioned and it is not particularly relevant to speculate on the two names or in which order they were presented to the prime minister. It was natural that there were those who would have liked Leonard in St Augustine's chair. When William Temple went to Canterbury Bernard Shaw had commented it was a 'realized impossibility'! Was there chance of another such impossibility? The answer is known. Robert Runcie of St Albans was the new archbishop of Canterbury. The forthcoming conflicts and controversies, confrontations and confusions, between Runcie and Leonard are such that this is an appropriate point to glance at the Runcie of 1979.

In almost every thought and action these two bishops were dissimilar and opposed, whatever surface appearances and superficial observations suggested. In some respects Runcie's image seems to have become the reality, so it is not easy to distinguish the one from the other. That is why it is essential to take a look at the man before the primacy consumed him. A revealing facial sketch comes from Wilfred De'Ath in the *Spectator* (22 March 1980): 'The face is a very interesting one: containing the elegance and worldliness of a civil service mandarin; a sweet, indulgent smile, and ultimately rather spiritual. It is a *lived in* face, bearing out his own repeated claim to have approached religion experientially rather than doctrinally ever since he was a young man.' Is it surprising that Leonard was going to clash with Runcie?

Apart from a curacy, Runcie's priesthood was served in theological college and university. The institutional and privileged atmosphere of such places dictated his outlook, affected his manner (and mannerisms) and stipulated his progress. He was good company, a raconteur and brilliant mimic. Was this a convenient façade to hide faltering foundations? He was usually reluctant to declare himself on any issue, so much so that there was the occasional whisper that a first-class mind that was open might be open at both ends. Although a member of some of the groups and cells in the Cambridge of the mid- to late 1950s, and intoxicated by the theological atmosphere, Runcie escaped offence and attack by being conspicuously absent from published symposia. 'A fence-

sitter', said a friend. There was an early habit of standing
nowhere in particular at the same time as embracing and
affirming the *via media* of Anglicanism. Newman's phrase has
become a slippery one. It has assumed an importance and
commanded an interpretation that was neither implied nor
intended. Newman's *via media*, the middle way between
popery and dissent, is far removed from the idea of the 'bridge
church'. When Newman used the magnetic phrase *via media*
in 1836 he was absorbed in his conflict with the Church of
Rome, which was to end nine years later in his dramatic
surrender. The Church of England stood then (and only just
remains standing now) for the great positive principle of a
non-papal Catholicism. It was Protestant, in the strictly
historical sense of that word, because it repudiated the papal
claim to be the universal bishop and infallible in all things.
(The former claim is less contentious today.) For Newman
Protestant and papist were, Protestant and Catholic were not,
in necessary antithesis.

In one sense, though not in all senses, Leonard is a priest
and bishop of the *via media*: Runice is an exponent of the
bridge church. At the Lausanne Conference on Faith and
Order (1927) the Anglican Church was recognized as the
bridge church, as the one Church which in any eventual
reunion of Christendom must hold the central position,
because in the days of Christian disunion it had always held
the middle way. It would be difficult to sustain that position
60 years on. The advocates of the bridge church spend so
much time on their bridges that they forget that bridges are
to cross; the realities are on either side. Those of the *via media*
are not much fussed for they consider their way is a distinctive
apostolic route.

The consequences of moving about on the 'bridge' are plain
to see. The claim was liberty; the result is anarchy. Freedom
to teach contradictory versions of truth is not evidence of
Anglican tolerance, but the precise negation of any authorized
Anglican teaching. The *via media* is a different way, one where
the tolerance and comprehensiveness of the Church are real
and precious but proved not by a limitless variety of teachings
but by the character of her standards and traditions. If it
sometimes appears to be both narrow-minded and broad-
minded as, for example, in its attitude towards sin and the

sinner, it cannot be accused like the bridge churchers of being double-minded.

What observations can be made about Runcie that will give some clues to his time at Canterbury? Although when bishop of St Albans he had taken a public position on certain controversial subjects (notably supporting proposals for allowing in certain cases a second marriage, after divorce, in church) his general reputation was as a skilled tightrope performer. He was generally liked and applauded in his diocese and in much of the wider Church. He was an attractive speaker, memorable in his phraseology. The danger was that the phrase might become a substitute for hard thought and deep conviction. Leonard of Truro was a thought-enlarging and spiritual preacher. Being under obedience he could be no other. He could not be called an exciting preacher. Runcie of St Albans could amuse, attract, stimulate and excite a congregation. But did he move them to repentance, or strengthen them in holy living or try to lift them from earth to heaven?

Runcie was more interested in preserving the Anglican communion than in propagating belief in the established Church of England. In this way he seemed to work from the outside, in. Those people who were later puzzled or angered at his apparent lukewarmness towards the Church and State link should have studied his lecture on 'The Future of the Diocese' given during the St Albans diocesan centenary celebrations in 1977 (published in *Cathedral and City*) where he said plainly, 'I hope that St Albans Diocese will be part of a disestablished Church.' In some ways Runcie with charm and grace, real or artificial, tended to be a compromising genius who would bow difficulties into a corner. Diplomat he had to be, as his co-chairmanship of the Anglican–Orthodox Joint Doctrinal Commission showed. The contrast between Runcie and Leonard is becoming clear. Their differences in outlook and 'inlook' are basic, substantial and unreconcilable. Leonard is serious, too serious for some, in a way that Runcie is not, and serious because of his unswerving sense of vocation.

Any man about to be made deacon is asked to answer a question which is the indispensable preliminary to all the rest: 'Do you trust that you are inwardly moved by the Holy

Ghost to take upon you this Office and Ministration, to serve God for the promoting of his glory, and the edifying of his people?' (*Book of Common Prayer*) 'I trust so' comes the answer, and on the assurance of that interior vocation the external commission is based. Here is the treasure in earthen vessels. On the one hand, it is a spiritual, a supernatural, a divinely-appointed ministry; on the other, it is entrusted to men and has to be fulfilled in the difficult and perplexing circumstances of life in the Church and in society. The sense of Leonard's divinely-given commission has never faded from his mind. It was sealed at his ordination as a priest and further strengthened at his consecration as a bishop in the Church of God. Any ambition he has, derives from his calling.

Another fundamental aspect of Leonard's relations with Runcie must be understood. Any disapproval and distaste he might have applies only to Runcie's beliefs or style, not to Runcie personally. Leonard does not criticize anyone personally in his public utterances or writings. He always tries to confine critical comments to what people teach or advocate. The difficulty is when the style becomes the substance. For Leonard the seeds of the differences in theological approach and pastoral style were planted at Westcott House. Runcie had been part of the gentlemanly High Church tradition of that College. As we have seen, this tradition entertained too many compromises and had elements which belonged to the gifted amateur for Leonard's liking. The Westcott atmosphere had been implanted and nurtured by B. K. Cunningham and was carefully preserved by some of his successors, notably Kenneth Moir Carey. It was in Carey's regime that a large number of Leonard's contemporaries on the bench of bishops passed through Westcott House, including Runcie and John Habgood (now archbishop of York), or were on the staff. Such men, while holding intellectually sensitive theological positions, were always aware of the diversity of Anglican opinion and, one has to add, in a Westcott manner.

While Leonard is loyal to his Anglican origins, his emotional and spiritual instincts, as well as his intellectual training, lead him to look for authority in both the biblical tradition of his Evangelical beginnings and the dogmatic world of Catholic teaching in which his thinking developed. At the same time – and this is crucial – he has kept his

151

distance from Roman Catholicism as such. He remains war
of some of that Church's teaching, particularly with regar
to the idea of earning merit. He has a habit of quoting th
lines in Toplady's hymn, 'Nothing in my hand I bring, simpl
to thy Cross I cling', which he maintains express both th
Catholic doctrine of grace, and the Evangelical doctrine o
justification. Leonard has always been wary of the excesse
of Roman Catholicism as exhibited in the later Middle Ages
during the Counter-Reformation and as in France in th
immediate pre-Vatican II years. There are aspects of mario
latry with which he is unhappy. As for indulgences, he doe
not understand them and thinks the concept nonsense. Bu
he can understand purgatory. The real influences on hin
come from the patristic age, and the people and writings o
the Caroline divines. He has always sought to live by a
Catholicism which while full-blooded is not specifically
Roman. Some of his supporters do not or will not understand
this. They want to be led by part of Leonard, but cannot take
him at full strength.

Leonard's conversion, as a young man, to Catholicism, was
absolute. Without leaving behind the Evangelical experience
he was set in a pattern of thought and action which has no
changed with the years. He looks for authority to the tradition
of the Church but is unhappy with the uncertain, confused, or
even contradictory Catholicism of the Anglican communion to
which he is determined to be loyal so far as circumstances
allow. He wonders if the tenets of Anglicanism are a bit
sophisticated for ordinary people. It is an interesting point.

Runcie was regarded as a man for the season. Seasons
change. Leonard does not change. His conception of his office
is so different from that of Runcie. Leonard represents to his
diocese (of Truro and now of London) the authority of the
whole Church, delivering the truth as it was received even
before the division between East and West, and appealing for
support to every Catholic bishop in every generation who has
handed on this deposit faithfully. The dimension in which he
thinks is different from that of merely the Church of England
or the Anglican communion. When the Crown appointments
commission was considering his name they would not see a
bishop for the season, or even a bishop for or of his time.
His pedigree showed something quite different and distinct.

Where matters of real principle are involved it is of supreme importance whenever the current of opinion is flowing strongly in one direction, that men of learning, integrity and spirituality shall be found to swim against it. That service Leonard had rendered at Willesden and at Truro and even more so at London. It is of minor consequence that he may fail to convert people to his opinion. There are moments in history when it is more important that a man should swim against the current than that he should turn the tide.

The resignation of Coggan and the nomination of Runcie was a distraction. Leonard was much occupied in other spheres. Following the failure of the Anglican–Methodist scheme for union, it was thought that a long period of reflective silence would be advisable before the Church of England embarked on 'unity' discussions again. Those favouring visible unity were unprepared for practical inactivity. The gentle pressures of a number of Churches resulted in the Churches Unity Commission in 1974 comprising the Church of England, the Baptist Union, the Churches of Christ, the Congregational Federation, the Methodist Church, the Moravians, the Roman Catholic Church and the United Reformed Church. The Congregational Federation comprised those who had not entered the URC. During the early stages of its life, the commission identified four needs if unity was to be achieved: to share one faith; to acknowledge one mutually recognized membership; to acknowledge one ministry; and to be ready to share one another's worldly goods. These were expanded into *Ten Propositions* (1976), not proposals for a scheme but propositions to test out the attitude of the participating Churches to a range of key issues to be faced by Churches seeking visible unity. These came before the Truro Diocesan Synod on 25 February 1978. By this time Leonard himself had joined the Churches Unity Commission initially during the latter half of 1977 in place of Canon Professor J. Macquarrie of Oxford, while he was on sabbatical leave.

There was a vociferous debate in Truro and it was clear that the clergy would vote against the ten propositions as an acceptable basis for continued consultations. They did: 41 for, 56 against, 1 abstention. The laity vote was little better: 42 for, 36 against, 1 abstention. Leonard voted in favour and was fearful that the vote would be seen as one against unity so he suggested an alternative motion saying that continued consultation 'must take doctrinal differences seriously and must seek to resolve them by a deeper and shared understanding of truth if it is to result in true unity'. This was carried.

For various reasons some of the participating Churches were unable to accept the ten propositions. Those that did, led to the establishment of the Churches' Council for Convenanting – Church of England, Methodist, Moravian and United Reformed; other Churches sent consultant observers. The chairman was Kenneth Woollcombe, former bishop of Oxford and then assistant bishop of London and canon of St Paul's Cathedral. The Council was given two years to prepare a covenant. The Church of England members who participated in the final preparation of the report were the bishops of Guildford (David Brown), St Albans (John Taylor), Durham (John Habgood – from November 1979), the Ven. Derek Palmer, archdeacon of Rochester; Canon Peter Boulton, vicar of Worksop Priory; Mr Keith Alsop, Mr Oswald Clark, chairman of the House of Laity of the General Synod and Miss (now Dame) R. Christian Howard.

Leonard's contribution to the council was not minimal. Regular in attendance and vocal in discussion he also contributed valuable papers: one on the theological biblical issues in the ordination of women to the ministry of word and sacrament. He prepared the basic draft for the 'consecration of a bishop', and when the working group substituted 'ordination' for 'consecration' so as to avoid conflict (for 'consecration' carried certain overtones) more than a word was changed. An emphasis and meaning was altered. Making episcopacy palatable for the Methodist Church and thinkable for the United Reformed Church was surely a prelude to disaster. In convenating it was not so much episcopacy in name which was at stake but what episcopacy was in fact. If bishops were little more than the existing moderators (URC), or if hundreds of superintendent ministers (Methodist) would become bishops, were the Free Churches and the Established Church talking about the same thing?

Despite large areas of agreement during the work of the council, and some changed attitudes, there were fundamental issues which would have to be resolved if those holding Catholic convictions in the Church of England (represented by Peter Boulton, Oswald Clark and Leonard) could be full participants in the covenant. The report was due to be published in 1980 and right up to and almost beyond the last moment it was not clear that there would be less than unanimity, even if there were hesitations. This was not, however, to be the case, for on 19 March 1980 Boulton, Clark and Leonard gave notice of their intentions to express reservations. It was a source of irritation and displeasure to other members of the council. Could they not have seen it coming?

In June 1980 the report, *Towards Visible Unity: proposals for a covenant*, was published. The proposals provided for the celebration of a national service in which representatives of the Churches would make promises to God and to one another (closely based on the earlier ten propositions), would together ordain at least one bishop and one presbyter from each of the participating Churches, while also praying for the blessing of existing ministries of episcopal oversight and of pastoral ministry, and then celebrate together the Communion, the sacrament of reconciliation. The national service would be followed by other regional and local services which would allow all ministers and congregations in the Churches to make a direct response to the covenant, and by the formation of agencies for joint decision-making in certain (if at first limited but crucial) fields. The covenant was seen as a decisive and irreversible step towards union. The report carried a 15-page 'Memorandum of Dissent' by Boulton, Clark and Leonard. Grave exception was taken to it by some members of the council. In a later pamphlet *The Failure of the English Covenant* there was a comment and innuendo: 'the Memorandum introduced new questions, hardly if at all raised before, which led many to wonder whether even if the questions at issue were answered new ones might still be raised'. The three dissenters maintained that they had raised their points consistently but had not been heard until they made moves to prepare the memorandum.

There was general recognition of Leonard's constructive contributions on such questions as the ministry, but there was the feeling too that no number of safeguards, qualifications or conscience clauses would persuade him to take the majority view on episcopacy, recognition of ministers, women ministers and rights of conscience. Who represented the Church? After *Towards Visible Unity* had been debated by the General Synod in July 1980, it was sent to the dioceses. Although it was stressed that this was not another scheme imposed from the 'centre', that is how it was perceived. There were outbreaks of enthusiasm for it but no one was putting the bunting out. In the Anglican–Methodist scheme the stone of stumbling was 'deliberate ambiguity'. The rock of offence for covenanting was to be unresolved anomaly.

For Leonard and those who would call themselves dissenters, the issues stretched beyond the recognition of women ministers in non-episcopal Churches or the deliberate reservations by the United Reformed Churches on the historic ministry of the Church. The nature of the Church would be altered by *these* proposals. Covenanting as a principle was right, but not these proposals, although it is doubtful if any set of proposals would have satisfied Leonard with these particular Churches, leaving aside the other Churches including the Roman Catholic Church. Boulton, Clark and Leonard published a pamphlet *The Covenant: a re-assessment*. The overall voting in the dioceses was 36 in favour (81.8%) and 8 against (18.2%). Bishops: 71 for (72.4%), 23 against, 4 abstentions; clergy: 1905 for (65.9%), 937 against, 49 abstentions; laity: 2036 for (72.1%), 742 against, 47 abstentions.) By the time the final vote came in the General Synod Leonard was bishop of London and devoted his presidential address to the diocesan synod on 13 March 1982 to the subject. It was one of those occasions where hungry sheep looked up and felt they were neither fed nor led. It was a misjudgement on the part of Leonard, the leader. He said: 'I conceive the duty of a diocesan bishop on such an occasion to be somehwat similar to that of a judge when he sums up at the end of a trial for the benefit of the jury. I do not believe that it is an occasion when the president should press his views. He has other opportunities and occasions to do that. Rather, like a judge, he must set out the points at issue and draw attention to the evidence which must be taken into account and assess what weight is to be given to it.' This was ever Leonard's way with controversial proposals. He had written and spoken much on covenanting, so his personal views were a matter of record. It is to them that seekers must look if they want to find why he dissented from the proposals.

By the time the General Synod debated the matter on 7 July 1982 the United Reformed Church had voted 69% in favour and the Methodists almost 80% in favour. When the Church of England voted the result was: bishops: 38 for (77.5%), 11 against, 1 abstention; clergy: 148 for (61.9%), 91 against, 2 abstentions; laity: 154 for (68.4%), 71 against. A two-thirds majority was necessary in each house: the vote was lost.

Articles had proliferated by the pro-covenanters, attempting to persuade or plead for the scheme's approval. David Edwards, dean of Norwich, had written a long open letter (published in the *Church Times*) to Leonard. Leonard had written a reply which was printed and circulated:

> I think our differences lie deeper than those about the details of the covenant proposals. The heading of your letter 'Please vote for the Covenant', your prayer for a miracle and a last minute change of heart, your reference to arguments which will appeal to consciences, all seem to me to reflect your belief that what needs to be changed is a personal attitude of will on my part and of those who cannot vote for the proposals. This is understandable, because you believe 'that the will of God has been shown to us in this matter' and therefore identify voting against the proposals as disobedience to the will of God.

'I do not believe that matters of truth can be resolved by majority vote' is a constant theme of Leonard's. It put a real burden on him to show how such matters of truth could be resolved. For some of his supporters it was a useful phrase for standing still (they would say 'firm') and doing nothing. Leonard knew he had to explore other ways by different methods.

When Leonard had been appointed chairman of the Board for Social Responsibility, the archbishop of Canterbury (Donald Coggan) had hoped it would not be too long before Leonard was in the House of Lords. There are 26 lords spiritual, including the archbishops. One of the bishops reads prayers whenever the house is sitting. This bishop is, therefore, theoretically available to speak on any matter which arises during his week of duty. But one of the main characteristics of the house's debates is their informed nature, so the bishop reading prayers may not be sufficiently expert on the subject of the debate to justify taking part in it. Many lords are working lords who have to research and master a brief. The quality of their best debates exceeds anything heard in 'the other place'. Woe betide the pompous prelate or preaching bishop. It can take time for a bishop to find his feet, and his mouth, in the house. The distance from Truro meant that Leonard had to be selective in his appearances. He made his maiden speech on 18 January 1978 during a debate on the Wolfenden Report on *Voluntary Organizations*. It was a short speech and well received, but did not signal his future reputation as a bishop who could defeat a government. While bishop of Truro, there were other speeches on blasphemy, government policy, nuclear weapons, the housing situation and the British Nationality Bill (1981). The Church had expressed criticism about this last bill, notably its reliance on racially discriminating immigration.

Gerald Ellison announced in June 1980 that he would retire as bishop of London on 30 April 1981. The Church and Crown appointments commission realised that the appointment to London was almost as important as that to Canterbury. Once again names were paraded, with Leonard's near front of stage. However, most of the diocesan hierarchy would not be in favour of Leonard. The area bishops were all Ellison appointees and he had, wrongly, appointed one after the announcement of his retirement. That was Bishop Mark Santer of Kensington. The other bishops were Geoffrey Hewlett Thompson of Willesden, William John Westwood of Edmonton, and James Lawton Thompson of Stepney. At St Paul's Cathedral Alan Brunskill Webster was dean. And little support could be expected for Leonard south of the river at Lambeth.

The vacancy in see committee in London went into action. Clergy and parishes were canvassed for their views and up to 70% favoured Leonard. The other percentage was divided between other possibilities. But had not this happened before, in 1973, and yet the prime minister's letter had gone to the wrong address. Brian Masters, vicar of Holy Trinity, Hoxton, a member of the standing committee of General Synod, was one of many priests and laity who knew that if they wanted Leonard they would have to do more than pray. They had lost him once and there would be no further opportunity. This meant that there would have to be activity in the corridors of persuasion. The more they padded those corridors the more they realized that another bishop and, with some of Leonard's opponents *any* other bishop, was favoured.

The Canterbury appointment had been quick. London was excessively slow. An appointment was expected early in 1981 but it was looking as if the postman would travel to the far North rather than to the utmost West. Any reading of the Statement of Needs of the London Diocese pointed West, not North. These are extracts from a December 1980 draft:

The diocese. The diocese of London is almost wholly urban. About three million people live within its boundaries not to mention commuters and tourists. Distributed across its 473 parishes are only about 70 000 people registered on parish electoral rolls. Within the boundaries of the diocese the largest single Christian body is the Roman Catholic Church. Other non-Christian religions also have substantial followings, some of which are increasing rapidly. In terms of its practice, following, prominence, and impact the Church of England is in real terms an insignificant presence within most of the diocese except for those occasions where it is represented by virtue of Establishment and for those Christian rites like baptism and burial which have survived in an industrialized and secularized society.

It is a diocese of extreme diversity at every level, racially, denominationally, culturally, and in terms of its wealth, housing, and employment. In particular the overlap between economic, social, and racial tensions pose increasingly acute problems for the future in which the social gospel of Christianity needs to be proclaimed and interpreted to the diocese from a firm and intellectually committed base of orthodox Christian belief and values.

Within the diocese the parochial structure of the Church of England is typically one of smaller rather than larger congregations, often isolated, which have chosen the churchmanship and/or the pastor that they like, rather than come together on a neighbourhood-loyalty basis. They and their priests or ministers often feel, acutely, the lack of a convincing spokesman for their basic beliefs and the lack of an inspiring leader who can apply those beliefs in the wider but day-to-day public domain where the voice of the Church of England seems to be largely lost. In this situation the qualities of the leadership required in the bishop of London are those of holiness, integrity, and intellect which can transcend party differences within the Church rather than ignoring them or glossing them over.

As a guardian of the faith once for all committed to the saints, he should have an unswerving devotion to the traditional Gospel of incarnation and redemption, as revealed in the holy scriptures and worked out through membership of the holy Catholic Church as the body of Christ.

There has been such speculation and innuendo about the London appointment that a few points need recording. Within the diocese, Leonard had strong support from Catholics and Evangelicals as well as from clergy and laity who would own no label yet wanted a pastoral bishop and a firm leader. The liberal and radical element in the diocese did not want Leonard. They saw him as a traditionalist (in the wrong sense), an opponent of the ordination of women, a wrecker of unity schemes, against reform in spheres of morality. The majority of the diocesan hierarchy did not want Leonard. St Paul's Cathedral did not want Leonard. In effect there was a 'stop Truro' movement which failed because it did not have a single equally strong candidate of its own. Opinion among Anglo-Catholics was not unanimous for Leonard. There were those who would have liked to have seen a daring appointment such as Dom Wilfrid Weston OSB, the young abbot of Nashdom. That was never a practical proposition.

After a great deal of deliberation the Crown appointments commission presented two names to Prime Minister Margaret Thatcher: said to have been John Stapylton Habgood, bishop of Durham, and Leonard. The voting on the commission was 7 to 5 by which neither name had a two-thirds majority. Thus the order in which the names were given to the prime minister was unimportant. There was no preference.

There the matter might have rested had it not been for the

exasperated diligence of Leonard's supporters who, hearing what had occurred, set in motion some political lobbying: not an activity of which Leonard would have approved. The archbishop of Canterbury would throw his weight behind Habgood, and the prime minister would know this. She had to be made aware that the diocese, excepting some officials, wanted Leonard. The prime minister would know more about Leonard than about Habgood. He had (at Willesden) been bishop of part of her own constituency. He was known to be against most of the liberal trends in the Church. He was said to be sympathetic towards Conservatism. She may have recognized that formidable even forbidding combination of unyielding conviction and steady vision which results in strength of purpose. Was she not like that herself? And she kept herself informed about Church affairs and its personalities. Of course, ecclesiastically she was unlikely to share a pew with Leonard. They would be unlikely to meet as pilgrims at the shrine of our Lady of Walsingham. Another way of looking at Leonard was that he was independent, not a member of the Establishment and was quite clear as to the Church's spiritual function in the State. This may have appealed too.

Whatever happened, the procedures agreed between Church and State over the question of appointments were followed in every detail. The commission may have preferred Habgood; the prime minister, after consultations with others and finally heeding her own judgement, preferred Leonard. It was even said that the queen was dismayed over the choice of Leonard and contacted the archbishop of Canterbury to see if the nomination could be reconsidered, but was advised not. Throughout the early months of 1981 there was a feeling of irritation that the appointment was so long delayed. Truro knew that London was at the least a possibility, but as time passed Leonard felt that he would remain at Truro.

While the vacancy in London remained unresolved, Leonard was asked whether he would let his name go forward (among others) as a nominee for the election to the archbishop of Cape Town, vacant by the resignation of Bill Bendyshe Burnett. He consulted a few very close associates who advised against it. They considered he was needed in England whether or not he moved from Truro. In any event Leonard

would have been uneasy about accepting such a call, because
the South African Government could have given him six
months as archbishop and then withdrawn his permission to
live in the country. However, the post soon delivered the
following letter:

10 Downing Street

20 March 1981

My dear bishop,
    The see of London will be vacant on 30 April on the
resignation of the Right Reverend Gerald Ellison, and it
is my duty to advise the Queen on the new appointment
to the see.
    I have received the advice of the Crown Appointments
Commission on the vacancy, and have considered my
recommendation with care. I have decided, if you are
willing that I should do so, to submit your name for the
succession to this See.
    I know the size of the task which I am asking you to
undertake. If, as I greatly hope, you find it possible to
accept my offer I shall have much pleasure in submitting
your name to Her Majesty for this appointment.
    Yours sincerely,
    Margaret Thatcher

Leonard accepted without delay. The announcement was
made on 30 March 1981 to a chorus of delight and dismay.
The Times sparked off controversy about the appointment
(Habgood v. Leonard) and the newspaper columns raged.
The displeasure of liberals within the Church was undis-
guised. It was a black day for them. The press conference
following the announcement was not to the press corps' taste.
This bishop would keep talking about God and theology!
There was a tremendous fuss about the supposed leak and it
was probably a leak rather than journalistic clairvoyance or
ecclesiastical conjecture. One bishop wanted an enquiry; he
held that the issue brought the queen into the ecclesiastical
wranglings of the Church of England. The excessive secrecy
with which such affairs are conducted encourages leaks, bad
conduct and confidence breaking. The archbishop of Canterbury regretted the proceedings over a London appointment
had been so protracted, but assured Leonard that there had

been much totally inaccurate gossip: 'I cannot say more than that, beyond assuring you that you have strong support here in London.'

The statements from both 10 Downing Street and Lambeth Palace confirmed that the procedure was followed correctly. Leonard himself was satisfied that the procedure complied with Prime Minister Callaghan's statement of 1976. Leonard's name must have been one of the two submitted by the Crown appointments commission, and the prime minister exercised the 'real choice' which it was intended should be retained.

Between Leonard's nomination and his enthronement his book *God Alive: Priorities in Pastoral Theology*, which was based on the 1980 Pastoral Theology Lectures given in the University of Durham, was published. Here was a theological book, Pauline and biblical, showing that 'the purpose of the Christian gospel and of the Christian life is union with God'. It was about spirituality. Was London ready for the consequences of having Leonard as bishop?

12

Belated Arrival

The formal election of Leonard to the see of London by the
dean and greater chapter of St Paul's took place on 3 June
1981. The appointment was confirmed by a majority. The
row over the appointment and the leaks continued unabated.
Fortunately the enthronement was not until 20 September in
the setting of a Eucharist. By this time the tempest had
subsided and the enthronement was perfect. Leonard did not
have to knock for admittance into *his* cathedral. The doors
were flung open and from that moment welcome, warmth, joy,
splendour and glory were the notes of the service. Leonard
responded to Alan Webster's welcome: 'Alan. Mr Dean, I
thank you. . . .' The cardinal and apostolic delegate were
there, friends from Free Churches, clergy from Truro. The
Agnus Dei from Mozart's Coronation Mass transported the
congregation to the heavens which was where they stayed as
Leonard opened his sermon with the following words:

> I am going to talk to you this evening about God and I
> will first tell you why. We are here as his people, his
> household the Church, the body of Christ, the company of
> those who are united to God in Christ by the Spirit, not
> just as a gathering of human beings for a purely human
> occasion. We are met to celebrate the Eucharist in which
> Christ renews us and in which by grace we become more
> truly his body. We are those who have been baptized into
> Christ, those who share his life and are, therefore, called
> to share his mission. As the Church, we have *no purpose nor
> meaning save that which is given to us by God.*

That last sentence is a permanent reminder both for himself
and for his people. It is the note of his priesthood and his
episcopate.

Would Leonard be able to pursue his chosen priorities or would he be engulfed and drowned by the work attendant on being bishop of London, who since Ellison's day no longer lived at Fulham Palace but, rather, in the centre of Westminster. The general secretary of the Protestant Alliance (Revd A. G. Ashdown) wrote to him on his appointment to London and was obviously worried about Leonard's leadership of Anglo-Catholicism. Leonard quickly unarmed (not disarmed) him:

Christians today have a specially grave responsibility both to witness to the Gospel by which we are enabled to obey the Divine Will, but also so to live that men and women are drawn to a life of holiness. . . . The one verse of scripture which we particularly need to remember today seems to be *Ephesians* ii: 8: 'By grace are ye saved: and that not of yourselves: it is the gift of God.' Man is trying to find ways of saving himself – and in spite of himself. As T. S. Eliot put it, 'dreaming of systems so perfect that no one will need to be good'. Alas, the Church and Christians are infected by this and suppose that less effort will suffice. It is the Gospel and grace which needs to be proclaimed'.

From the start, Leonard was determined to care pastorally himself for the London episcopal area, the cities of London and Westminster. 'I am sure that this is right, apart from the fact that, being the kind of person I am, I cannot work as a bishop without a pastoral area of my own.' What do some of the clergy of his area say? The Revd Ian MacKenzie, rector of St Mary, Bryanston Square:

Many of us would say that he is precisely what London has long needed. He is a bishop with the necessary dignity of the office, a man of principle and generosity of mind (a rare combination), both a 'prince of the Church' and a pastorally minded bishop. His concern for his clergy is obvious and much appreciated. He is kindly. He reminds us of essentials and priorities and the great things of Christian vocation. He knows that the priestly office is 'both of so great excellency and of so great difficulty' and administers his pastoral care of and concern for the clergy accordingly. He is not a 'yes man' to the powers that be.

I have the distinct impression that Dr Leonard tests all things by the measure, 'is this to the honour of God first and therefore to the true dignity of humankind following on inseparably?' and acts accordingly. Certainly many of us feel – even those fully trained and qualified theologically – that we have never risen from 'sitting at his feet' and gone on our way without being enriched in those things which make men wise unto salvation. He is a bishop in the mould of the Nicene Fathers . . . and as determined.

Canon Peter Delaney, vicar of All Hallows by the Tower, has known Leonard for 20 years. He first met Leonard when he was an archdeacon

and in his precise and tangible way [he] was conscious of how a young priest needed support and help and how he could possibly give it. His combination of humour and extreme discipline was something that touched me from the beginning. . . . His personality has always fascinated me as it has been a personality based on academic, scientific examples of thought, but committed to the risk and expression of artistic interpretation. I can remember him clearly coming to a group that I had of young people sitting cross-legged on the floor and answering questions well into the night and then the following day seeing him at an area synod in which he hardly knew one and continued in this rather distant guise, which he puts on sometimes to protect himself and which I think he is trapped in. . . . I think [Bishop Graham] suffers, as do most public figures and particularly Anglican bishops, from the problems of the public image which is created, either by them or those around them and the deeply private and personal aspects of their lives which exist in a tension with that public image.

He is a man of deep personal prayer and is very much nurtured on the images of people like Ignatius Loyola and Francis de Sales, though curiously simple in the Englishness of how he interprets biblical criticism and his own personal development of prayer. He is a man that one can gain access to and he takes his responsibility towards his own clergy very seriously indeed, moving heaven and earth in order to see them and be supportive of them.

The vicar of St Mary's, Bourne Street, Revd John Gilling, who is at one end of the ecclesiastical spectrum, comments that

> because of his commitment to and love for the Church he often appears rather cold and forbidding. But he has a vein of fun in him that comes out among friends. So when he preached at our centenary in 1976 he had St Mary's congregation rolling about with laughter. He has far too much to do in his present job, but he feels in conscience bound to try to do it all. This means there are sometimes delays in correspondence etc which makes it appear he is not getting on with the job. But when a pastoral or other crisis happens no one could be more kind and gentle and thorough.

The rector of All Souls, Langham Place, Revd Richard Bewes, who is at the opposite end of that same ecclesiastical spectrum remembers when

> [Leonard] had come as a guest to the Senior Evangelical Anglican Conference at Swanwick in the early 1980s and it was my privilege to interview him one evening in front of about 400 delegates. We covered a wide area: ethics, revelation and liberalism, evangelism, education and the Church. Never lost for a word, what came across from him during those 45 minutes was his tenacious hold upon the great fundamentals of the revealed faith. . . . He made it plain that he had never refuted the Evangelical beliefs [of] the centrality of the Cross, the authority of Scripture and the personal nature of faith in Christ. He has gained a reputation for being something of a maverick; upsetting the conventions doesn't bother him overmuch, if what he feels he is doing is right. I admire and look up to him for his generosity of spirit, his courage in controversy and his care and concern for us clergy and our families.

Another view comes from the Revd Dr Martin Israel, vicar of Holy Trinity, Prince Consort Road, South Kensington.

> His rather extreme views made public in the media belie a man who is the soul of compassion. As a man he is immediately approachable, and has the knack of making

himself rapidly conversant with the difficulty of the person who has asked to see him. Unlike many traditional bishops (fortunately fewer today than even a decade ago) there is no film of authority that tends to separate [them] from the man in the street. He is constructively conservative in church ... but is never afraid to attack authority when what he sees as injustice is in danger of being done.

My own interests include among many other things the paranormal dimension, and I am one of the advisers on psychic matters in the diocese. Graham Leonard is remarkably well clued-up in this matter, neither dismissing it as a psychological aberration nor fearing it as the work of the devil, as do many fundamentalistic clergy. He is a valued patron of the Churches' Fellowship for Psychical and Spiritual Studies. [He] has no difficulty in accepting the 'miraculous' aspects of the Bible, and especially the Gospels, in a wider framework of the potentialities of human personality, supremely witnessed in the life of Christ. I personally esteem Bishop Leonard for his integrity. Much of what he advocates ... is extremely unpopular, but he knows where he wants to lead the Church. ... His conservative witness is a useful antidote to much emotionally biased radical thinking that so often tends to throw out the baby with the bathwater. I admire the man immensely.

These few reflections relate to Leonard in relation to his clergy. He has the softest of hearts. He is almost too reluctant to be hard on the sinner. Compassion and forgiveness flow from him. A priest who has done many years of faithful service transgresses: what does Leonard do? He does all in his power to help the man and restore him to wholeness and, if necessary, asks the parochial church council to have him back and for *them* to show their compassion and forgiveness. But there is rigour about the Church's moral teaching. This was made clear over his view on the report *Marriage and Divorce*. He was alarmed at the way in which the Church had acquiesced in the steady erosion of the Christian understanding of marriage in the country. When the matter came before the General Synod in March 1984 Leonard was a foremost critic

of those who advocated and pressed for remarriage in Church
after divorce using the normal marriage service.

In the General Synod debate he had asserted:

> I believe that there are many in the country who are now
> looking for a bold affirmation by the Church of the meaning
> of true marriage, of the responsibilities which it brings; of
> the care for children which it lays upon those who under-
> take it; of the duties of loyalty and faithfulness; of the
> determination which is required to love rather than to give
> up. At this very moment, we are being told that within one
> year you can tell whether a marriage is going to work or
> not. What a travesty of love that is.

Any bishop of London has to chair or attend an impossible
number of meetings and committees, and some of them are
impossible too! Throughout his priesthood and episcopate he
has been in demand as a chairman. What is a general view
of him as chairman over the years, for he has not much
altered? Some admire his quick grasp of the core of an issue,
and his refusal to let woolly thinking survive long enough to
form the basis of any actual decision-making; they admire the
sparkle with which he conducts business, and his ability to
survive graciously even the most violent attacks on his views.
Others find his habit of leading constantly from the chair very
frustrating and destructive of *real* discussion of the matters at
issue. They can also be irritated by his glorious self-indul-
gence in personal anecdote to illustrate a point (or not, as
the case may be) linked to his desire to get through every
agenda item as quickly as possible. Equally there are those
that think the personal anecdote is helpful. As a chairman
of any major committee or board his approach has always
illustrated integrity and professionalism, for example, he will
not allow other issues, like the ordination of women, to
obtrude into his relationship with committee members.

Here I have strayed into something important, the matter
of integrity. Leonard has an overriding concern for truth.
This is why subjectivism and indifference are anathema to
him. Yet his integrity is such that this concern, this belief,
does not lead him to join the ranks of those who would
indoctrinate rather than educate. That is why he disappoints
some of his ardent followers. There is an unwillingness to

manipulate others, no matter how good the end or how laudable the purpose. He is activated by motives other than that of self-interest. The purpose of his life is not found in himself but in obedience to God. On the issues for which he is a leading voice he is not one who will bludgeon people into accepting his argument or views. How irritating that is for those who want to be led and whose consciences reign but do not rule.

The side of Leonard that is business-like (and knowledgeable) in matters such as finance, is not generally seen. Sir Douglas Lovelock, First Church Estates Commissioner, has some reflections:

I suspect that I see an untypical side of Graham Leonard: that is to say that I do not have official meetings with him when he is concerned with doctrine, for example, the furore about the bishop of Durham, or about the ordination of women, but primarily in connection with financial or administrative issues. What follows is of course written purely in my personal capacity. I say later what my impressions are. They reinforce my feeling when we first met, that there are two Graham Leonards: one the 130th bishop of London, conscious (with reason) of the prestige that office endows upon him, with a strong sense of history and perhaps even a tiny touch of pomposity. The other is the totally unassuming down-to-earth man of business with whom I find it a pleasure to deal.

My main contacts with him are as a colleague on the commissioners' board of governors, in his role as chairman of the Churches Main Committee, which brings together the various denominations to consider problems of common interest (usually ones with a financial flavour), and as chairman of the Board of Education who every year appears before the Joint Budget Committee, which I chair, to see how much money he can wheedle out of us.

He is an excellent chairman: crisp, orderly, no nonsense, who keeps the discussion to the point and ensures that a conclusion is reached. Finance is not his natural scene, but he deals with it very well. His naturally high intelligence would enable him to master any subject he gave his mind to. His capacity for hard work is astonishing. He once showed me his diary and I doubt if there are more than three or four busier ones in England. The combination of national and diocesan responsibilities is formidable. Obviously, his life is very well organized and he knows how to single out what is really important.

As I have indicated, all I know of him as a theologian and purveyor of doctrine is what I hear him say in synod and elsewhere and in his frequent writings. Once again, I see a contrast between the analytical approach see him display in the activities we jointly participate in, and some of his other views. For example, I understand the arguments which he and others adduce about the ordination of women as prejudicing the unity of the church, (even though I do not share them), but I cannot for one moment see how he can persuade himself, as he evidently sincerely has, that they have anything to do with salvation. It is as though on certain subjects the heart takes over from the head.

There is something else too. With the intellectual and personal maturity, and the gravitas which he brings to his office, there is still the delightful schoolboy not far beneath the surface. There is about him a certain innocence, a certain simplicity that is quite unexpected the first time one encounters it, and yet continues to reveal itself time after time. It is there when he asks, after a speech or address, 'Was that all right?' It is as if he needs reassuring on such occasions that he has put up an adequate performance. The schoolboy innocence reveals itself most markedly when an expression of glee crosses his face having just made a telling point, or won a particular vote or been asked to attend some prestigious function. It also reveals itself in the trust he puts in people that he believes have put their trust in him, whether they be cabinet ministers or parishioners. This characteristic, coupled with his speed of decision, occasionally impetuous, has led to some strange appointments and, it must be added, to some extremely good ones. William Temple was said to have this 'innocence' too and he was said to have made some misjudgements of people. But, as with Temple, this trust in people, and an underlying *interest* in people, is also a great strength and a source of undoubted charm. His charm is gracious, not oily. According to Mrs Mark Hood,

He is a rare mixture: a man of steel with a tender core, a cool and calm man fired by passionate beliefs, a sophisticated and urbane scholar who never lost his schoolboy enthusiasm and wonder. He can grasp the intricacies of theological arguments yet retain a wonderfully simple and trusting personal belief. He is Anglican and is impatient with people who overlay true Anglican practices with others.

Everyone else I know wastes time, energy and personal resources, but he never wastes anything. He is a conserver. He loves music, his books, his garden, and pottering at his work-bench. . . . I have always been able to take any problem to him whether my concern has been my sick child, my injured husband, a moral dilemma in nursing, or grief over a friend. He listens carefully. He pays infinite care to details and talks through a problem. He rarely offers advice. He has a horror of manipulating people and argues logically. When arguments fails he never resorts to emotional appeals.

Myths start by inaccurate reporting or through misunderstanding. Leonard has often been referred to as the present prime minister's favourite bishop. Then if he appears to be opposing the Government on issues another bishop takes his place. In his dealings with the Government Leonard manifests a very pragmatic balance between flexibility and consistency. Once he has committed himself to a public statement he will not go back on it, yet he will sometimes be seen to be reinterpreting it in some way or other. There is a balancing act in his relationships with the Tory party. He is in sympathy with many of the aims of the party, and yet there are times when he has felt their actions in power to have been misconceived. He has been prepared to say so and yet he has (even then) been anxious not to give the impression that he was simply Tory bashing as some of his fellow clergy and fellow bishops seem to, or are supposed to, enjoy doing. However, he will never have modified, or even moderated, his position simply out of any partisan loyalty. It will be because he will have identified some new factor in the situation which has challenged his original position.

One position which commended him to the Conservative

Government was his consistent belief in the need for the nuclear deterrent. Following publication of the report *The Church and the Bomb* (1982) from a working party chaired by the bishop of Salisbury (John Baker), Leonard contributed chapters to two books: 'The Morality of Nuclear Deterrence' (in *Unholy Warfare*, 1983) and 'A Fragile Peace' (in *The Cross and the Bomb*, 1983). He also wrote an article in the *Reader's Digest* (April 1983): 'In Defence of the Bomb'. Leonard, as chairman of the Board for Social Responsibility, had the unenviable duty of introducing and intervening regularly in the General Synod debate (10 February 1983) which was conducted at a high level and was televised for all to see. He guided the synod towards the resolutions which happened to accord with his view which was the majority view. It was his last series of speeches as chairman of the board. Leonard's view was in essence simple: 'Nuclear weapons have introduced a new dimension into international relations. The principles underlying the Just War are not altered, however. A Christian government, no matter how great the threat from another power, must never barter away justice and freedom, simply to survive. Nor is it morally responsible to allow nuclear weapons with all their evil potential to be entirely in the hands of those who have no scruples about their use.' *The Church and the Bomb* concluded that Britain should abandon her nuclear weapons unilaterally. This was a view Leonard could not share: 'As a Christian, I believe that negotiating disarmament from a balance of power is the best way of preserving peace because that process is based on valuing human life above mere survival.' There was a sting to Leonard's belief: 'We must not imagine that the existence of nuclear weapons, the product of man's ingenuity, can absolve us from living in accordance with our moral nature.' The recovery of moral sense 'begins with repentance in every aspect of our life and not simply with the repudiation of one result of our sinful condition.'

In the pamphlet war which followed the proclamation of the bishop of Durham's opinions, Leonard was in demand by television, radio and the Press to give an opposing view – or rather, his version of the truth. He was deeply concerned with the aftermath of what became known as the 'Jenkins Affair'. He wrote a preface to *Easter at Durham* by Murray Harris,

173

warden of Tyndale Hall; and contributed the Saturday article
in *The Times* (15 September 1984) on 'The Coherence of the
Life of Jesus'.

The Church of England avoids confrontation whenever
possible. Confrontation does not bother Leonard. There is
nothing new about it and one can see a surplus of it by
looking at the Church in Corinth in biblical times. The bishop
of Norwich (Maurice Wood) called for Jenkin's resignation
and to that Evangelical voice it was hoped the Catholic voice
of Leonard could be added to join in the hounding of Jenkins.
Those who approached Leonard were surprised at his
immediate refusal and failed to understand him in one absolutely vital regard. This has been touched upon in an earlier
chapter. Christian moral teaching has always been based on
two fundamental truths. The first is that a person must always
follow his own conscience. The second is that every person's
conscience is always in need of correction. His convictions
had never wavered and he held them very strongly. He could
say to a fellow bishop concerning Jenkins, as he wrote to
Bishop Colin Winter of Damaraland-in-exile (26 July 1973)
who asked for advice whether he should continue or resign.
The circumstances were entirely different, but the principle
is the same:

> I hold to [the] principle, which I think is relevant, namely
> *Conscientia semper sequenda*. I believe it is morally wrong to
> say to a man, 'If I were in your position, I would resign'.
> That is to ask him to violate his own conscience. Either he
> must be allowed to follow his conscience, or if those in
> authority over him judge his conscience to be so misin-
> formed as to justify his removal from public office, they
> must take steps to remove him and be prepared to justify
> this publicly. I have always found it impossible to justify
> Archbishop Fisher's attitude to Bishop Barnes, when he
> said that if he, Fisher, had found himself in Barnes' position
> he would find it impossible to continue as a bishop. Barnes
> obviously did not, and thought he was right. Fisher could
> have attempted to persuade him to see the error of his ways
> and inform his conscience, and may have done so, but if
> he did and failed he should have either accepted Barnes'
> position or taken steps to remove him.

The unsatisfactory nature of the Church of England's disciplinary procedures, then as now, and the uncertainty about the court's interpretation of the Church's formularies was an additional problem. Leonard thinks that the best way to combat opinions that he finds unpalatable or heretical is by the proclamation of the truth. Coupled with the unsatisfactory disciplinary machinery is a General Synod which virtually claims to be infallible.

Following the February 1985 debate in General Synod on the nature of Christian belief, at which Leonard spoke, it was felt that something should be tackled by the bishops. At the bishops' meeting in June 1985 it was agreed that a small group of bishops should be asked to prepare a report. The bishop of Salisbury (John Baker) was chairman and the archbishop of Canterbury invited Leonard to be one of a group of five. The other bishops were St Albans (John Taylor), Bristol (Barry Rogerson), Chester (Michael Baughen) and Birmingham (Hugh Montefiore). This group eventually produced *The Nature of Christian Belief* (1986). Bishop Michael Baughen notes that his

closest connection with Graham Leonard was when we found ourselves on the small group of five bishops commissioned with the task of producing the report *The Nature of Christian Belief*. Under the bishop of Salisbury's superb chairmanship the group of five met frequently and was involved in a very considerable amount of discussion and revision of drafts, etc. I found the meetings enormously stimulating. Different theological view points were represented round the table but there was never a moment when people did not listen to one another and seek to understand what was being said so that the resultant report, prior to its being submitted to the whole House of Bishops and receiving some amendments, was one where the five different opinions could fully agree. Particularly at this time, it was the agreement which Graham Leonard and I share so fully on the basis of scriptural authority and of divine revelation which showed itself. Here we found ourselves locked in strong agreement reaching back to the absolutes of God himself and not simply to relativity of thinking. This is not to say that this was not reflected in other bishops round the table but it was particularly something where Graham Leonard and I found a deep rapport. It is a rapport that has continued since then in other gatherings and meetings.

The statement by the House of Bishops accompanying the report was fully endorsed by Leonard and repays reading to those who say the Church of England has not made up its mind about the faith of the Church:

As the House of Bishops we are united in our adherence to the apostolic faith which the Church of England has received and in which it lives. That faith is uniquely revealed in the holy scriptures, and set forth in the Catholic creeds, and to it the official formularies of the Church of England bear witness.

We affirm our faith in the Resurrection of our Lord Jesus Christ as an objective reality, both historical and divine, not as a way of speaking about the faith of his followers, but as a fact on which their testimony depends for its truth. As regards belief that Christ's tomb was empty on the first Easter Day, we acknowledge and uphold this as expressing the faith of the Church of England, and as affirming that in the resurrection life the material order is redeemed, and the fulness of human nature, bodily, mental and spiritual, is glorified for eternity.

We declare our faith in the affirmation of the Catholic creeds that in Jesus Christ fully God and fully human, the second person of the Blessed Trinity is incarnate. As regards the Virginal Conception of our Lord, we acknowledge and uphold belief in this as expressing the faith of the Church of England, and as affirming that in Christ God has taken the initiative for our salvation by uniting with himself our human nature, so bringing to birth a new humanity.

We accept wholeheartedly our mutual responsibility and accountability as bishops for guarding, expounding and teaching the faith to which God has led us to commit our lives, and for doing so in ways which will effectively 'proclaim it afresh in each generation', while at the same time distinguishing in our teaching the ideas of theological exploration from the beliefs which are the corporate teaching of the Church'.

Leonard has always been associated with some strictly Anglo–Catholic organizations such as The Society of Mary of which he is superior general. The secretary of the Society observes that 'the bishop's interest and help to the society derive from his own personal devotion to our Lady', and adds, 'We have always been encouraged by his lead on important Catholic issues. However, many of us felt disappointed when he went ahead with the ordination of women as deacons'. Leonard's position on the ordination of women as deacons has been consistent. For many years he advocated the restoration of the diaconate to its primitive place and form before the question of whether women should be admitted to it was considered. When, however, this had not happened and the issue arose he said that, whereas it was clear that women had never been ordained to the priesthood in the Catholic church, the same could not be said of the ordination of women as deacons. He also regarded the diaconate as a distinct order rather than as a stepping stone to the priesthood. While recognizing that the ordination of women as deacons would be confusing and could lead to the wrong expectations, he felt he could not refuse to ordain women deacons on principle.

Pilgrimages have played an important part in his life. He has been an honorary guardian of the shrine of our Lady of Walsingham since the mid-1970s. In 1982, and again in 1985, he led two large pilgrimages to Lourdes (taking in the shrines of Ars and Rocamadour). Important ecumenical links were forged as a result of these visits and Leonard invited the bishop of Tarbes and Lourdes to visit him in London in 1986 and he took him on the national pilgrimage to Walsingham. What do pilgrimages mean to him, and what does his presence on them mean to other people? The bishop of Moray, Ross and Caithness (George Sessford) has some reflections:

During the 1970s and early 1980s the pilgrimage movement offered to Graham Leonard two new opportunities to link together glory and compassion. He so often remarked that the very proper abhorence of triumphalism could so easily lead to an apologetic faith with little confidence and few signs of glory. The Walsingham pilgrimages and the

Lourdes pilgrimages helped him to express so clearly the glory and joy of Catholic faith and worship hand-in-hand with enormous compassion for the sick and handicapped. Even when time was so precious and the pressures of an extremely demanding bishopric weighed heavily on him, he insisted on setting proper time apart for preparation and rehearsal before public worship. Nothing slip-shod and unworthy was allowed. All must be done in decency and with prayerful rehearsal.

When at Lourdes, with so many things to do, so many formalities to be observed with the French Church, and so much protocol to attend to, constantly at every pilgrimage his concern was for the *sick*. They were the important ones. When one in a wheelchair apologized for being a 'nuisance' and delaying the group he said, 'nonsense – you are why we are here!' The sick and suffering had the priority, and his own prayers for the pilgrims continued long after their return home, as so many can testify.

Once at Lourdes our timetable had to be amended and certain items had to be missed out. He was due to preach at the pilgrimage Mass in St Joseph's chapel. One possible way of saving time was suggested – the omission of the sermon; Graham's response was immediate: a smile and 'yes, that would be delightful', but then a serious look 'yet I've prepared the words and I really do have to utter their message.'

When the bishop of Tarbes and Lourdes came to England Leonard ensured that he experienced the complete Church of England and not just a few Anglo-Catholic centres and this meant sung Matins at St Paul's Cathedral as well as solemn High Mass at Walsingham. The visit was a joyful encounter. A former administrator of Walsingham, Canon Christopher Colven, remembers vividly the 1981 celebrations of the jubilee of the shrine's restoration:

His particular emphasis on the theology of the Incarnation does I think make Walsingham's holy house a very special place of affirmation and devotion for him. . . . [He] was staying overnight and presiding. In the morning before the main Mass, he took himself off into the village just to wander round and talk to the crowds as they began to arrive; he wanted to be among the ordinary pilgrims instead of having an hour or two to rest. In 1985 . . . the bishop hosted a dinner for the guests (from Lourdes) which was held in the college dining room during which Bishop David Hope, as master of the College of Guardians, invested Mrs Leonard as an honorary dame of the Order of our Lady of Walsingham . . . Bishop Graham was obviously delighted that Priscilla's place close to him had been recognized in this way, and she was moved and pleased too.

Leonard regards the healing ministry as an integral part of the ministry of a bishop or parish priest. He says 'The spiritual realm is almost as real to me as the physical and I see the two are constantly interacting.' When he visits the sick or those who are troubled mentally he almost always offers the laying on of hands, sometimes with annointing. He cannot recollect any occasion (except where there was a refusal of penitence or an indication that there might be, and he has given the person the benefit of the doubt) when healing of some kind, whether physical and/or mental and/or spiritual did not result. There have been occasions when the result has been particularly evident. During a pastoral visit to a parish in Cornwall, he laid hands on and annointed a young teenage boy who had bone cancer and had had to take to his bed permanently. He recovered and later was accepted fit to serve in the army.

Leonard himself had a trouble-free medical record until in 1984 a tumour was diagnosed on the salivary gland in his neck. A tricky operation was necessary because the nerves are interwoven there and he could have been left with permanent paralysis. It was not known whether the tumour was malignant or benign. He had to prepare for the worst possibility in practical ways with Priscilla and to prepare himself spiritually in ways in which he had been helping other peole throughout his ministry. The tumour was benign. Writing to American friends, Gordon and Peggy Heath, after the operation he said: 'I found my first stay in hospital as a patient a valuable experience, spiritually as well as physically. I prepared myself by a general confession and by being annointed and found myself ready to put myself into the hands of God and other people.'

179

Leonard has also always taken the reality of the paranormal seriously and has therefore exorcised places and, very rarely, persons. There are numerous examples of the effectiveness of this ministry. In his experiences many disturbances arise from troubled (not evil) spirits for whom a requiem is the proper remedy. On one occasion in Harrow a blind woman was living in a new bungalow with a concrete floor and she complained of an evil smell and sense of evil which came fairly frequently. The social worker was a youngish rationalist who thought that being blind the woman must have left food about but the place was spotless. The social worker decided to spend a night with her and had the same experience and would not spend another night there. Leonard carried out an exorcism and there was no further trouble. It transpired that the bungalow had been built on the site of a house with a distressing history. On another occasion in 1973 following a Requiem in a vicarage where manifold disturbances and 'presences' has been encountered, all of 50 to 60 candles in the church were found to be lit – but not by human hands.

In the diocese of London itself, the area system is now established and considerable powers and responsibilities are delegated to the area bishops. With regard to appointments, the diocesan bishop remains patron of livings in the bishop's gift. However, appointments to them are discussed at the regular bishops and staff meetings and the diocesan accepts an agreed nomination from the area bishop concerned. All but one of the area bishoprics has changed since Leonard's appointment. This has enabled him to select his own bishops: people according, more or less, to his own viewpoint but with their own distinctive characteristics.

Leonard is more a metropolitan than a diocesan bishop and the Church should think again about a metropolitical see – taking in the diocese of Southwark and a portion of the Chelmsford Diocese. In the 1967 report *Diocesan Boundaries* five dioceses for the Greater London area were proposed – London, Southwark, Barking, Croydon and Kensington.

Any bishop of London has to reject many more invitations than he is able to accept. The City dinner season is such that the bishop could be dining out almost every night of the week. Gerald Ellison was well known at City dinners. Perhaps he was involved in Freemasonry; Leonard is not. This makes a difference in the City where a fair number of leading figures in the civic and social scene (including clergy) are deeply involved in masonic activities. Leonard rations his City dinners and occasions. By City standards he is not an attractive speaker. The City is on the whole too pragmatic for his academic and doctrinal approach.

All his sermons begin with the phrase 'My beloved in Christ'. For him to say this to some City congregations, with an impassive stoney face, a large mitre and with no outward expression of love for his people, does not always endear him to his listeners. The fact that he reads many sermons from a carefully prepared text, while demonstrating a remarkable ability to think clearly and commit it to paper, perhaps reduces the personal impact. Yet it is his teaching which draws people and by which he is remembered rather than any after-dinner humour. Once he undertook a series of six lunchtime services at St Mary Woolnoth when he expounded the letter to the Ephesians. Here was the bishop teaching his people, and there was a sense of power in his exposition. He enjoyed it; the people appreciated it. (He could not complete the series due to illness.) When he delivers a lecture, for example to the Institute of Bankers, his theme and argument are closely argued to such a degree that the closest attention is necessary to follow and understand the views being expressed. Leonard makes no attempt to seduce an audience before launching into his theme. He is too serious for that and assumes he is addressing an intelligent and thoughtful group of people. Again he avoids emotion to make his firmly held convictions clear to an audience.

Leonard has many City friends but the impression he makes in general terms on the City is not great. Why? In his interview with Anthony Clare *In the Psychiatrist's Chair* he said he did not wish to push himself or to reveal his own personality too much. Certainly he would not parade his virtues. In the City this is a disadvantage where people do push their personalities in order to make an impression.

Leonard's travels overseas continued unabated. In 1982 he visited Jerusalem with Sir Donald Logan and Archdeacon R. A. Lindley representing the Jerusalem and the Middle East Church Association to acquaint themselves at first hand with the problems and need of the Anglican diocese. While in

Jerusalem Leonard was installed as an episcopal canon of St George's Cathedral. He met the Greek, Latin and Armenian patriarchs, the apostolic delegate and the custos of the holy places who were well disposed to the Anglican Church. That visit was in September. Two months later he went to Egypt to visit the Coptic Pope Shenouda III on behalf of the archbishop of Canterbury. Priscilla went with him and they had one glorious day at the monastery in the desert where the pope was then in exile. Between the two visits he was leading the Lourdes pilgrimage.

In 1983 there were two visits to the United States, one in May where he gave addresses to the Evangelical and Catholic Mission Congress in Milwaukee when he also received an honorary degree at Nashotah House. In October he was in Long Island, New York, and Philadelphia for the 150th anniversary celebrations of the Oxford Movement. In November he was in Jamaica representing the archbishop of Canterbury at the centenary celebrations of the provinces of the West Indies.

Six visits overseas were made in 1984. First, in January, to attend and preach at the installation of Samir Kafity, an Arab, as bishop in Jerusalem, followed by a private visit to Jordan. In April he was in New York and Greenwich and Lourdes in May. August took him on a three-week visit to Zambia where he conducted a clergy retreat and spoke and preached to congregations giving them and the Church in Zambia a much needed apostolic fillip. He strayed over the border to visit Victoria Falls and Livingstone in Zimbabwe. There were 'quiet day' addresses in Ballymeena, Ireland, in September, followed by a week's engagements in the United States, addressing the Church Pension Fund, attending the 250th anniversary celebrations of St George's Church, Schenectady, New York and receiving an honorary degree at Siena College a Roman Catholic institution administered by Franciscans.

1985 was lighter in terms of overseas visits, with the Ars, Rocamadour, Chartres and Lourdes pilgrimage in July, and the centenary celebrations of the Copenhagen chaplaincy in September. The following year he conducted a Lenten Mission at the University of King's College, Nova Scotia, where there was also a theological conference. He was in

Ireland in June to preach at the 350th celebrations of St Columb's Cathedral. He spent part of May abroad in 1987, first in Los Angeles, speaking and receiving an honorary doctorate at the Simon Greenleaf School of Law, and then to Canada for a theological conference in Charlottetown and another conference in Philadelphia. He returned to the United States to give the 42nd John Findley Green Foundation Lecture at Westminster College, Fulton, Missouri on 'The Tyranny of Subjectivism' to which we return in the final chapter. In an earlier chapter we saw how deeply involved he was with the retreat movement. Interest and involvement has never wavered and two 1988 retreats conducted by Leonard took him overseas: in February to Fort Worth in America and in March to Brussels for some of the clergy in the diocese of Europe.

One overseas visit has been omitted. It took place in 1986 and the name of the place has entered Anglican history: Tulsa.

13

The Wisdom of Foolishness

It is not much of a place, on the road to nowhere, hardly
worth a second glance and certainly not worth a detour. The
name, Broken Arrow, has a romantic ring but that is all.
Broken Arrow, some eight miles from Tulsa, Oklahoma,
would have remained unknown and undiscovered had it not
been for St Michael's Episcopal Church and the bishop of
London. Tulsa (Broken Arrow) has entered the ecclesiastical
history books and is likely to be more than a footnote to the
history of the Anglican communion in the latter part of the
20th century.

The Episcopal Church of America [ECUSA], formerly
known as the Protestant Episcopal Church of the United
States of America, had a faltering history in Oklahoma. At
the opening of the 19th century there were few missionaries
and their work was hampered by the absence of a local bishop
who was needed to confirm the baptised and converted, and
to ordain priests. The first missionary bishop to Oklahoma
and Indian territory was Francis Key Brooke, who was consecrated on 6 January 1893. Under him the Church grew both
in numbers and influence. It was not until 1937 that sufficient
money was raised to enable it to become a diocese in its own
right. Since then there have been three bishops, Thomas
Casady, Chilton Powell and, since 1977, Gerald Nicholas
McAllister. Bishop Casady led Oklahoma to diocesan status
in the darkest days of the Great Depression. His successor,
Powell, led it into the era of ecclesiastical ferment in ECUSA.
The rot set in during the 1970s; Leonard had noticed signs
of deterioration when he made his first and long visit to the
USA in 1970.

ECUSA has failed to show the glories of the Anglican
communion's *via media* and made comprehensiveness a term

of abuse. The Church is torn apart by schism, and the *via media* of Anglicanism stands exposed to formidable criticism and some obvious objections. It seems to hover and halt between two opinions and to endorse conflicting ideals. The zealots of 'tradition' find it disloyal, and those of 'progress' find it disappointing. But 'progress' overpowers and tramples on its adversaries, thus the distinctive character of Anglican Christianity is being obscured, and, some people feel, possibly even destroyed. The result is a paralysing incoherence and lack of discipline within the Church itself, and a grievous loss of influence in Christendom. The progressive zealots are agitators for the ordination of women to the priesthood and episcopate, for changes in the liturgy and the introduction of 'inclusive' (not gender specific) language; they support every liberal political position on offer and advocate a moral revolution often devoid of ethical content. The recently published report of the ECUSA House of Bishops *Sexuality: a divine gift* (1988) against which even some liberal bishops have protested, demonstrates how far morality has been secularized in that Church.

Chilton Powell of Oklahoma was in the vanguard of liturgical reform and was known as the 'father' of the *Book of Common Prayer 1979*. He was chairman of the national liturgical commission which supervised the often controversial work of prayer book revision. Gerald McAllister, a native Texan, was a parish priest in San Antonio before moving to Oklahoma. He had voted for the ordination of women to the priesthood in 1977. Six months after his consecration as bishop, McAllister attended a meeting of the House of Bishops at Port St Lucie, Florida (30 September to 7 October 1977). It was a vital meeting, for the bishops had to face the fact that some sixty parishes in the United States had voted to secede from the parent Church and several bishops were involved in civil court suits against breakaway churches. At that time only one Oklahoma parish, St David's, had joined the secessionist movement. The House of Bishops was concerned with the activities of Albert Chambers, retired bishop of Springfield, Illinois, who was a kind of episcopal spiritual adviser to breakaway Episcopalians and administered the rite of confirmation in breakaway churches. His action was unanimously decried by the House of Bishops but Chambers, who attended the meeting, was unrepentant.

The presiding bishop, John Maury Allin, had an important question for his fellow bishops:

> Can you accept the service of a presiding bishop who, to date, is unable to accept women in the role of priests? . . . If it is determined by prayerful authority that this limitation prevents one from serving as the presiding bishop of this Church, I am willing to resign the office. The ministry must be offered voluntarily as the offering can only be accepted voluntarily and never upon the demand of the minister.

The result was that Allin continued in his office as presiding bishop.

In a statement on *Conscience* prepared by the theological committee of the House of Bishops, it was affirmed 'that no bishop, priest, deacon or lay person should be coerced or penalized in any manner, nor suffer any canonical disabilities as a result of his or her conscientious objection to the 65th General Convention's action with regard to the ordination of women to the priesthood or episcopate'. Many priests were to learn that there are more subtle ways of coercing and penalizing people who cannot in conscience accept a prevailing view particularly by use of the system of canon law which operates in ECUSA.

Unlike the situation in England where ecclesiastical courts are statutory courts, subject to the same constitutional restraints and rules of evidence as the secular courts and subject to judicial review, those in ECUSA are essentially domestic courts with no right of appeal beyond the Provincial Court of the Church. While there are national canons, they are supplemented by diocesan canons, which should conform to the requirements of the traditional canons. These can (and do) permit practices that would not be permitted in England and which would seem to offend natural justice: for example, the bishop prosecutor may appoint the president and some members of the court. Under the canons, the bishop can issue a 'pastoral directive' relating to any matter, however minor, to which the canons refer. If a priest refuses to obey such a directive the bishop can turn it into a 'godly monition'. If the priest refuses to obey that, he becomes liable for trial, though he can ask for the case to be dealt with by the bishop without trial. It would seem that, if the matter goes to trial, the sentence is usually 'deposition from holy orders' and not mere censure or deprivation from office. Such a sentence is very rarely given in England and only then for a very serious offence of gross immorality such as to make it necessary for the man to be prevented from exercising any element of his priesthood.

In 1969 a priest named John C. Pasco moved to Tulsa charged to found a new congregation in the south-eastern Tulsa area. Pasco had served first in the diocese of Connecticut, moving to forces' chaplaincies in the United States and in Germany and then in a mission at Pryor, Oklahoma. Following his move to Broken Arrow, Tulsa, in 1969, St Michael's began its life. As a mission, the gathered community, the body of Christ, met in homes and city parks for fellowship and worship before finding a temporary home at the Skyline Terrace Nursing Center. Within its first year the church moved to Grissom Elementary School and then in an imaginative departure St Michael's shared the building at a swimming club owned by a private corporation with St Michael's Presbyterian Church.

It is important to realize that the congregation and its pastor were given the charge to take on the character of the people attracted to its membership. In 1969 there were many defections from the Episcopal Church following the growing liberal progressive policies advocated and adopted by its leaders under the presiding bishop, John Hines. St Michael's was not to attempt to attract its members from existing churches, but rather to reclaim to the altar the 'drop-out Episcopalians' and others with no allegiance to any church. So it was that St Michael's grew as traditionalist and conservative because this was the nature of those who needed a parish.

In 1972 the bishop of Oklahoma, Chilton Powell, and his council formed a committee under the chairmanship of Mr Malcolm Deisenroth to 'assist' St Michael's. Deisenroth was a Tulsa banker and geologist and prominent Episcopalian. He was opposed to the formation of St Michael's yet appointed the committee that was to 'look into the situation', that is, the Church's existence. The committee met during the spring and summer of 1972. On 19 September Pasco received a telephone call from the chairman of the diocesan council on missions who advised that they had decided, 'there was no room in Oklahoma for a traditional Episcopalian church'. It was the first time that a label 'traditional' had been attached to St Michael's. The events of the following days (in Fr. Pasco's words) are worth recording:

21 September 1972. At the meeting of the bishop and council in Oklahoma City, the Deisenroth Committee made its report which included false allegations such as that there were only two families active in St Michael's, there were actually 91 active communicants. The report recommended: (1) that St Michael's interests in property be sold to the Presbyterian Churches; (2) that the proceeds of the sale be given to the diocese to satisfy the church's debt to the diocese. (3) that St Michael's Episcopalian Church be immediately dissolved; (4) that Pasco be given the 'opportunity' to seek employment elsewhere. At the conclusion of the report and recommendations, two members of the council asked Pasco to respond. He rose to do so. It was immediately moved to go into 'executive [closed] session' and Pasco be excused from the meeting. Deisenroth seconded the motion, and it was passed. Pasco was excused, and in his absence, the report and its recommendations were adopted.

22 September. The bishop telephoned Pasco to say they really wanted St Michael's to 'die'. Therefore Pasco was not to speak with, visit, or minister to (even at the point of death) any member of St Michael's. Pasco responded that he could not obey this unless it was a Godly admonition. The bishop made it so.

23 September. The bishop telephoned Pasco to say St Michael's could have one last service on the next day (Sunday) to observe prematurely the patronal festival.

30 September. The bishop telephoned Pasco again and restored him as pastor of St Michael's members, and to say the church would be allowed to meet in a mission church in a neighbouring town, but said that this did not void the decision of the bishop and council decisions.

5 October. The president of the standing committee informed the bishop and St Michael's that only the standing committee and not the bishop and council can dissolve a mission. Therefore, St Michael's could continue until their decision.

October and November. Numerous requests were made by St Michael's [members] to be allowed to rent, accept invitations to use, or lease property in Tulsa where its members lived. These were all rejected either by the bishop, the executive committee or the finance committee. Finally, in late November, when it was apparent that the intent of the diocesan officials was to kill St Michael's by banishment, the vestry voted to lease, without diocesan permission, a warehouse and make it their church. Moving to it, the church thrived, and one year later the bishop and council 'retroactively' approved the lease.

On Palm Sunday 1979, following the Eucharist at the warehouse, members of St Michael's carried the church furnishings to an address in South Garnett Road, Broken Arrow, to establish the parish in its present location where initial services were held on Maundy Thursday. The buildings and land were owned by St Michael's Church Foundation, a private corporation supported by Episcopalians and other non-Episcopalians and chartered to provide a church with facilities. Between the November 1976 election of Gerald McAllister as bishop of Oklahoma and his consecration in April 1977, Pasco met with McAllister telling him that while he had not supported his election he would support him as bishop. This did not mean that Pasco lowered his voice against the reform of the prayer book, the ordination of women to the priesthood and the political stand of leading bishops.

St Michael's mission became a parish in 1981. Pasco was rector. The story continues in 1983 (again in the words of Fr. Pasco):

March 1983. The bishop visited St Michael's for Eucharist and confirmation. The service was fully in accord with the traditional form of the '79 BCP, using the 'traditional idiom'. A copy of the service was sent to the bishop more than three weeks prior to the date of service; he voiced no objection to it. At the service, the bishop preached on the prodigal son with the implication that St Michael's was a prodigal who should return to him. The bishop used *ad lib* words in administering confirmation. At the rear of the church, after the recessional hymn, within hearing of the congregation, he proclaimed loudly, 'This service was pure butchery!'

May. The rector returned from an out-of-state conference to find the deacon of the parish teaching new concepts and practices which the rector had specifically directed would not be taught or practised, and using the '79 prayer book in one of its alternative ways which the rector had specifically directed would not be used. In discussion with the deacon, the rector was informed that the deacon worked for the bishop and was under his orders, not those of the rector. The rector released the deacon from further service in the parish.

8 May. The rector met with Bishop McAllister to discuss situation with the deacon. The bishop denied any complicity. In discussion, he alleged that the rector was 'unhappy' in the Episcopal Church and that he as bishop would help him out of it. The suggestion was made of an arranged early retirement, or of assistance to Fr. Pasco to become a member of the Anglican Catholic Church. The rector responded that he was born, baptized, confirmed, married and ordained in the Episcopal Church, was absolutely loyal to it and its legitimate authority, and would not leave it voluntarily or allow himself to be driven out of it. The rector also told the bishop that he should rejoice that St Michael's provided a place where traditionalist Episcopalians could be retained at the altars of the Church. The bishop allegedly responded that the Episcopal Church would be 'better off without them'.

April–May. The rector received repeated reports from various clergy of the diocese alleging that 'the bishop was saying he was going to "do something about Fr. Pasco" etc'.

When the attack came which led to the present position it was less to do with God than with mammon. In 1984, during the diocesan comptroller's routine audit of a St Michael's parochial report signed by Fr. Pasco, alleged financial irregularities came to light and the subsequent discovery was made of the independent foundation. This resulted in Pasco's trial before an ecclesiastical court for violation of canon law and his eventual deposition as a priest.

The steps leading to this event are too tortuous to be retraced here. Unfortunately, it is all too common for American bishops to appear in law suits which are financial in origin (often to do with church property), and complex in content. The diocese placed the whole of its emphasis on 'financial irregularities'. In a letter to the parishioners of St Michael's ('Dear Fellow Episcopalians.. . .') the bishop noted that

> investigations revealed that while St Michael's overall income (church and foundation) was increasing, every year its share of the diocesan budget (which is basically the cost of operation of the diocese and the mission and ministry which we do together) was decreasing.

> It soon became apparent that Fr. Pasco was himself directing and encouraging others to channel their giving into St Michael's Foundation. These funds have been extended on behalf of the parish and the result of this irregularity has been that St Michael's has not been paying its fair share of our joint ministry and mission. An independent auditor found that pledges are made to and received by both the parish and the foundation. Father Pasco and your senior warden have acknowledged that members who cancel their pledges to the parish will be offered other alternatives for their giving. In this way, these members may support the parish indirectly without supporting the diocese or the national church.

> I might pause here to observe that this exchange reveals clearly that Fr. Pasco and some of your parish leadership have forgotten that the basic unit of the Episcopal Church is the diocese. It is not the individual congregation. St Michael's was started by the diocese of Oklahoma as a mission. It has received a minimum of $110 000 from the diocese in clergy support from other congregations and individual Episcopalians such as yourselves. It was given a building and a large cash contribution from Malcolm

Deisenroth because it was a needy congregation. It was
also given $50 000 by the diocese towards the construction
costs and improvement of the building.

It is a fact that St Michael's would not even exist and
probably would not have land and a building if it were not
for the diocese of Oklahoma. It is sad to observe what the
leadership of St Michael's is doing in relationship to the
diocese which created the congregation and sustained its
life for many years. Even more distressing is the apparent
fact that the title to your church property is held by a
foundation which, despite its name, is not owned by St
Michael's Episcopal Church, and its Articles of Incorpora-
tion express no allegiance or accountability to any part of
the Episcopal Church, including St Michael's Episcopal
Church. This is contrary to the canons (the laws) of the
Episcopal Church at both national and diocesan level. . . .
Fr. Pasco has repeatedly attempted to portray himself as a
defenceless martyr against the unbridled power of the
bishop's office.

Is it fanciful to think that this was all? In various dioceses
in America priests and congregations who were not accepting
the 'new look' of the Episcopal Church were being isolated
and barred. This is how the 'continuing Churches' came
into being. There was a new conformity, a narrowing of
the comprehensiveness of the Church. Admittedly there were
some dioceses which were all or nearly all of one form of
churchmanship opposing one or more, but rarely all, of the
changes. Most usually opposition to the ordination of women
to the priesthood was the issue uniting the parishes, yet on
other matters they were divided amongst themselves.

Pasco found himself in agreement with all the traditionalist
positions, and against each and every modernistic trend. He
and St Michael's had become a permanent and pervasive
sore on the back of the diocese of Oklahoma. It was not a
sore that would heal. With such an abrasion the only cure is
to remove it. There was provocation in plenty. From 20
to 22 March 1984 the Foundation for Anglican Tradition held
a consultation in Tulsa, with St Michael's as host parish.
The Foundation is devoted to the defence and proclamation
of the faith and order of the Church as grounded

in scripture and the 1549–1928 books of common prayer. Throughout 1984 the financial investigations were taking place, and there were many meetings between Pasco and/or officers of St Michael's and diocesan officials.

On 2 November 1984 McAllister sent letters to all clergy instructing them to inform delegates to the diocesan convention that St Michael's was reduced to a mission and its priest, wardens and vestry removed. The following day McAllister gave 'permission' to Pasco to conduct the 4 November services as a 'supply priest'. On the same day, in his 'capacity as rector of diocesan missions', McAllister appointed the Revd DeWitt Boyce as vicar of St Michael's *mission*. But St Michael's congregation stood solid with their rector. At the diocesan convention the actions of the standing committee, diocesan council and bishop were approved without dissent by over 400 delegates.

Pasco and his wardens had written to the presiding bishop, John Allin, who requested a meeting, 'in a mutually acceptable location, said meeting to include the bishop, the standing committee, and you and your wardens. Leave emotional "hot heads" at home', stating that they would 'pray in silence to begin the meeting.' The presiding bishop also said that, failing mutual agreement, St Michael's should be prepared to 'accept the limitations of separation [from the Church] as peacefully as you are able'. But separation was unthinkable to St Michael's people. Pasco summarises the meeting on 29 November thus:

St Michael's members and the bishop's delegation (himself, asst Bp William Cox, standing committee, including 'vicar' Boyce) at the Quarterhorse Inn in Stroud, Oklahoma. The bishop refused to begin the meeting or discuss any matter because St Michael's delegation had 29 (including rector and wardens). The bulk of the delegation were members of the vestry. St Michael's has never had a 'closed' meeting, and this did not seem the time to begin having them. The presiding bishop's letter said the meeting was 'to include' the rector and wardens, not limit the delegation to them. However, the bishop maintained that the presiding bishop limited the meeting thusly [*sic*]. At the impasse, it was suggested by one member of St Michael's that the meeting proceed, but with all from St Michael's except the rector and wardens sitting silently and just listening. The bishop refused. It was suggested that we at least begin with the first item on the presiding bishop's agenda, praying silently, but the bishop refused even this request, and departed.

Pasco held then, as he holds now, that it is the Episcopal Church which has departed from him and not he from it. Pasco did not want to join one of the breakaway churches.

St Michael's was isolated. Where could they turn for episcopal support in the Anglican communion to maintain the traditional historic faith and its expression in worship?

On 30 November 1984 Pasco wrote to Bishop Graham Leonard of London,

> As one charged with the care and nurture of souls in this parish of the One, Holy, Catholic and Apostolic Church, I write you, one of our Lord's chief shepherds, to assist in preserving us from the grievous sin of schism. There is no bishop in this land to whom we may turn. The recent public declarations of the Archbishop of Canterbury approving the ordination of women to holy orders makes appeal to him at this time inappropriate. We are in present spiritual danger. We turn to you in this our immediate peril, heartened by your stalwart defense of the faith and expressions of support for us and all who remain firm in that faith. . . . We regard departure from the Church, schism, as a most grievous sin, and have no intention of so wounding the Body of Christ. At the same time, the schism will be no less real by the Church casting us off. Our bishop and the presiding bishop make no provision for our continued physical union with the One, Holy, Catholic, and Apostolic Church. For this reason, we appeal to you, as a bishop of the Church, so to provide for us, lest we be as sheep without a shepherd, souls starved for lack of union with the Church.
>
> We do not presume to suggest to you what form our union through you to the Church should take. We know of no precedent for our request, but we also know of no precedent for separating the faithful from the Church. Therefore, from our despair, from our spiritual hunger, and from our anxiety for the souls of the faithful, we ask you to guarantee us union with the Church through you, a true

bishop of the Church. Pending resolution of a specific form, it is our request that you now allow a declaration that the priest and laity of Saint Michael's Parish are united with the One, Holy, Catholic and Apostolic Church through their unity with you.

Leonard did not reply in writing to this letter. He had entered hospital on 11 November for a serious operation on his neck which was followed by three months' convalescence. However, he managed to convey Christian greetings to Pasco and St Michael's via Mrs Gordon A. T. Heath, chairman of the International Council for the Apostolic Faith. Fr. Pasco continued to plead with Leonard for a declaration that he was in communion with them. On 15 April 1985 Pasco received a statement from Lionel E. W. Renfrey, dean and assistant bishop of Adelaide, Australia, that he regarded himself in communion with Pasco and his congregation. On 17 May 1985 Leonard sent a telegram to Pasco: 'Have considered your request most carefully. Regret for theological and canonical reasons unable to accede. Continuing consultations and will write. Prayers being offered here for you.'

In 1985 two sets of court proceedings, ecclesiastical and civil, were in progress. Yet there were still attempts at negotiated reconciliation, to no avail. Meeting at St Dunstan's Episcopal Church, Tulsa, on 23/24 September 1985, the ecclesiastical court of the diocese of Oklahoma found Pasco guilty of four charges brought against him by the standing committee and the bishop of the diocese. The charges were violation of vows of ordination by refusing to leave St Michael's on bishop's order; violation of General Convention canons by officiating in the cure of another minister without the permission of that minister, that is, De Witt Boyce who was McAllister's replacement for Pasco; conduct unbecoming a member of the clergy for participating in and being president of St Michael's Foundation; and 'immorality' inasmuch as all these by definition so constituted. On 27 September William Cox, assistant bishop of Oklahoma, notified Pasco of the court's verdict and again McAllister wrote to say Pasco was inhibited.

Earlier, on 18 September, Pasco had written to the archbishop of Canterbury (Robert Runcie) asking him to intervene, but Terry Waite (secretary for Anglican communion affairs) replied (on 28 October) quite properly saying that the archbishop had no jurisdiction in the matter and was not free to intervene.

Immediately after the verdict Pasco hosted bishops or official representatives of the 'breakaway' or 'continuing' Church as well as from the Episcopal Church at choral Evensong for the feast of St Michael and All Angels (29 September). Representatives of the Anglican Catholic Church (8 bishops, 7 dioceses, 178 parishes, 1 seminary), the American Episcopal Church (8 bishops, 5 dioceses, 90 parishes, 1 seminary), the United Episcopal and the Reformed Episcopal Churches attended. These Churches were divided among themselves, and Pasco did not want to join any one of them. They were in no way part of the Anglican communion as Pasco regarded himself.

At the ecclesiastical court hearing in September Pasco had called out denying the court's authority over him. He appealed against the decision of the diocesan court to the Court of Review, province viii. This court met on 14 March 1986 at Cathedral House, Kansas City, presided over by Arthur A. Vogel, bishop of Western Missouri, with three priests, two attorneys and one lay person from dioceses in the review other than Oklahoma. Pasco attended and his attorney, Pat Williams, spoke briefly in his defence. After four hours of deliberation the appeal court upheld the verdict of the lower court. Pasco and his attorney left the hearing before the verdict was delivered.

In March 1986 Leonard was in America for a meeting of 'traditionalist' Anglican bishops and clergy from all over the world. The meeting was in Fairfield, Connecticut. Among other matters, the gathering considered the implications that might follow the consecration of the first Anglican woman bishop. Other bishops present were John Hazlewood of Ballarat, Australia, and Robert Mercer of Matabeleland. Leonard managed to have some conversation with Pasco at this gathering. On 25 April 1986, following the verdict of the appeal court, the diocese of Oklahoma issued its sentence of deposition on Pasco: 'Therefore, I pronounce Sentence of Deposition from the sacred ministry upon the above named priest, depriving him of all right to exercise the gifts and spiritual authority as a minister of God's word and sacraments conferred upon him in his ordination to the diaconate and priesthood, effective immediately, releasing him from all ministerial obligations.'

The deposition was signed by Bishop William J. Cox, countersigned by two priests and recorded by the registrar. McAllister indicated what this meant for Episcopalians:

> First, a deposed priest is no longer a member of the clergy in the Episcopal Church. A deposed priest cannot legitimately celebrate the Eucharist, confer the blessing, or pronounce absolution.
>
> Second, we are Episcopalians and members of the Anglican communion through our membership in the diocese of Oklahoma and the Protestant Episcopal Churh the United States.
>
> Third, neither I nor the standing committee of the diocese wish the separation of any person from the Episcopal Church. If those who have remained at St Michael's, Tulsa, are separated from the Episcopal Church, it will be done only by their own actions. We urge them to seek the honest and prayerful counsel of an Episcopalian priest.

Pasco cabled Leonard: 'McAllister declared my deposition Friday. I refuse to accept. Await your guidelines.'

Pasco had not been slow to broadcast Leonard's interest. That is easily appreciated for who would not, in Pasco's position, claim the attention of the bishop of London? McAllister was well aware of Pasco's trumpeting, and wrote to Leonard (29 April 1986) seeking his help to put the record right: namely, asking Leonard to clarify the 'relationship' between Pasco and Leonard as bishop of London; in short, to disown him. As far as McAllister was concerned, Pasco had chosen to obscure the issue of church discipline, practical responsibility and simple honesty by dwelling on emotive and divisive issues – traditionalism versus modernism, conservatism versus liberalism.

Leonard had not been as inactive as the record to date suggests. He had been evaluating the position and taking advice. With the deposition of Pasco the time for action had come. On 3 June 1986 he wrote to Pasco enclosing a carefully worded document. In his letter to Pasco he wrote

First, I have made it clear that my action follows your deposition and the removal of St Michael's from ECUSA. I could not support the action of any bishop who attempted to establish a relationship to a priest or priest or his people as long as they were recognized members of a diocese and under its bishop.

Secondly, I have avoided the word 'jurisdiction', which has many legal overtones which could lead to great difficulties. I am not making any claim to have jurisdiction over any territory or buildings in the USA. Rather I am giving a dispossessed priest and his people a relationship to a bishop. The word 'communion' seems to me to express all that needs to be said.

Thirdly, I have made it clear that I have acted not as bishop of London, but as a bishop. I have two reasons for doing so. First, I have to retire at the latest on May 8th, 1991, and my successor may well not share my views. Secondly, the former jurisdiction of the bishop of London is a matter of legal debate, both with regard to its origin and to its subsequent history. To appeal to that might well be challenged. Thirdly, I believe it is important to affirm the rights of a bishop *qua* bishop.

If you seek advice from me, I shall confine myself to saying that such and such an action would have my episcopal approval. I do not and cannot claim to direct you.

The Declaration read as follows:

To the Revd John C. Pasco and the faithful of St Michael's Church, Tulsa. Grace and peace be to you in our Lord Jesus Christ. Whereas the Reverend John C. Pasco is no longer regarded as a priest by the Episcopal Church of the United States of America within which he was ordained a priest in the Church of God, and whereas St Michael's Episcopal Church, Tulsa, is neither a parish nor a mission in the diocese of Oklahoma and therefore of the Episcopal Church of the United States of America, and whereas both Father Pasco and the faithful of St Michael's are earnestly desirous of continuing in the fellowship of the One, Holy, Catholic and Apostolic Church within the Anglican tradition, and whereas according to Apostolic faith and practice, such fellowship requires communion with a bishop, duly consecrated, and whereas Father Pasco and the faithful of St Michael's are deprived of such communion.

Now we, Graham Douglas Leonard, consecrated bishop in the Church of God on the feast of St Matthew, 1964 in St Paul's Cathedral, London, by Michael, Lord Archbishop of Canterbury and ten other bishops, and presently Lord Bishop of London, do, by virtue of such consecration and of our episcopal office in the Church of God, not by our occupancy of any particular see, hereby declare for our lifetime that you are in communion with us within the fellowship of the One, Holy, Catholic and Apostolic Church and that we do recognize the priesthood of the said Father Pasco and the congregation of St Michael's as faithful Anglicans, and promise you such spiritual and pastoral assistance as is within our power to give.

Invoking the blessing of Almighty God and praying for the grace of our Lord Jesus Christ and the guidance of the Holy Spirit, we have subscribed this declaration on the first day of June in the year of our Lord one thousand nine hundred and eighty six and in the twenty second year of our consecration.

+ Graham Londin

Together with his letter and document, Leonard enclosed a paper on the Anglican communion which traced with remorseless logic the developments which threatened the unity, if not the dismemberment of the communion. Here are a few headings, sufficients to illustrate that logic:

(1) There has been a growing emphasis and insistence upon the autonomy of individual [local] Churches within the Anglican Communion. (The 1978 Lambeth Conference recognized this relating to the ordination of women.)
(2) This recognition of autonomy has gone side by side with a view of the competence of national synods or conventions, which is based more upon an understanding of the powers of assemblies, having its origins more in the philosophy of the Enlightenment in the 18th century than in the theology of the body of Christ.
(3) The belief in the omnicompetence of synods and conventions . . . has gained support from the increase in

nationalism in recent years, which has put great strain upon the coherence of the Anglican communion.

(4) Likewise, it has been intensified by developments in theology and in New Testament scholarship. . . . The effect is to minimize the significance of the particularity of the Incarnation and to justify interpretation of the scriptures by the cultural outlook and attitudes of today, whereas the traditional belief of the Church is that it was 'in the fulness of time', i.e., at the time of God's plan and choosing, that the Incarnation took place when it did.

(5) Both the belief that synods are autonomous and the relativist attitude to scripture have led to the adoption of moral stances which many find impossible to reconcile with the teaching of our Lord.

(6) The virtual abandonment of the *Book of Common Prayer* has meant that it is no longer a unifying influence in the Anglican communion. Moreover, changes of doctrine expressed in some of the new liturgies mean that they do not provide any substitute.

(7) Whereas holy baptism and holy Communion had both been a basis of unity, with unrestricted intercommunion and recognition of ministers, the ordination of women meant that this was no longer the case as far as holy Communion was concerned.

(8) In so far as the priesthood derives from the episcopate, the ordination of women diminished the role of the historic episcopate as a basis of unity.

Copies of these items were sent to the archbishop of Canterbury and the bishop of Oklahoma. To each he made it clear that he had declined to take any action as long as Pasco and St Michael's parish were part of the diocese of Oklahoma. Now that Pasco had been deposed and St Michael's no longer was a part of ECUSA Leonard felt free to act. In his declaration, so carefully worded, he was not acting as bishop of London but as *a bishop* concerned in the Church of God within the Anglican communion. In a telling sentence in his letter to McAllister of Oklahoma (4 June 1986), the full consequences of which may be realized at the 1988 Lambeth Conference, Leonard, in referring to the autonomy of Churches, wrote:

I respect that autonomy, though I believe that the continued existence of the Anglican communion depends upon some way being found by which it is exercised to take account of the Anglican communion as a whole. An impossible situation arises if one Church exercises its autonomy and then demands that other Churches relinquish their autonomy and accept what it has done.

I cannot accept your statement that 'obviously [Fr. Pasco] cannot function as a priest in the Anglican communion because he has been canonically deposed'. I certainly cannot regard myself as bound by the decision of a diocesan court in the USA.

Leonard explained why he found it difficult to accept the decision of the court. The constitution of the court was so ordered and composed that its independence was in question. It compared extremely unfavourably with ecclesiastical courts in England and with secular courts in either England or America. Moreover,

A bishop would take particular care not to express any opinion publicly on a matter that was to come before [the court] whether on his initiative or of someone else. I find it extraordinary that you, while prosecuting, could make statements about his guilt in letters to the diocesan council etc. In this country, such action would be regarded as gravely prejudicial to the trial even though the bishop could have not had a hand in appointing a member or members of the court. Both national and diocesan canons state that the property and material affairs of the parish shall be in the hands of the vestry and that the treasurer shall be responsible for the funds. I do not understand why action should be taken against a rector who has the same rights as other members for what is the responsibility of the vestry.

My surprise over the fact that he was found guilty of 'immorality' may simply arise from difficulties over language. In this country, such a word is used only for grave offences which are clearly defined, such as adultery, sodomy and embezzlement. It would be inconceivable that it would be used for the offence of which Fr. Pasco is said to be guilty. . . .

I am very surprised by the freedom with which depo-

201

sition is used as a sentence in ECUSA in a way which I have not experienced elsewhere. For serious offences in this country deprivation is the usual sentence which carries with it inhibition for preferment until the archbishop and bishop concerned remove it. Deposition is very rare and its use is confined to cases of gross immorality in special circumstances. . . .

I am surprised that there is no appeal beyond the provincial court, and that there is no provision, as in this country, for judicial review by the civil court.

Although the publicity given to Leonard's declaration was substantial, both Canterbury and Oklahoma buried their mitres in the pews. Did they think the declaration was merely unwise and eccentric? Did they choose not to see any consequences? It was a *pastoral* relationship and thus pastoral care was necessary. Some American universities may award degrees by post, but the Church could not administer its sacraments by cable. Pasco had candidates who had been prepared for confirmation. What could Leonard do? He considered whether he could ask a retired United States bishop to act for him. Bishop Albert A. Chambers, formerly of Springfield, had declared himself in communion with Pasco and his flock. But Leonard could not put an American bishop in that position. Retired bishops in the Episcopal Church, unlike retired bishops in England and almost everywhere else in the Anglican communion, are still members of the House of Bishops and subject to discipline. Such was the ruthlessness with which the canons were applied that Leonard thought Chambers (or any other bishop he might ask) would be in real dangers of being deposed from the episcopate.

The pressure on Leonard's own time was such that he could not see an early possibility of going to St Michael's. In the circumstances he decided to send his own bishop suffragan, Charles John Klyberg of Fulham. The arrangements were made in July 1986 for him to visit Tulsa between the 7 and 15 October. John Klyberg, with his ripe sense of humour, would appreciate that the public announcement was made on the feast of the Transfiguration. The confirmation was fixed for 12 October.

Runcie of Canterbury had chosen to remain silent

regarding the June declaration. Indeed, he had sympathy with Leonard's attempt to give spiritual support to a parish which was in danger of joining a dissenting Church. But support implies providing sustenance. And sustenance means sacraments. Perhaps Runcie thought the problem would go away or at least be resolved without conflict or collision. The American bishops under their new presiding bishop and primate, Edmund Lee Browning, were at fever pitch about Leonard, and when Runcie was in the United States during August 1986 he was persuaded that he had to take a stand in the interests of the Anglican communion. He had a series of meetings with the presiding bishop and arranged to see Leonard on 10 September at Lambeth. He wrote a letter in advance, expressing his disquiet that the bishop of Fulham was going to Tulsa. Fulham was London's suffragan and might this not conflict with the oft-repeated emphasis that Leonard was not assisting Tulsa as bishop of London? Whatever Leonard argued to the contrary, that is how the public would see it.

The meeting between Runcie and Leonard was one of mutual mistrust, however superficially mannerly it was in the best English tradition. Nonetheless, it was what is called a 'frank exchange', and Runcie asked Leonard to consider three points: (1) the implications of exercising episcopal ministry either first hand or delegated within the USA without the approval of the presiding bishop and the bishop of the local area; (2) the appropriateness of support for a parish whose status was still unclear; (3) the implications of acting as bishop of London or the implications dissociating bishop of London and bishop in the Catholic Church in order to operate liturgically and sacramentally in the USA without the approval of the presiding bishop. It was widely recognized that a serious dispute was in progress between Runcie and Leonard. After the meeting, Leonard said he would respond to Runcie's questions and Runcie hoped he would do so quickly as he was being pressed for statements.

Earlier, on 29 August, Leonard had written to the *Church Times* indicating that he would devote his October 1986 diocesan *Newsletter* to fundamental issues which faced the Anglican communion: namely, the relations between doctrine, church order and communion. This he did at length, leading

GRAHAM LEONARD

up to his view that the duty of a bishop to be guardian of the
faith 'is not one which he is called to exercise only in his
jurisdiction'.

Leonard replied to Runcie on 24 September answering the
points he raised and changing his mind on one aspect of the
dispute: 'I accept that to ask the bishop of Fulham to go
would be open to misunderstandings and could be taken as
an exercise of my jurisdiction as bishop of London, though I
did not see it in that light. I also think, on reflection, that it
would be unfair to ask him to do so.' Runcie had only a few
sentences of relief before the appearance of five words;
succinct for Leonard, apocolyptic for Runcie: 'I propose to
go myself.'

In his October *Newsletter* and in correspondence Leonard
made a distinction between the consecration, mission and
jurisdiction of a bishop. 'Consecration is, of course, to an
order within the body, not to a function, whereas mission and
jurisdiction relate to functioning as a member of that order.
I do not believe that the functions of mission, e.g., guardian-
ship of the faith, pastoral care including sacramental minis-
trations, are only to be exercised as part of the functions
stemming from jurisdiction, which is essentially concerned
with government.'

At this time the House of Bishops of ECUSA was meeting
in San Antonio, Texas, and on 25 September unanimously
passed a statement expecting the primate and houses of
bishops of the other branches of the Anglican communion to
'challenge, correct, and discipline any bishop ... who
attempts by his physical presence or his episcopal office to
enable a deposed priest of our Church or a removed vestry
to circumvent the canons'. The thought of Runcie and the
English House of Bishops challenging Leonard is singular.
No one had yet answered Leonard in substance or detail. As
for correcting and disciplining him, the imagination is
stretched to breaking point. That such a request should come
from the American House of Bishops was extraordinary. For
them – and many bishops elsewhere – the game was up.
Whatever the pretensions of the Episcopal Church with its
large number of bishops and dioceses, it is a sideshow as far
as North American religion is concerned. Its numbers make
it border on being, technically, a sect. The liberal American

Church and establishment had trampled over the traditionalists far too long. Now the liberals were squealing, as well they
might – and not only in America.

Leonard found it difficult to understand why, over the last
20 years or so, those who had broken the rules in a liberal
direction had by and large gone unscathed – certainly publicly
– whereas those who had sought to stand for traditional
Anglicanism were penalized:

> To take a few examples. What happened to the US bishops
> who performed the illegal ordinations at Philadelphia in
> 1974? Nothing. Charges against them for violating the
> canons were withdrawn. What happened to Mervyn Stock-
> wood when he went to do in the USA what he was not
> allowed to do here, i.e., take part in the ordination of
> women. Nothing. What happened when in 1981 Elizabeth
> Canham did in principle what I am now accused of doing,
> namely to perform sacramental ministration in the territory
> of another diocese? Nothing to support me in the difficult
> position in which I was placed. What happened when a
> US bishop divorced his wife to marry the divorced wife of
> one of his priests and goes on the television at Christmas
> to ask his people to drink to their health? Nothing. What
> happened when immediately after the General Synod has
> *not* passed the Women Ordained Abroad Measure, a
> woman priest celebrates in Southwark? Nothing. What
> happens when without any notice, a Methodist minister
> celebrates at an ordinary service in Lincoln Cathedral or
> when a woman priest gives the blessing at a Sunday sung
> Eucharist? Nothing. It always seems to be those who
> believe they must stand for traditional belief and morals
> who get criticised publicly. However that is the stuff of
> martyrdom and while we must not seek it, I suppose we
> must embrace it when it comes.

Leonard had made his decision and was prepared to accept
the consequences. He sent a long response to the American
House of Bishops asking: 'Do the canons express the
traditional faith and order of the Church or some local departure from it which cannot be said to reflect the mind of the
universal Church?' The Episcopal Church had become a law
unto itself in the Anglican communion and was arrogantly

trying to be a law to everyone else. It selected traditionalists for its contempt and, in its own way, persecution. Actions belie words. Leonard continued:

> The presiding bishop in an interview on his election, said 'that he tried not to tolerate any ideas of ins and outs, no outcasts'. He said that 'the Church needed to affirm each and every one in his or her uniqueness. . . . All must have a chance to contribute and be affirmed'. Does not this extend to traditionalist Anglicans? In the context of the ordination of practising homosexuals he said 'I do not believe we should put anybody down. I don't believe you should legislate against people'. What about legislating against traditionalists?
>
> In the new prayer book of ECUSA much of the male imagery of God has been eliminated from the prayers and the psalter. Has any protest been made against the introduction to the form of service prepared in Hawaii for Church Women United, of which ECUSA is a member, and circulated for use in the USA in which the Hawaiian women lament that they have had to replace their traditional god by a Christian God and call for an end to the use of the Cross as a symbol of conquest and an addition to a flag?
>
> Full communion does not now exist in the Anglican communion as there is no longer the necessary full interchangeability of ministers. It cannot be restored simply by everyone accepting what everyone else does. The question has now to be asked, 'What is the doctrinal basis of the Anglican communion?' Meanwhile, some bishops will feel that if that question is to be taken seriously, they must care for those who seek to witness to its traditional roots in scripture, reason and tradition.

Runcie made it clear that he considered Leonard's approach wrong and unwise. Few people could be found to support Leonard in public. The English liberal Establishment had closed ranks and erstwhile supporters of Leonard went into hiding. The bishop of Birmingham (Hugh Montefiore) proposed that the issue should come before the House of Bishops of the General Synod on 21 October, which was a week before Leonard was due to visit Tulsa (the revised date).

Naturally, Leonard had been taking counsel over the past months – legal, constitutional and theological. He had been helped with historical precedents where a bishop had cared for those who were dispossessed because they wished to remain faithful to orthodox belief and practice. During the Arian controversy in the fourth century, orthodox laity who found themselves oppressed by Arian bishops sought the pastoral care of the nearest Orthodox bishop who did not hesitate to provide it. And there were more recent precedents. It was natural that Leonard would seek an opinion from one of his examining chaplains. Canon Dr Gareth (Garry) Vaughan Bennett, fellow of New College, Oxford. Advice was given. What Leonard did not immediately realise was that Garry Bennett was also giving Runcie the benefit of his opinion. In sum Bennett's view was 'Frankly, I do not think that Graham Leonard has any precedents on which to take action'.

A paper entitled *Episcopal Jurisdiction* was prepared for the English House of Bishops and carried Runcie's signature. In it an attempt was made to appeal to the unity of the Anglican communion. When the House of Bishops met, the only evidence of unity was that of uniting against Leonard. The exact details of Tulsa seemed irrelevant. Whether the matter be one of heresy, neglect of duty or financial dishonesty it was said that the proper authority to judge must be first within the diocese concerned and then within the province concerned. It should not be the function of a single bishop in another province to call in question the canonical procedures or to seek a reverse the effects of their sanctions. Leonard's contention that he was acting in his right as a bishop of the whole Catholic Church to uphold sound doctrine was not accepted. A single bishop is never in the position of judging the cause of another bishop even in his own province, much less in another. A diocesan bishop is called to account by his metropolitan acting with other bishops of the province. And Leonard was, in a way, being called to account. But few bishops appeared to have the effective ammunition. Hugh Montefiore of Birmingham, who had much admired Leonard as chairman of the Board for Social Responsibility and respected his known pastoral care, had the courage of his convictions and made a case against Leonard and Tulsa.

Other bishops were voluble behind the scenes but not to Leonard's face. Runcie did not know what to do. Yet there was a real question as to the measure of communion which existed between the Church of England and the Episcopal Church of America. This was not really faced and in so far as it was faced the answer was dodged. What would the archbishop and his fellow bishops do for the artificial unity of the Anglican communion? How could there be full communion when one Church had taken the new step of ordaining women to the priesthood and the Church of England did not allow women priests to minister as such here?

After debate the House of Bishops (1) agreed that a bishop of the Church of England should not exercise episcopal care over a priest and congregation situated in a diocese of another province except with the consent of the proper authorities of that province; and (2) invited the archbishop of Canterbury to take any further steps he thought appropriate to promote full understanding with the House of Bishops of ECUSA on this matter and on the pastoral issues involved. The voting was 47 for, 1 against and there were 2 absentions. The bishop of Edmonton (Brian John Masters) voted against and the two abstainers were Bishop Eric Kemp of Chichester and Leonard himself.

And still it was hoped Leonard would change his mind. For months this had been a major issue before the Church. Runcie had made public his disapproval. And yet, even yet, despite being given every opportunity by Leonard (to the extent of Leonard asking, 'Are you forbidding me to go?') Runcie did not, or would not, issue a command. Runcie should have known that personal appeals as man to man, Runcie to Leonard, would have no effect. He needed to act and speak as the archbishop of Canterbury to the bishop of London. Leonard is a man of obedience. Runcie's advisers should have known that that was the way to deal with Leonard. Then Leonard would have had the difficult task of wrestling with his conscience on a different plane. But Runcie didn't, and Leonard went! Here is his report.

I arrived at Tulsa at about 9 p.m. on Wednesday 29 October and was taken immediately to meet the members of the former vestry of St Michael's, when it was a parish. I was impressed immediately by their good sense, moderation and ability. They ranged from business men in very responsible positions to simple folk. As was evident later in the congregation, there was no trace of triumphalism, nostalgia for the past, nor aggressiveness. They clearly held Fr. Pasco in high regard and were distressed by the charges which had been made against him. . . .

I telephoned Bishop McAllister (the next morning) and asked if he would like to speak to me which he said he would. Our conversation was polite but not at all productive. He said he regretted my coming and that I had not contacted him before doing so. I reminded him that I had written at length to him in June but that he had not replied and had been reported as saying that I had said nothing of substance and merely sent him a copy of the Fairfield Statement (which I had not done). He admitted that I had written at length. When I asked him why he had not replied, he said he saw no point in doing so as I seemed to have made up my mind. I said I had expected him to question and correct anything I had written with which he did not agree. He then began making various specific points of which I will mention but two. I said I could not understand how he maintained that the diocese knew nothing of the Foundation until 1984. He admitted that they did (and Fr. Pasco's attorney tells me that he did so in the course of the legal action [that] the diocese is taking to gain possession of the property). But [he] maintained that when the diocese made the loan and grant to the parish, Fr. Pasco endorsed the cheques so that they were paid into the Foundation. I questioned this as I had copies of the letters from the diocesan comptroller saying that the money was being sent direct by bank transfer to the account of the Foundation. [Leonard might have mentioned that he had seen photocopies of cheques from the Foundation to the diocese and accepted by it].

The bishop then said that the congregation had not been expelled but was still part of ECUSA. I quoted the diocesan spokesman as saying that it was not. I also referred to the letters received from incumbents by Fr. Pasco saying that they had been instructed not to transfer members of their parishes to St Michael's as it was not part of ECUSA. . . .

I then saw Bishop Haden, the retired bishop of Northern California, at his request. I had previously met him at the Lambeth Conferences of 1968 and 1978. He had come to Tulsa, in spite of his age, to show support for me. He is still a retired bishop of ECUSA, but is giving pastoral care to the congregation of the Church of the Holy Communion, Dallas, which has left ECUSA because it is unwilling to accept the uncanonical order of the bishop there for them to use the new prayer book. In this case, there is no litigation as the bishop has agreed that the congregation should have the buildings.

Bishop Haden spoke at some length of the pressure which is put on priests and congregations in ECUSA who wish to remain traditional Anglicans in worship and doctrine. What distressed him particularly was the way in which they were told to go or allowed to go, without thought of their pastoral care. Some of the leaders in the Church of the Holy Communion at Dallas had come with him and asked to see me. I told them that I could not enter into any relationship with them as long as Bishop Haden was available and until the effects of my visit to Tulsa had been evident and ascribed. They said that their main concern was for a priest to serve them. But that if anyone went, action would probably be taken against them. . . . I then briefly saw John Pasco's attorney, who gave me the information I mentioned (in para 2). . . .

After lunch there was a press conference. . . . I was impressed by the general attitude of the Press present, who seemed more concerned to gain information than to stir up controversy. I then had a welcome rest before the service, which was very moving. What I said earlier about the former vestry was also evident, with no sense of having won or asserting independence. It was a joyful if sober act of worship. I was impressed by the candidates who ranged widely in age and ability, and who were supported by their families. They had clearly been very well instructed. There was evidence of a very well-organized Sunday school using good modern material. I avoided anything controversial in my sermon, and preached on the Love of God. The 'bunfight' was no different from those in this country except that some of the congregation who came up to thank me were weeping.

I knew that photographers were to be taken up to the Offertory but I had not realized that TV shots were being taken for England.

I was surprised when at the notices Fr. Pasco said that the governor of the state had made me a territorial marshall of Oklahoma and gave me a scroll to that effect. It apparently gives me power of arrest.

On Friday I was flown to Philadelphia in the private jet of a businessman, an Episcopalian, not a member of St Michael's, but a supporter of Fr. Pasco and the congregation. The parishes I visited in Philadelphia are traditional and flourishing. Although they disagree with the bishop of Pennsylvania on a number of issues, they all have a good working relationship, for the simple reason that he does not threaten such parishes and accepts that they have a place in the diocese. He retires in February and they wonder if this situation will continue when the co-adjutor takes over. They all say they would find the position very difficult if a woman were consecrated bishop.

What I did learn, though not by direct questioning, was that Bishop McAllister does not enjoy the confidence of the community at large. Indeed, it was clear that he has a reputation for changing his line to suit the situation. I learned that since he became bishop 15 priests have left the diocese, though Fr. Pasco is the only one to have been tried. The others have chosen to leave before or without trial. It is, under the ECUSA canons, possible for a priest to ask for his case to be dealt with without trial.

Whatever controversy occurred before and after the visit, the reason for going must not be forgotten, namely 21 baptized souls seeking the grace of the Holy Spirit in confirmation. When Pasco met Leonard at Tulsa airport Leonard declared, 'Well, John, I'm here. They said I wouldn't come. They just don't know me'.

Leonard returned to a uniformly hostile reception. Bishops were angry and bewildered. The secular and Church Press were antagonistic. The kindest observation was that Leonard had made a colossal error of judgement. The more common remark was that he was a wrecker of Anglican unity. The *Church Times* editorial (7 November 1986) held that

> The real tragedy of Tulsa is that the bishop of London has given no sign at all that he really cares about the feelings of those American Anglicans who, disagreeing with him, yet constitute the vast majority; and judging by the reported comments of the bishop of Stepney, not enough signs of being careful about the unity of his own diocese. Presumably he will remain in office; but for most Anglicans, who want unity, respect for his office and respect for his conscience will not be accompanied by respect for his wisdom.

And a leader in *The Times* (November 1986) asserted:

> For him to step in where other Anglicans have feared to tread must be seen as a provocative act rather than a healing hand. He may not be subject to the discipline of the archbishop of Canterbury, but to have crossed the Atlantic in direct defiance of a specific request that he should not is to embarrass Dr Runcie and create unnecessary trouble.

It was a strange observation from a newspaper that often gives the appearance of relishing opportunities to make the archbishop of Canterbury uncomfortable.

Leonard wanted to give a personal report to Runcie and the two met for an hour and a half on 7 November. Once again Runcie recognized Leonard's pastoral concern for a deposed priest and his congregation but still disapproved of Leonard's decision to visit Tulsa for the purpose of administering confirmation. Questions of episcopal collegiality had been raised and undertakings for the future were under consideration between archbishop and bishop. It was natural that there were those in the Church who wanted to interpret the meeting as a carpeting for Leonard. Sufficient has been written here to show that that was never a possibility. Runcie was anxious to limit damage; Leonard wanted the issues to be faced. There was no real meeting of minds or wills. The two men were thinking and acting on very different levels. In one sense they had to. Runcie would be president of the 1988

Lambeth Conference involving the whole Anglican communion, as well as just 'primate of All England'.

There was an attempt to have the matter debated in the General Synod on 11 November and Runcie referred to the time he had spent in trying to limit the damage caused in the Anglican communion by Leonard's action. He made the point that 'There is an inherent authority in bishops acting collectively both within and between provinces. A bishop exercises his authority as a member of a college of bishops – symbolized through the laying on of hands of his brother bishops at his consecration. This inherent authority is recognized in our communion – for example, the final decisions about ARCIC have, by the agreement of all the provinces, to be made by the Lambeth Conference.' Even that statement would be questioned by Leonard. Douglas Brown, a well-known and respected ecclesiastical correspondent, wrote an article in the *Church Times* (14 November 1986) wondering if Tulsa had been 'a gesture of a strong, committed and defiant leader of rigid orthodoxy' or 'was it largely unaccountable and ill-considered exhibitionism by an over-romantic traditionalist'. Douglas Brown closed by grappling with the possible motives of Leonard:

> He is not, I think, basically a flamboyant or publicity-seeking person, if perhaps more than a little prelatical. He is not generally given to ill-considered, extravagant or headline seeking utterances. He should have made his point over Tulsa and the American situation generally in other ways than by his sensational transatlantic journey. He was in breach of that Catholic order he espouses. Yet he is within himself a symbol of his own position.
>
> Not for nothing did he call one of his books *Firmly I Believe and Truly*. He witnesses in his own manner to traditional beliefs and values: traditional order, theology and dogma set against the surge of pluralism, of rationality replacing the transcendent and numinous. Is it a surge that he and others who broadly think like him can contain, or is there no remission? The only hope for some less anxious future seems to lie with the Lambeth Fathers of 1988.

The Tulsa controversy continued until well into 1987 throughout the Anglican communion and remains unresolved. The amount of publicity in press, radio and television (including some very bad tempered programmes, though not involving Leonard himself) was massive and wide.

The legal proceedings were not settled until 29 January 1987. From the tone and content of the statements put out by the diocese of Oklahoma and St Michael's it was not immediately obvious that there had been agreed court settlements in which the diocese withdrew its charges of fraud and deceit; Pasco dropped his libel and slander suit. It was not obvious because the diocese agreed to a settlement *after* it had presented its case in court. Pasco and the parish were therefore precluded from responding in court, whereas the case of the diocese alone has received publicity. A financial settlement was agreed whereby St Michael's would pay the diocese $106 000. In turn the diocese withdrew its claim to St Michael's land and buildings.

For Leonard the position is little different from when he first offered spiritual help. As a bishop of the universal Church, not as bishop of London, he felt a duty to support St Michael's. Many Americans were taken aback by Leonard. They expected a turbulent firebrand. Instead they found an intensely spiritual mind, a personal devotion to our Lord, and sympathy with all that (in the best sense of the word) is Evangelical, namely the ardour of a living faith and a strong conviction, and firm loyalty to the unalterable Gospel. These are the characteristics of this intrepid champion of catholicity. Nevertheless he preserves his independence and gives the impression of being at heart a solitary, despite a companionableness.

As for collegiality and his relations with Runcie, it is important to remember that over Tulsa as in other matters Leonard believes that the episcopate represents the fatherhood of God. It is an episcopacy that takes into account the responsibility of every bishop for the witness that his Communion gives to the world. Leonard has kept before him, has to keep before him, an impossibly high ideal, the kind of ideal which the preacher, Dr R. C. Moberley, put before Charles Gore when he was consecrated bishop of Worcester in 1902: 'Direct pastoral leadership in spiritual things is the true function of a bishop. With your consecration upon you you have to be a fountain to all the diocese, and to its thirsty

places, of spiritual hope and spiritual life, so that wherever
you go, something is felt of the manifestation of God.' Leonard
had based his action over Tulsa on the traditional distinction
between orders and jurisdiction. He asserted that the purpose
of holy orders is to enable the Church to live in faithfulness
to the apostolic Gospel. Jurisdiction is a juridical and administrative arrangement which developed after the Church
became 'legalized' in 303 AD and has been regarded as subor-
dinate to the claims of revealed truth. He quoted Archbishop
Laud: 'much evident it is, that the 'succession' which the
Fathers meant is not tied to place or person, but is tied to
'verity of doctrine'. . . . So that if the doctrine be no kin to
Christ, all the 'successors' become strangers, what nearness
soever they pretend of.'

14

Before the Deluge

In 1963 Archbishop Ramsey set up a commission 'to examine the question of women and holy orders'. This reported in 1966 with *Women and Holy Orders*. The commission was chaired by Gerald Ellison, then bishop of Chester, and contained a powerful and representative membership. The commission examined and presented the facts and arguments without advising the Church what it ought to do in the future. This was the start of the debate. At the 1968 Lambeth Conference the bishops debated the subject and affirmed its opinion 'that the theological arguments as at present presented for and against the ordination of women to the priesthood are inconclusive'. In a resolution on the diaconate the conference was said to recommend 'That the diaconate, combining service of others with liturgical functions, be open to men and women remaining in secular occupations'. . . . The words 'and women' were not in the original resolution passed by the conference and had been added by one of the conference's chief agitators for the ordination of women, Archbishop Coggan of York, in consultation with one or two officials. The conference had another resolution: 'That those made deaconesses by laying on of hands with appropriate prayers be declared to be within the diaconate' (221 for, 183 against). A new body with a new factor slipped into Anglicanism and has helped to change its character. The Anglican Consultative Council [ACC] was established and acts as a mini-Lambeth except that it seeks to dictate corporate change in a way that the Lambeth Conference never did. It cannot actually dictate anything, as its name suggests and its constitution embodies. But there are ways of bringing to the forefront of debate and decision subjects which are of little or no interest in some provinces of the Anglican communion yet are issues of paramount concern in others and usually pushed forward by articulate agitators in the westernized parts of the Anglican communion. At the first meeting of the ACC at Limuru, Kenya, during February and March 1971 the council made its own agenda from 1968 Lambeth Conference resolutions that called for further application or study.

The ordination of women to the priesthood was regarded as an urgent matter for some provinces and the ACC decided to pursue this in time for its meeting in 1973. Meanwhile it passed a resolution on a specific issue:

> In reply to the request of the council of the Church of South-East Asia, this council advises the bishop of Hong Kong (Gilbert Baker), acting with the approval of his synod, and any other bishop of the Anglican communion acting with the approval of his province, that, if he decides to ordain women to the priesthood, his action will be acceptable to this council; and that this council will use its good offices to encourage all provinces of the Anglican communion to continue in communion with these dioceses.

This was carried by 24 votes to 22 and it is not without significance that the Archbishop Michael Ramsey voted against. Thus 51 members of a worldwide Anglican Church, while not legislating, were certainly doing more than consulting. The ACC was a power house.

Between 1968 and 1978 the nature of the Anglican communion changed fundamentally. The 1968 Lambeth Conference had provided power to the machinery, and the ACC of 1971 flicked the switch enabling movement. By the time of the 1978 Lambeth Conference the Anglican Church of Canada, the Episcopal Church in the United States of America, the Church of the Province of New Zealand as well as the diocese of Hong Kong, had ordained women to the priesthood, or admitted women to the presbyterate as stated in the resolution. Eight other member Churches of the Anglican communion had either agreed or approved in principle or stated that there were either no fundamental or no theological objections to the ordination of women to the historic threefold ministry of the Church.

Before considering the 1978 Lambeth Conference and the period since, we must look at Leonard's reasons for opposing the ordination of women to the priesthood. Many opponents simply don't like the idea but have no theological reasons to sustain them. It is easy to misrepresent his views. He has written and spoken so much on the subject that it is necessary to look at the kernel of his position. In his shortest statement Leonard wrote (April 1986):

> There are two basic reasons why I cannot accept that it is right to ordain women as priests and bishops, whose role is to represent Christ as head of his Church:
> First, I believe it undermines and questions the way in which God himself has taught us how to speak of him and know him. I do not believe that it was by accident, but by God's deliberate choice that he chose to reveal himself in a patriarchal society and became man in Christ, as a male. The highest role ever given to any human being was given to a woman, Mary, when she responded to God's call to be the mother of Christ. We cannot disregard these facts to suit our ideas today.
> Secondly, the Church of England claims to have continued the ordained ministry as given by God and received from the universal Church. I do not believe it has the right or power to alter it fundamentally without destroying that claim.
>
> In my judgment, the whole approach (and the arguments) of those who press for the ordination of women questions and undermines the revealed nature of the Christian faith, as given by God, not devised by man.

In his paper to the Churches' Council for Covenanting (published in the *Epworth Review*, January 1984) Leonard set out the theological and biblical issues in words which he could have used at any time in his life and priesthood. Why many people find Leonard difficult is because he judges contemporary thought by biblical revelation rather than judging biblical revelation by the extent to which it matches contemporary thought. The Feminist Movement of the period is not one which should influence the subject. It has done so, particularly in America and to a lesser extent in England. Feminists hardly begin to understand Leonard.

We live in a world in which diversity is often assumed to

imply superiority or inferiority. Scripture reflects the fact
that the pattern on which the universe operates is one of
diversity in unity. . . . The present idea which is so
common, that if you are to be equal to someone you must
be identical, is I believe a travesty of the way in which
creation actually operates. This pattern is recognized and
accepted in the scriptures. You will remember the passage
in 1 *Corinthians* xii where St Paul speaks of the various
organs in the physical body and uses them to illustrate
what he is saying about the body to which St Paul appears
to allude are properly expressed in the word 'subordi-
nation'. Today it is a very unpopular word, being associated with domination and aggression and as contrasting
with that natural love which in human society and the
Church should characterize the relations between the
various organs in the Church.

I pass to the question of the Incarnation. If men and
women are equal, complementary but not identical, then
it cannot have been a matter of indifference as to which
sex God would choose in which to be incarnate. Since we
believe that God is the creator of the universe, we would
expect that whatever choice he made would match the
nature of man as created male and female, and this I
believe he did in being incarnate as a male. . . .

In view of what I said about the Incarnation it does not
surprise me, therefore, that this ministerial priesthood has
been restricted to those who are masculine, i.e., those who
psychologically and physically represent because they are
men, not because they are virtuous, not because they have
certain abilities, but because they are men. They represent
the Divine initiative, the Divine begetter. . . .

I do believe that the images through which God chooses
to speak to us through the scriptures are authoritative and
are not disposable. For that reason, I get very worried
when I hear it suggested that we must, for example, cease
to speak of God as Father.

In conclusion I want to say first this: For a great many
years it was the tradition of the Church not to ordain
women to the priesthood. If that is to be changed, then I
must have compelling reasons for it. So far, I have not
heard those reasons, but on the contrary, I have heard

arguments such as that about speaking of God as Father which appear to me to question the biblical revelation.

Let us return to the 1978 Lambeth Conference. When it opened Leonard called a meeting of those bishops he knew to be opposed to the ordination of women and they continued to meet at regular intervals during the conference. The average attendance was about 50 but nearly 150 were in association with the group. From the outset it was clear that any question of securing a repudiation of the ordinations in the USA, Canada and elsewhere was out of the question. On the contrary, the real danger was that a resolution approving the ordination of women unconditionally would be put to plenary session when it would have some chance of success. Moreover, there was no kind of agreement among the opponents as to what attitude should be adopted in the event of a 'green light' resolution being carried. Leonard noted that

> Some would have left for the wilderness, some would have soldiered on, withdrawing into a cocoon – easier to do in some overseas provinces than in England. Some would have reluctantly accepted it. Some would have gone over to Rome or Orthodoxy. Some would have sought to achieve some kind of uniate status with Rome or Orthodoxy. It was evident that in a straight vote on the pros and cons the opposition would have been hopelessly outvoted and disintegrated beyond any hope of action.

The speeches of two observers were unhelpful. The strident and threatening tones of Archbishop Athenagoras (Orthodox) was ill received and thus lacked persuasion, whilst Bishop Cahal Daly (Roman Catholic) managed to make the official position of his Church clear at the same time as saying Lambeth need not worry too much for there was a good deal of sympathy from Roman Catholics in general. The American bishops who were against the ordination of women had a difficult task but instead of the strength of their position coming through they presented a negative and sterile attitude. What could Leonard and his group do?

It seemed therefore that the best which would be achieved while avoiding the worst would be to work for (a) a recognition that though member churches were autonomous they must act with the whole Anglican communion in mind; (b) a recognition of opponents as having an honourable and wholly accepted position in the Anglican communion; (c) some control of the exercise of the ministry of those women who have been ordained; (d) the intention to continue ecumenical dialogue; (e) a warning about the consecration of women to the episcopate.

The resolutions as presented to the conference embodied these points. As a member of the group which struggled to produce them I would have felt bound to vote against if any one point had been defeated in plenary session. In fact, they were strengthened rather than weakened and as no part was omitted I felt bound to vote for the resolutions, though in doing so I did not weaken in my opposition to the ordination of women. The wording of resolution 206.7.2 is significant in that it explicitly recognizes that those who have taken part in the ordination of women to the priesthood believe that their ordination has been to the traditional priesthood. It does not commit others to that belief. . . . I judge that what was achieved was the best of a bad job, if not a very good best.

The effect of the resolutions on the November (1978) debate in the General Synod is as follows:
(a) The Church of England is still free to make its own decision. This decision will have considerable effect in the Anglican communion as a whole.
(b) The Church of England must consider the effect in the Anglican Communion and on ecumenical relations.
(c) The position of opponents must be openly and honourably faced. The implications of resolution 206.5.2 are very significant. It is very important that those who cannot accept it make their position known clearly and unequivocally to the proctors in convocation as members of the House of Laity.
(d) The arguments in principle can still be put, but they will have to be made in the context of why it should not happen in England rather than on the bare principle of whether it should happen anywhere.
It follows that the opponents should not slacken their efforts but rather the reverse.

What the eventual outcome will be is difficult to discern.

There is evidence that those women who have been ordained are not finding it easy to get appointments in those member churches where parishes call their ministers. It may be that we are faced with a period comparable to that faced by the Church between the Council of Ariminum in 359 when in the words of Jerome 'the whole world groaned and marvelled to find itself Arian' and the Council of Constantinople in 381 when orthodoxy was reestablished and that in the words of Gamaliel 'if the undertaking be of men it will fail'.

What was most evident at Lambeth was the need for a recovery of theology in the Anglican communion. While the establishment of the Doctrinal Commission and the reaffirmation of the function of bishops by Lambeth is significant, the urgent need is for clear, direct theological teaching in the parishes, without which, however hard some bishops try, pragmatism will win the day.

Leonard was already well established as the leader of the opposition and at the request of the standing committee he made the major speech opposing the motion in the General Synod (November 1978) to remove the barriers to the ordination of women. The thrust of his case was as usual concerned with obedience. The tradition of the Church witnesses to the fact that the initiative is with God and we respond with obedience 'which is the only way to true freedom and fulfilment'.

For such a break with tradition we should expect overwhelmingly compelling reasons. Indeed I think that the question was wrongly put in the first place. We should not have been asked whether there were no fundamental objections. Rather we should have been asked to search scripture and tradition for compelling reasons for reversing the universal practice of the Church for nearly 2000 years. Such reasons have not been forthcoming. On the contrary, I find that the arguments used lead me to question the rightness of an action which needs such arguments to justify it.

We are entitled to ask the advocates to convince us by sober and weighty argument, consonant with Anglican tradition, that beyond all reasonable doubt it would be theologically and morally right *as Anglicans* to proceed.

For I speak as a convinced Anglican accepting that the Church of England is both Catholic and Reformed. When I admire Rome it is when she is faithful to scripture and the tradition of the undivided Church. When I admire the Reformed Church it is when they are faithful to scripture and the same tradition. I do not appeal to Rome or Constantinople or Geneva as such, I appeal as Anglicans have always appealed, to scripture and tradition and reason, tested by scripture.

The full motion before the General Synod asked for legislation 'to remove the barriers to the ordination of women to the priesthood and their consecration to the episcopate'. The voting was as follows: bishops: 32 for, 17 against; clergy: 94 for, 149 against; laity: 120 for, 106 against. The following year the question of enabling women ordained abroad to exercise their priesthood in England in certain circumstances came before the General Synod and again was defeated in the House of Clergy: bishops: 26 for, 10 against; clergy: 87 for, 113 against; laity: 110 for, 65 against.

The protagonists had no intention of taking 'no' for an answer. Indeed, they renewed their efforts with campaigning fervour. The Movement for the Ordination of Women [MOW] was well organized, published an abundance of literature attractively produced, had a travelling exhibition and provided an array of speakers who knew how to put their case convincingly. Among its leaders were the bishops of Southwark (Ronald Bowlby) and Manchester (Stanley Booth-Clibborn). The bishops of Salisbury (John Austin Baker) and Lincoln (Simon Phipps) wrote pamphlets. The moderator was Mrs Monica Furlong. Other bishops began to say openly that they supported the ordination of women.

Catholics looked to the leadership of Leonard and Bishop Kemp of Chichester, yet the Catholic movement seemed unable to mobilize itself. As long ago as 1973 when Leonard was at Willesden the Catholic societies met to see how best to conduct a campaign. Leonard was concerned that efforts should be made to carry Evangelicals with them. But they were as divided as Catholics. For example, George Carey, the principal of Trinity College, Bristol, and now bishop of Bath and Wells wrote a pamphlet for MOW on *Women and Authority in the Church*. There were mainstream Catholics and Evangelicals who were equivocal on the issue. They were the ones that each side needed to convince.

Women were growing impatient, encouraged by visiting women priests from America. The dean of St Paul's Cathedral, Alan Webster, was a leading supporter of MOW, his wife was its executive secretary. Elizabeth Canham, an English woman who had gone to America and was ordained priest in the diocese of Newark by Bishop John Spong, perhaps the most liberal bishop in the USA (certainly the most controversial), visited England in January 1982, and celebrated the Eucharist in the deanery of St Paul's. The event was reported in the *Church Times*. She had been made a deaconess by the then bishop of Southwark, Mervyn Stockwood. When she was ordained to the priesthood Stockwood, by now retired, had gone to America and participated in the ordination. Leonard was understandably shocked at the celebration in the Deanery and made a statement to the London area bishops' council on 12 January. The law, both of the Church and of the land, had been broken. Women ordained abroad were not allowed to perform any ecclesiastical function in the Church of England, whether privately or publicly, without the authorization of the archbishop of Canterbury and the bishop of the diocese concerned.

> It may be argued that she acted in a private capacity but the Eucharist, even if celebrated privately in a house or intended to be purely private is an ecclesial act, that is, an act of the Church and cannot be regarded as a private devotion. Such action may well be embarrassing to the priest who has the cure of the place in which it occurs, particularly bearing in mind that he has taken the oath of canonical obedience.

There was a furore. Spong of Newark was a liberal subversive. In 1980 he had 'chaired' a bishops' ad hoc committee on clergywomen. One of the proposed solutions to be considered was to offer women in other parts of the Anglican communion a move to the United States where they would be screened like any other resident of a diocese, and, if accepted, practise their priesthood there until the situation changed in their country and synod when they could return home. A pool of priestesses would thus be available to splash themselves wherever they were needed and in due course of time cause a flood. Such action undermines the autonomy of the provinces of the Anglican communion. It was subverting the authority of sister Churches over their own households. Leonard sent a copy of his statement to Spong and to the archbishop of Canterbury. The latter criticized the illegal celebration; the former supported it and issued a long statement saying, *inter alia*, 'Part of the vocation of the Anglican communion is to witness against sexual oppression and sexual prejudice in all branches of Christianity. To court unity by preserving prejudice and oppression is an unworthy goal of any branch of this Church of ours.'

Leonard – and on this occasion Runcie too – were accused of legalism over Elizabeth Canham. That could not be sustained. It had less to do with law than with discipline. The registrar of the diocese of London, David Faull, provided a legal note in the course of which he said:

> Of course people's consciences are troubled on both sides of the argument, and I have great sympathy with that. But the Church of England has made its disciplines clear, contrary to the advice of many of its bishops. But for bishops, clergy or laity to ignore those disciplines is simply to move towards anarchy and disunity. It is not therefore a minor event, nor is the letter of the law being applied as Bishop Spong suggests. At the present time it is the mind of the Church of England which overseas dioceses are being asked to respect.

Anarchy was always a possibility if the women did not get their way, and if this was a sample outbreak then the Church of England would have to rethink the matter.

The most distasteful and disgraceful aspect of the Canham celebration was the part played in it by the dean of St Paul's. Alan Webster is too intelligent not to have known what he was allowing in his own home, and did not apparently have the courage of his convictions readily to admit his agreement to what had happened. Canon Douglas Webster, a canon residentiary of St Paul's, and supporter of the ordination of women, wrote to Spong on the inappropriateness of Canham's visit, sending a copy to Leonard:

> You ordained Miss Canham to work for two years as a priest in your diocese. Well and good. Everyone here assumed this is what she would do. But in little more than a month she was back in England and intent on showing that she could now do what many another gifted woman in England longs to do but is not yet permitted to do. This was hardly tactful or sensitive. Moreover, it is reported that she had a programme to take private Communion services up and down the country. What possibile theological or pastoral justification is there for this? She was not going to places where no priest was available or to people cut off from the sacrament. At St Paul's Cathedral there are seven full-time priests and there is a daily Eucharist. There was no pastoral need for such a service in a nearby private house. Theologically it was even more open to question on the ground of motive. It had every appearance of a gimmick, designed not to feed the faithful but to promote a cause. This, I respectfully submit, is an unworthy and improper use of the sacrament. Furthermore there was obviously no intention of holding a quiet service of fellowship between people with a shared concern. Maximum publicity was sought and the choice of the world's most prestigious deanery ensured it.
>
> I am convinced that this kind of behaviour, far from promoting the ordination of women over here, will delay it. Your criticisms of the Church of England and the Establishment may well be true. They are not specially helpful or relevant. On this particular matter, as on Church unity, opinions are deeply divided. We have to live and work with one another, to love and respect those with whom we disagree. We also have to live with our history, and this can be difficult. Changes come more slowly but they do come.

Over the Canham issue Leonard received sympathy from unlikely quarters but Alan Webster had support too, including the bishop of Stepney (James Thompson). The affair was a deviation, not a setback. The campaigns moved inexorably onwards.

On 15 November 1984, before a full house and packed galleries, the General Synod debated the following motion: 'That this synod asks the standing committee to bring forward legislation to permit the ordination of women to the priesthood in the provinces of Canterbury and York.' Leonard had contributed an article, 'Why women priests would be divisive', to the *Guardian* of 12 November. Here he introduced a new ingredient: The Church would split and energies would be absorbed when 'the Church should be looking for renewal in faith and life to commend the Gospel to a nation which so desperately needs it'.

The background paper for the debate *The Ordination of Women to the Priesthood: a further report* was prepared by Miss Christian Howard a leading supporter of MOW. She had prepared two earlier reports. Leonard did not speak and his own position was not reflected in the debate. Catholics who spoke gave the impression of seeking simply to stall rather than defeat. When voting came this time it was carried in all three houses. The victory was not unexpected at this stage. In the next stage the percentage in all three houses would have to be 67% or over.

In the January 1986 issue of *The Voice* (the diocesan periodical for Newark, USA), Bishop John Spong shared a dream with his diocese: 'I cherish a dream and entertain a hope that the diocese of Newark, which frequently by God's grace has been a leader in the Episcopal Church, might now be called to the vocation of providing for the Anglican communion its first woman bishop'. In the letter Spong referred to Leonard. 'As the moment draws nearer when episcopacy will open to women, opponents are beginning to recycle all of the arguments of the past and to make dire threats of chaos and schism. The bishop of London, Graham Leonard, thinks so little of the Church decision-making processes that he threatens to encourage a division of the Church of England into two separate bodies if his point of view opposing women is not sustained.' Spong also wrote: 'The discredited biblical argument continues to be heard from no less a person than Pope John Paul II.'

The diocesan convention of Newark was due to meet on 1 February when it was anticipated that the diocese would call for an assistant or suffragan bishop. Under the canons of the

Episcopal Church in America the call for the election of a suffragan bishop is the exclusive prerogative of the diocesan bishop. When news of this reached Leonard he wrote to the archbishop of Canterbury (29 January 1986) expressing more than his concern. Was this a 'trailer' to action by Spong and his diocese for the consecration of a woman bishop so that the primates were presented by a *fait accompli*? It was understood that the preferred candidate was a woman archdeacon in the diocese. Of course, the House of Bishops could withhold their consent but could this be relied on? Would Spong go ahead uncanonically as was done in 1974 at Philadelphia over women priests? The Philadelphia bishops 'got away with it' and it had the desired effect of securing *post hoc* canonical approval and those who had acted uncanonically were allowed to go unscathed.

Leonard made his position quite clear to the archbishop. 'I would not be able to remain silent if a woman bishop were consecrated uncanonically, and would feel bound to say that I could not longer be in communion with bishops who took part.' Runcie was in a difficult position for whilst he might find himself in a similar position to Leonard he had to be careful lest he was accused of interfering in the affairs of another province.

The worst did not happen. However, Leonard wrote again to Archbishop Runcie (4 March) extending his promise or threat (as differently viewed) not only to possible uncanonical action resulting in a woman bishop, but also to any consecration of a woman, even if carried out under ECUSA canons, following approval by the primates. This time he knew he would not be alone, for individual bishops in many provinces, particularly Australia, West Indies, Japan, South Africa and Scotland had indicated their support for him and within a year the number of provinces concerned increased. Leonard continued: 'Some, like myself, would (I know) have to reconsider very carefully whether we would be able to be present at Lambeth in 1988 if women bishops were among those invited, since their very presence would indicate acceptance of them.'

The gravity of the position was recognized by both archbishop and bishop, the former wanting to halt precipitate action before Lambeth 1988. But what difference would that really make? Some provinces had decided that women bishops were a natural stage after women priests (to the logic of which position Leonard would agree) and ultimately there would be women bishops in some provinces whatever was said at Lambeth. The real question is whether that would signal the beginning of the end of the Anglican communion. Again, logic says it will.

Before the July 1986 General Synod was a motion for the final approval of the draft Women Ordained Abroad Measure. The decision would be final and irrevocable and had to be defeated. Leonard wanted it to be defeated in the House of Bishops and efforts were made to persuade the few wavering bishops. Leonard thought he could count on twelve episcopal votes. After a short debate the Houses divided and the motion was lost: bishops: 28 for, 12 against; clergy: 128 for, 95 against; laity: 147 for, 88 against with a total of 6 absentions.

On 8 July synod debated the report *The Ordination of Women to the Priesthood: the scope of the legislation.* A group chaired by Professor J. D. McClean of Sheffield, including members identified with the various shades of opinion within the synod, prepared the report. Since it had been published it had received a rough passage because it set out in painful detail the options facing the Church if it moved forward towards women priests. It was not itself a set of proposals. By this time a few priests and some laity were *in extremis* about the direction the Church was taking, of which the prospect of women priests was simply the biggest among many departures from Catholic order and theological truth. Leonard invited those 'who believe [that] the ordination of women to the priesthood would imperil the doctrinal position of the Church of England' to write in confidence to a priest in Oxford giving their names to be included in a register. Over 20 000 names have been registered. The uncertainty has been too much for some and a trickle of priests have left for the Roman Catholic Church and a few will be ordained by that Church.

The next major hurdle, or stepping stone, was set for 1987. The report, *The Ordination of Women to the Priesthood* due to be debated at the February session of synod, came from the House of Bishops. The bishops spelt out the safeguards that would need to be brought into any legislation to allow the ordination of women to the priesthood. They envisaged a transitional period when parishes, priests and bishops who could not accept the ordination of women would have a power of veto. Final compensation was recommended for the objectors. There were many other possibilities for temporary agnosticism or opposition. But once a province had started ordaining women priests, it would be 'anomalous' to appoint a bishop actively opposed to the ordination of women. What the bishops rejected as 'legally undesirable and theologically unacceptable' was any suggestion of setting up a non-territorial 'diocese' to accommodate opponents of women priests. 'Parallel jurisdictions in full communion are only tolerable where there is reciprocal recognition of sacraments and ministries together with the possibility of interchange of ministries.' Leonard signed the report because he believed it accurately described the situation which would obtain. This was made quite clear in the bishops' theological group in the House of Bishops, of which Leonard was a member, when some bishops said they could sign the report but could not sign any appended motion which actually encouraged the synod to proceed.

Leonard prepared a statement on Sunday 8 February which was not made public until 10 February when he had read it to the bishops' theological group on 9 February. The accounts of the report which had appeared in the Press were misleading in that they tended to refer only to the temporary safeguards to provide for those who, while unhappy about women priests, could soldier on for their lifetime or those who, being agnostic, wanted safeguards for a while. There was no or little reference to what was proposed for those who would be unable to continue in a Church of England in which women were ordained to the priesthood.

The report recognizes that some would find it impossible to remain within a Church of England in which women were ordained to the priesthood. It states that once the archbishop of Canterbury, together with the college of bishops of the Church of England, has proceeded to ordain women to the priesthood 'those who could not remain in communion with the see of Canterbury, would need to find

other ways of continuing their existence within the
universal Church and would be entitled to explore such
ways. It is realised that some who could not accept the
ordination of women would claim that they represented the
traditional faith and practice of the Church of England and
would therefore believe themselves entitled to a share in its
resources.

The report accepts division and separation as an inevitable consequence of any synodical decision to legislate for
the ordination of women to the priesthood and accepts the
departure of those who cannot agree to it.

On 9 February *The Times* leader was headlined 'Are Women
Priests Worth a Schism?' It suggests that

the only prospect of a resolution lies in a trial of strength
between opposing forces, with the consequent risk of serious
injury to either or both.

Christian Churches should not shrink from painful sacri-
fices in the name of truth and justice, though it is understandable that they should want to postpone them as long
as possible. But the issue of schism has now to be faced
properly. It is no longer a supplementary question arising
subsequent to the principle of women's ordination; it has
become the primary question itself.

Allowing for a leader writer's licence, the clear point is made
that the issue of women priests had to be faced but if there
was to be a schism it would not be over that issue alone.
What Leonard had done was to draw attention to an element
in the report that had been neglected in the media and
correspondence.

There was fury that once again Leonard had captured the
headlines and dictated the pace of the debate. Archbishop
Habgood of York accused Leonard of having failed to make
his intentions known during the House of Bishops'
discussions. He was asked to explain what his statement
meant. Leonard could easily reply that it meant what it said.
Other bishops were furious too, the bishop of Birmingham
(Hugh Montefiore) suggesting: 'I think resignation is a matter
for him to consider.' The archbishop of Canterbury's letter
in *The Times* (11 February) was less direct than his northern

counterpart. 'It is worth recording that the bishops voted for the report unanimously and that the house included those with the strongest views for and against the issue of principle'.

Some of the archbishop's staff were more direct when talking to the Press, even if they thought it was off the record. In a 'Spotlight' article in *The Sunday Times* (15 February) reference was made to the 'crisis over Leonard'. 'Runcie will not tolerate what he considers arrogance and deceitfulness. He has yet to speak publicly on Leonard's recent activities but the church propaganda machine is already moving into action, quietly ridiculing Leonard as a man with delusions of grandeur.' The last observation was fatuous: Leonard was four years from compulsory retirement. The observation about 'arrogance and deceitfulness' was different. One is an opinion, the other refers to actions. Leonard pursued this rigorously with Runcie, who denied using the words and gave Leonard an open letter to that effect. They came from an over-enthusiastic staff member. Meetings with Runcie were amicably tense, not acrimonious. In a sense it might have been better had there been more plain annoyance, a less 'laid back' approach, from the archbishop. But what passed for frank cordiality probably disguised deep disquiet and exasperation at the least. Leonard would not let his quarry escape. Attempts by others to encourage mutual animosity were mischievous even vicious.

Leonard was accused of having a double 'constituency': that is, of being in the House of Bishops and of being a loyal Anglican. Quite so. However, what should happen when a member of the House of Bishops believes a particular action will draw the two into conflict? Leonard would retort: is not his duty to Anglican formularies, to conscience and to God? It is surprising how often Leonard returns to the 39 Articles and the *Book of Canman Prayer*. When he was ordained priest he promised that he would teach 'nothing as required of necessity to eternal salvation but that which we shall be persuaded may be concluded and proved by scripture', words which reflect what is in the articles. If women are ordained priests they become part of the structure of the Church and for Leonard they cannot then be ignored. Their acceptance becomes part of what is required as necessary to salvation. This kind of writing and talk irritated some of Leonard's episcopal colleagues, but few failed to answer him in *those* terms. Perhaps they should have tried in order that some genuine debate could have taken place. However, they took the view that he was beyond persuasion just as MOW proponents were blind and deaf to their opponents' views.

In an article for the *Daily Mail* (19 February) with the provocative headline 'Why I am prepared for the break-up of the Church of England', Leonard repeated his case. 'If the Church of England is split by the issue of ordained women I will not be leading the division but responding to the inevitable consequences of a fundamental change which the Church has no right to make unilaterally.' It was said that as many as 2000 clergy would have to leave the Church of England with Leonard. And what of the laity? Their voice has been quiescent in those parishes whose churchmanship is neither wholly Anglo-Catholic nor wholly Evangelical. They share with Leonard the view 'that there are many in the Church I love who think and feel as I do, deep down in their hearts, that they could not continue if women were ordained'.

Leonard lost some support when he ordained women deacons in St Paul's Cathedral on 22 March 1987. One area bishop, Brian Masters of Edmonton, refused to participate. Leonard had always seen the diaconate as a separate order, and not as a year's probationary period before priesthood. Incidentally, in his charge, given on 18 March, he referred to 'the role of spiritual direction to which many women are called. When I was bishop of Truro I recognized this', and he arranged for training in this sphere with the result that there are now many women helping others in their spiritual growth.

A group of bishops produced a first class report which came before the General Synod in July 1988. The bishops were those of Newcastle (Alec Graham), who was chairman, Bristol (Barry Rogerson), Southwark (Ronald Bowlby), Birmingham (Mark Santer), Wakefield (David Hope), Doncaster (Michael Persson) and London (Graham Leonard). Consultants were Canon Christopher Hill of Lambeth, Dr Mary Hayter and Mrs G. G. Pinnock (one of Leonard's examining chaplains). Nigel Barnett of the General Synod Office acted as secretary. Also before the synod was a draft measure. The bishops' report provided the background for debate and the voting took place on the Priests (Ordination of Women) Measure where only a nominal majority was needed even though two-thirds will be eventually required. The voting showed a Church very substantially divided on the issue: bishops, 28 for, 21 against; clergy, 137 for, 102 against; laity, 134 for, 93 against with 1 abstention. Overall figures: 299 votes to 216.

In fact the Constitution of the General Synod provides for a special majority only at the final approval stage, hence only 50% at general approval. Attempts have been made to vary this which Leonard thinks will eventually be successful.

It is not completely clear which way the Church of England will move, although the sky is cloudy for opponents of women priests. Leonard would never lead a break away movement and is unimpressed with the internal squabbles of such Churches. If the Church of England ordains women to the priesthood, Leonard would not be able to do anything which would imply acceptance of women priests, nor could he act in the name of a Church which did so. He will have had to retire before it can happen, but what deeply concerns him is the advice which he should give to those who have their priestly ministry before them and share his position. What distresses him is the common assumption that they are the dissentients, whereas, in his view, it is those who wish to ordain women who are 'innovators' and it is those who hold fast to Scripture and tradition who remain Anglicans. For the moment Leonard remains the most reliable brake on this issue, and the best accelerator for directing the Church to its main work in today's world.

15

Prophet among Propitiators

Leonard reaches compulsory retirement (70) on 8 May 1991. It is neither feasible nor desirable to contemplate the organisational shape or ecclesiastical temper of the Church in even such a few years time. It *is* possible, and necessary, however, to record how the climate in the Church has changed over the past years. There are no longer bright periods with scattered showers, thundery in places, rather a persistent drizzle of liberalization with foggy patches to confuse the faithful and severe hailstorms bombarding the Church with anything that is new. The prefaces to *Crockford's Clerical Directory* have provided an opportunity for a commentary on Anglican affairs. Anonymity gave the author the chance to survey the Anglican scene with a wide-ranging lens. The author's eyes see what they want to recognize.

During the past two decades through the archiepiscopates of Ramsey, Coggan and Runcie, the Prefaces have supported most movements for reform and the ascendency of liberal thought and action. There have been opportunities for the derogatory aside or double-edged reference to Leonard. For example, the *Crockford's* author described *Growing into Union* (written with Mascall, Buchanan and Packer) as 'polemical and abusive, very free in its moral condemnation of other theological views and very self-satisfied with its own. . . . The most arrogant theological work in the last 20 years'. In another Preface, this time on women and priesthood, the author noted that 'One of the opponents was the Bishop of Truro, a leading wrecker of Anglican–Methodist reunion although a clever man and an idealist. To him, the proposal amounted to "a criticism of the way in which God made the world".'

By 1985 the new establishment was liberal, overbearing

and cocksure. Leonard was labelled a traditionalist, which was meant in a negative, even derogatory way. His ideas and way of thinking were regarded as either obscure or outmoded and increasingly irrelevant. The spirit of the day was against Leonard. And it was that spirit which had infected the Church's leaders. They did not recognize it as a fever leading to delirious decisions, but as a mind-enhancing drug showing them the true vision of 'The Future Church'. The danger is that some of them have made fashion into the final criterion of truth, which is absurd. As with any drug user, they have deluded themselves that they have the future on their side. Their word is the last word. In history nobody has the last word except God. In matters of opinion and of taste and fashion the judgement of history is provisional and contingent. The liberal case, argued from progress, is tendentious and precarious. In a paradoxical way the liberals have become the new intolerants.

The choice of the *Crockford's* author and of the people who select him are crucial matters. In some measure he should be a historian, but the ecclesiastical historian has his own preferences and perceptions. David L. Edwards, now provost of Southwark, has admitted to being the author of several *Prefaces*, and his personal views are well known through his many publications and articles. When the 1987 directory was due, it fell to Derek Pattinson, secretary-general of the General Synod, and J. E. Shelley, secretary of the Church Commissioners, to select the author. They chose someone who could be expected to review the Church's life, work and personalities in a rather different way from David Edwards. As soon as pre-publication copies of the Preface were available, it was clear that there would be more than a fuss on publication: there would be major controversy. It is interesting that a copy was sent to the bishop of London's Press secretary (Revd Norman Hood) from the Press and Public Affairs Department of the General Synod ahead of copies going to all diocesan bishops. One wonders why.

Leonard received and read his copy on 1 December. On the eve of publication (2 December) news of the contents of the Preface was broadcast: prior to a deluge of reporting and comment on 3 December. It is now a matter of history that the Preface was one of the most cogent and pungent polemical writings that had appeared for many years. Instead of attacking traditional policies and people who, it had been said, were endangering Anglicanism, the writer emptied his armoury on the liberal Establishment of the Church, the predominating tendency, militant in its own way and very un-liberal in its dismissal of opponents. A polemical writer exaggerates to make his point. The bench of bishops is not as monochrome as the author implied. Yet his corrosive criticisms of the Church and its liberal Establishment can be sustained.

The author singled out the archbishop of Canterbury for slight praise and major blame. Not everything the author says can be upheld, but there is more than enough to sustain his case. Runcie is described as having established himself as a notable holder of the primacy; as having intelligence, personal warmth and a formidable capacity for hard work; as being one who listens well and has built up a range of personal contacts among clergy and laity far wider than that of any of his predecessors:

His speeches and addresses are thoughtful, witty and persuasive. . . . His influence is now probably at its height. It would therefore be good to be assured that he actually knew what he was doing and had a clear basis for his policies other than taking the line of least resistance on each issue. He has a major disadvantage in not having been trained as a theologian, and though he makes extensive use of academics as advisers and speechwriters, his own position is often unclear. He has the disadvantage of the intelligent pragmatist: the desire to put off all questions until someone else makes a decision. One recalls a lapidary phrase of Mr Frank Field that the archbishop is usually to be found nailing his colours to the fence. All this makes Dr Runcie peculiarly vulnerable to pressure-groups.

In a rare synodical moment of self-revelation he [Runcie] once described himself as 'an unconvinced Anglo-Catholic' thought it is the latter part of the description which should not be taken too seriously. His effective background is the elitist liberalism of Westcott House in the immediate post-war years and this he shares with Dr John Habgood, the archbishop of York. In particular it gives him a distaste for those who are so unstylist as to inhabit the clerical ghettoes of Evangelicalism and Anglo-Catholicism, and he certainly tends to underestimate their influence in the spiritual life and mission of the Church. His clear preference is for men of liberal disposition with a moderately Catholic style which is not taken to the point of having firm principles. If in addition they have a good appearance and are articulate over the media he is prepared to overlook a certain theological deficiency. Dr Runcie and his closest associates are men who have nothing to prevent them following what they think is the wish of the majority of the moment.

Then there is an unlikely observation, that Leonard, not the archbishops and their ilk, was a representative of mainstream Anglicanism.

Most exposed of all is Dr Graham Leonard, the Bishop of London, whom the Press love to portray as the Archbishop Lefebvre of the Anglican communion. He has not always been particularly adroit in the presentation of his case and he has a predilection for popish ecclesiastical outfits, but all this should not obscure the simple fact that his ideas on faith and order place him securely in the mainstream of Anglicanism. A series of small books which seek to offer a modern spirituality based on a traditional theology make him one of the few bishops able to speak to those who feel the spiritual emptiness of so many Church publications.

After reading the Preface Leonard telephoned 'the only man in the Church of England who could have written it'. The number he dialled was that of one of his examining chaplains, Canon Gareth (Garry) Bennett. Bennett denied that he was the author, which puzzled Leonard as style and content pointed in that direction. Leonard believed Bennett's denial. The media campaign to hunt the author was without parallel for this kind of publication. Who knew? One person who knew the identity of the author was the Revd Philip Ursell, principal of Pusey House, Oxford, a friend of Bennett's who had been taken into his confidence. On the eve of publication Philip Ursell saw Garry Bennett during the evening and writes: 'He seemed quite pleased and not over-concerned with the stir he was causing. "It's amazing what a chap can do from his little semi-detached house in Oxford", he said at one stage. And again, "Of course, they will suspect it is me" he said, "but they'll never know for certain".' On the morning of publication (3 December) Leonard spoke to Ursell. '[Leonard] was very pleased about his favourable mention but told me he concluded that it couldn't have been Garry's writing because (a) Garry had denied authorship, (b) they had had such a serious disagreement over the Tulsa affair.'

The *Crockford's* Preface opened the curtains on a Church blighted by bitterness. The Church of England has always been a bit cantankerous, but now the temper is corrosive, eating away at people, personalizing every issue. The spirit is not Christian. Is it imagination, or has this bitten deeper and faster since the growth of the pseudo-democratic General Synod? Garry Bennett poked the Church where it hurt. The institutional Church is in a mess. The liberal Establishment bears a heavy responsibility for its condition. The prevailing note of the Church of England and, to a different extent, of the Anglican communion, is one of uncertainty, speculation and misgiving. Reckless innovation and theological perversity have held sway, attracting eager, effervescent and uncritical attention. If the Preface was more strident than anything Leonard had written, it echoed his sentiments, although he would not have brought personalities into public debate. Within six days of publication, Garry Bennett was dead: he had committed suicide. It is rarely appropriate and never easy to speculate what, at the penultimate moment, drives someone over the edge of the precipice into the darkest of valleys below. Various pressures coming from different directions merge, and the mind snaps. Attacks on the 'anonymous' author had been as direct as had been Bennett's own comments. Archbishop Habgood of York was much quoted for describing the Preface as 'scurrilous . . . sour and vindictive'. These and similar comments were directed at someone as yet unknown who was not a journalist specializing in sensationalism but a careful scholar well known in the upper echelons of the Church.

On 15 December there was a solemn Requiem Mass in New College Chapel, Oxford. It cannot have been lost on many of those present that there was a time when such a Mass would not have been said for a suicide victim. Yet such a service was wholly appropriate. The concelebrants were those bishops to whom Garry Bennett had a canonical relationship: Colin James of Winchester (the visitor of New College); Eric Kemp of Chichester (where Bennett was prebend of Exceit); Leonard (for whom he was an examining chaplain). The priest concelebrants were the members of the 'Saturday lunch', founded in Oxford by Ronald Arbuthnot Knox: eight priests who rotate as hosts on the eight Saturdays of term. This was very much a regular part of Bennett's social life. During the last six years there had been only two guests: on one occasion Michael Ramsey, and on another, Leonard.

In his address, the Revd Geoffrey Rowell, chaplain and fellow of Keble College, commented that

> God created Gary [sic], our friend and brother, in his image and likeness. He gave him gifts of deep and simple faith and sharp intellect, of historical perception, of sensitivity combined with firmness, of love felt if not always easily shown, of wit and of wisdom: and for these we give thanks. When pain and darkness drove him to a hell of despair, the God we trust met him; there was the God who in Christ crucified went down into the darkness. To that God we now commend him. . . . There are many pains and griefs here today – pains 'counter and keen' – of loss, of anger, of guilt; the pain of one alone, bearing accusations and striving to know what was right; the pain he felt in belonging to a Church which could seem ruled by trend and not the tradition handed on; the pain he felt and shared with others in the Church that apostolic faith, and ministry, and sacraments, were threatened, not so much by changes in ministry, about which there may be debate, but by the way those changes were pursued, and by the lack of concern for the bonds of ecumenical friendship and the character of historic Anglicanism by those who pressed for them, come what may, and sure that they were right. There are other pains also which others feel, but these are ones felt here and now. All this pain must be recognized and acknowledged and brought before God in our prayer today and in the Church in the months ahead.

One final observation on this tragic and traumatic affair was recorded by Fr. Philip Ursell: 'Garry told me on the

Thursday night [the day of publication, 3 December] that his greatest temptation to "come clean" had been that morning when Bishop Graham had been on the telephone to him saying what a splendid essay it was: any distance between them which still remained after their Tulsa disagreement could have been completely patched up by Garry admitting he had written the Preface, but somehow he had managed to resist'. We may only speculate about the possibilities had he spoken.

All this gives a sharper edge to Leonard's exchange at a press conference on his return from Tulsa:

'Have you broken the law?'
'No.'
'What have you done then?'
'I've upset the club.'

It must not be thought that Leonard stands apart or aloof from all or most of his fellow bishops on all matters. On some he has strange allies, even if he or they may not want to recognize each other as allies. Surprisingly, Leonard still has sympathy with the idea of a national Church. Some of his views are not dissimilar to those of Habgood of York, although they express them in different ways, and Leonard would not go as far as embracing Habgood's identification and advocacy of 'folk religion'.

What of Leonard's approach to political, economic and social affairs? Is there a specific approach that is Christian? In general terms, yes; in party political terms, no. Leonard thinks it is necessary for Christians to accept a distinctive quality of life for themselves without seeking to force it upon those who do not profess Christian belief. He has never seen social concern and personal holiness as alternatives. Of course, Christians and Churches must be occupied with the structures and forces which shape society. But this is of use only if the Christian is committed to a distinctive quality of life. If not, Leonard considers that Christians

are not equipped to bring a Christian mind to bear upon such political and social structures and social forces. In the absence of such a mind the vacuum is filled by an uncritical acceptance of secular trends. . . . They become ready prey to worldly motives of envy, bitterness or resentment which corrupt their otherwise laudable intentions. Christians who are conscious of the moral content of discipleship tend to express their concern in terms of sweeping condemnation – rather than be primarily concerned with embodying Christian moral behaviour in their own lives. Christians must be concerned, for example, to live chastely before they preach chastity.

For Leonard, the difficulty is that people think the role of politics is to provide human happiness understood in material terms. It does not matter which political view is being paraded for salute. In an introductory talk on the 'Christian and Politics', given by Leonard at the Christian and Conservatives Conference at Westminster Chapel on 1 February 1983, he said plainly that

The Church must insist in the last resort that the problems we face are caused by the kind of people we are. We face problems of violence, poverty, bad housing, war, because men are violent, grasping, envious, unjust, greedy and bitter. The problems we face are not, in the last resort, simply caused by ignorance, bad administration or bad planning. The Church must also insist that while we must be concerned with education, better planning and administration, they can only help us to be better and make it harder for us to be bad.

In general terms, despite occasional unctious words to the contrary, the entire process of life has been secularized and the thought of God has been banished from the considerations that determine action. Governments are secular and their procedure is earth-born and earth-bound.

Leonard has not needed to worry about this. Ideological politics are something of which he is wary, to the point of avoiding them. When giving expression to his view he turns, as he does on many issues, to his favourite poet, T. S. Eliot (C. S. Lewis and Charles Williams are other favourite writers):

What makes me suspicious of any kind of political system which is supposed to supply the answer is, it is actually going to be operated by fallible and sinful human beings.

T. S. Eliot's superb verse says it all, when he speaks of
men who
    'constantly try to escape
    from the darkness outside and within
    by dreaming of systems so perfect that no one will need
      to be good'.

Leonard dispenses praise and criticism across the political
spectrum and not, as is often said, to the Tories alone. Giving
an address at the 200th anniversary service of the Board of
Trade at St Margaret's, Westminster, on 28 February 1986,
he noted that 'One of the more disturbing characteristics of
our society at the present time is the way in which people are
treated as less than human, being seen as the means of profit
on the one hand or as the object of amelioration on the other.
I refer to both aspects because it is as easy to dehumanize
people by making them the means by which we discharge the
claims of our consciences as it is by treating them as no more
than economic units.'

There are four ways in which Leonard has sought to influence Government legislation. First, by personal acquaintance
with members of Parliament of all parties, with some cabinet
ministers, and with the prime minister herself. There are a
few occasions for informal contact, the more important for
being unrecorded. Secondly, his membership of the House of
Lords provides opportunities for contributing to debates in
which he has an interest as bishop of London: for example,
the London Docklands Bill (1986); or simply as a Christian:
for example, the Sunday trading, abortion or blasphemy bills.
A third means of influence comes through his chairmanship
of an undervalued and little publicised body, the Churches
Main Committee. It is a body (set up in 1941) as a reaction
on the part of the Churches to the provisions of the first War
Damage Bill. In practical terms the committee has concern
for all secular matters, other than education, of interest to the
various Churches in the discharge of their ministry. Most of
the Churches are members, including the Roman Catholic
Church. In this ecumenical setting Leonard is held in high
esteem as its chairman, leading the committee towards a
consensus with the minimum of irrelevant debate. From his
early years with the National Society to this committee, his

enjoyment, with only intermittent frustrations, of summarizing views in the form of a plan for action, is noticeable. By meetings and by letters with the prime minister or the appropriate minister, he pursues his subjects with effective and restrained vigour. Recent issues have included the question of value added tax on church building work, the maintenance of the ecclesiastical exemption from listed building control, and the Government's proposal to introduce a community charge that will impose a severe additional financial burden on the Churches.

The fourth way in which Leonard seeks to influence legislation is that which gives him the highest profile. As chairman of the Board for Social Responsibility he was the Church of England's spokesman on anything that came before the board. In 1983 he relinquished the chairmanship for that of the Board of Education. He came to that board at precisely the time education was facing dramatic change. The Government's Education Reform Bill has found its most effective opposition not on the Labour benches in the House of Commons but in the House of Lords, and led by Leonard. This bill comprises some of the most radical and comprehensive reforms in the educational system for many years. The secretary of state for education and science, Kenneth Baker, is one of the most enlightened and civilized members of the present Government. He combines intellect with independence, vision with determination. He is also a churchman. Leonard (very ably aided by Colin Alves, general secretary of the Board of Education) has established a rapport with Kenneth Baker by correspondence and personal meetings.

The Church was generally unhappy that the minister was not proposing to give religious education a place in the proposed new core curriculum. (Religious education was the only subject guaranteed under the Butler act of 1944.) Seldom has a bishop been so closely involved with an intricate piece of legislation, stage by stage, clause by clause, hour by hour. Behind the scenes and in the debating chamber of the House of Lords, Leonard has shown himself to be consummately skilled at persuasion and politics. He has constantly held a position that had the best chance of success without losing sight of his target. Some of the peers who were militant for

Christian education might have lost everything had it not been for the reconciling hand of Leonard.

The Government made major concessions to Leonard and where they could not be persuaded to concede on matters of importance to Leonard and those peers who thought like him, amendments were proposed by Leonard and he won. The Government suffered many defeats. Yet Leonard did not indulge in adversarial politics. The bill returned to the House of Commons in 1988 somewhat mauled by the Lords. The Government accepted the substance of his amendments which will be to his lasting credit – a bit of history. Religious education, which was made compulsory under the Education Act of 1944, had become very unsatisfactory being often either neglected or lacking in any real content. It will now have to have specifically Christian content as was always intended, while the presence of those of other faiths in the country will be recognized in the agreed syllabuses which have to be prepared by each local education authority. Worship in schools will be wholly or mainly of a 'broadly Christian character'. In schools where pupils are non-Christian there can be collective worship of a kind acceptable to parents.

At the end of the third reading on 7 July 1988 the Chief Rabbi, Lord Jakobovits, spoke for many inside and outside the House when he joined in praise of Leonard's 'enormous skill, ingenuity and persistence'. One of Leonard's critics on other issues referred to this as 'his finest hour'.

The mutual respect between minister and bishop despite the latter's fervent and successful opposition to parts of the Education Reform Bill have been shown in a surprising and pleasing way. Leonard has accepted Kenneth Baker's invitation to be a member of the Polytechnics and Colleges Funding Council, one of the two new bodies set up under the bill. Thus the Church is represented on a national body concerned with general education policy and not just with the Church's interest. Leonard had previously decided to resign as chairman of the Board of Education and of the standing committee of the National Society to take effect from 31 October 1988.

If education has captured the headlines, AIDS and homo-sexuality have seldom been out of the news of late. On AIDS, Leonard's view is clear:

AIDS is the natural consequence of sin, because we have disregarded the way we were made. . . . The Church as a whole hasn't come out clearly on homosexuality, and I believe that is wrong, but then I also believe that fornication is wrong. AIDS is not a purely homosexual problem. It is a heterosexual problem in Central Africa, where they do not even have a word for homosexuality. Promiscuity is the cause. (*Daily Mail*, 13 December 1986)

Leonard blamed the Church's leadership from the 1960s onwards for failing to speak fearlessly unpalatable truths against the spirit of the age. And he used the word 'we' rather than 'they'.

On homosexuality the pastoral heart may obscure the clear gaze occasionally. Homosexual orientation is one matter; promiscuity is another. The 'gay' culture that is prevalent in some places has similar features to those found in heterosexual society: casual relationships, parties for 'pick-ups', promiscuity, 'missionary' endeavours on the part of strong-minded homosexuals seeking to persuade the immature, excessive drinking etc. This culture is known in the Church, has been known in some theological colleges, and finds a focus in the diocese of London. It has become a commonplace to say that some of the best priests are homosexually orientated. That may be correct. If so, they are mature and well integrated. The danger comes when a group of homosexual clergy find themselves in, or are driven into, claustrophobic, clannish cotories which easily become the locus of promiscuity.

Leonard is not an investigator. If allegations are made about promiscuous activity, heterosexual or homosexual, he asks for the evidence. And evidence it must be. Two men, or two women, sharing a house is not evidence, and indeed should not lead to innuendo and false conclusions. 'I hold to the traditional belief and believe physical homosexual practices to be incongruous with the Christian faith. In trying to help, counsel and understand homosexuals I have never concealed that belief. . . . I have known priests, whom I think have been of homosexual orientation, but who have been models of devoted, disciplined and sensitive pastoral care. I have, however, never knowingly ordained anyone who has been a practising homosexual.'

246

On another moral issue, that of the remarriage of divorced people in church, Leonard has four times led the fight in Synod against those who would alter the Church's ruling. Again he found himself on the opposite side of the battlefield from Robert Runcie, for this is an issue on which Runcie has consistently argued for a change. On each occasion the Leonard battalions won.

Leonard's position has never varied for, as he says:

The problem is not divorce, for which it is possible to repent. The problem is remarriage which involves repudiation of the original vows. I do not see how the Church can endorse that, which in any case involves the Church in saying that there can be a limit to loving. I do regret that the Church of England has no mechanism for deciding whether a marriage is null and void *ab initio*. If I am convinced that an original marriage was null I find some way of indicating that the person can marry with a clear Christian conscience, but I have never approved of the use of the marriage service. The real problem in the Church of England over getting a proper nullity procedure is that some of us would want it on strict grounds of nullity whereas others want it on the basis that a marriage can 'die'. This idea I regard as incompatible with the Gospel which gives the pattern of love as being to the end.

None the less there are those who feel that Leonard's heart is too inclined to be generous. His stand over the question of authority, and of the defence of what he believes to be the Catholic faith, has always been central to his life, though he is a strangely adaptable person when given proper information and left to make a *pastoral* decision. There can be no limit to pastoral care. That is why he could never allign himself with the bigoted Christian moralizers whose hearts are hard. It is often said that Leonard is not a good judge of character. But pastoral situations call for the penetrating tenderness of the priest rather than the appraising coolness of the 'judge'. Such tenderness does not exclude directness and toughness where appropriate and includes insight and understanding.

Crises lead to strange alignments. However, they are not true alignments as Leonard is aware. There are those who purport to support him but do so for their own militant advance rather than for what he stands. The new breed of 'Christian' dictators, with fanaticism in their eyes, who combine rigid biblical fundamentalism with a punitive morality linked to dubious political involvement do not begin to understand the faith as preached and lived by Leonard. They would be shocked and find unacceptable the demands he would make on them in terms of Christian obedience and the implications of the sacraments. Hating the sin and loving and forgiving the sinner is something they do not seem to understand in practice.

Yet this is all of a piece with a man who is vulnerable and easily hurt, while at the same time giving the impression of being able to rise above it, though some of the wounds have left scars which have lasted a long time. There is a self-doubting side to Leonard that is quite self-contained, but it is there. He is self-contained too in his personal religious practices. He says Mass daily in his private oratory with his wife Priscilla as his congregation. He would say his oratory is packed each day, for we believe in the communion of saints. For meditation he usually turns to the desert fathers, but above all he ruminates on biblical passages. And he is always reading a recently published book, so his bookshelves and his mind are never in danger of gathering dust.

Although Leonard has produced millions of words, he has not yet written many books. It was a long time before he would agree to a book being published. He was conscious of not being an academic, and was fearful of reviews. Of his four books, *The Gospel is for Everyone* (1977), *God Alive: Priorities in Pastoral Theology* (1981), *Firmly I Believe and Truly* (1985) and *Life in Christ* (1986), *God Alive* is the most important, and *Firmly I Believe* the most helpful. The one has rightly been described as 'an unconscious apologia denying his false reputation as a harsh rigorist'; the other is a simple yet spirited exposition of the Catholic essentials, justifying his reputation as a rigorous defender of the faith.

Leonard is seen as the leader of a movement of thought that extends far beyond particular controversies. On 18 September 1987 he stood where Winston Churchill once stood, giving the 42nd John Findley Green Foundation Lecture at Westminster College, Fulton, Missouri. The title of his lecture was 'The

Tyranny of Subjectivism'. He explained his main thesis in these words:

> First, I believe that many of these problems have arisen because the West has lost its soul. Secondly, I believe that this has happened because it has rejected the one essential belief which marked it for centuries, namely that man, by his very nature, has to be obedient to an authority over and above himself. Thirdly, that the rejection of such authority leads not to freedom but to tyranny: a tyranny which springs not, as in past centuries, from a fundamentalist approach to truth, but from the bestowal of absolute authority on the expression of what individuals or a group believe to be self-evident truths, but which, in fact, only reflect contemporary fashions.

When he approached the realms of theology he said:

> For a number of years I have been suggesting that within all the Christian Churches, a fundamental realignment has been taking place, gaining momentum since the Second World War. It cuts across existing denominational divisions, as is often evident at ecumenical gatherings. I believe that in time it could acquire the dimensions of a second Reformation.
>
> To put it in very basic terms, it is a realignment between those, on the one hand, who believe that the Christian Gospel is revealed by God, is to be heard and received and that its purpose is to enable men and women to obey God in love, and through them for creation itself to be redeemed. On the other hand are those who believe that it can and should be modified and adapted to the cultural and intellectual attitudes and demands of successive generations, indeed, originates in them. To the former the scriptures are of unique authority as witnessing to the events of God in history which brought the Church into being, and as serving to speak of God's revelation to successive generations to enable them to discern how the truth of the Gospel is to be expressed in different times and cultures. The Creeds are accepted as serving a simple purpose by distilling the essential meaning of the biblical revelation. To the latter, however, as one scholar has contended, since both

249

scripture and tradition have lost their authority, all decisions in Church matters must be made simply in the light of 'appropriateness' and 'expediency'. Significantly he gives no indication of the criteria by which 'appropriateness' and 'expediency' should be determined. In practice, they are determined by the cultural outlook of the present day, the assumptions and prejudices of which are accepted without being brought under Christian judgment'.

The Fulton Lecture received very widespread attention and there has been much analysis and comment from supporters and critics alike. The archbishop of Canterbury made a partial retort in lectures in America in January 1988 (published as *Authority in Crisis? an Anglican response*). But the two minds (Leonard's and Runcie's) do not meet in argument. Their temper, habit and manner of thinking are too different.

One body which has been active in upholding the revealed faith, biblical teaching and the apostolic ministry is the International Council for the Apostolic Faith based in Greenwich, Connecticut, under the energetic chairmanship of Mrs Gordon A. T. Heath (*Life in Christ* was dedicated by Leonard to Gordon and Peggy Heath). The Ash Wednesday 1988 Declaration of Unity, Witness and Mission originated from this body and had the immediate and still growing effect of encouraging bishops from all over the Anglican communion to declare themselves. There are already some surprising results. By July 1988 the archbishop and every bishop in the province of Papua New Guinea had signed; four of the seven bishops of the Scottish Episcopal Church have signed: Aberdeen and Orkney, Glasgow and Galloway, Argyll and the Isles, and Moray, Ross and Caithness; a third of the bishops from South Africa have signed: Bloemfontein, George, Kimberley and Kuruman, Lebombo, St Helena and Swaziland. In the Anglican Church of the southern cone of America the bishops of Argentina and Uruguay, Northern Argentina, Peru and Bolivia have signed. In England the diocesan bishops of London, Winchester, Chichester, Gibraltar, Leicester, Portsmouth, Truro and Wakefield have declared themselves. No names appear from Wales, Ireland, Canada,

New Zealand or some of the African Provinces. The declaration states:

> We accept the revelation of God in the holy scriptures as the ground of faith and the source of all authority in the Church, and as being the rule and ultimate standard of faith and morals. We believe in God the Holy Trinity and in the Incarnation, Death and Resurrection of the Lord Jesus Christ as set forth in the Catholic creeds and defined by the general councils of the undivided Church.
>
> We accept the two sacraments of Baptism and the Eucharist, ordained by Christ himself, as generally necessary to salvation. We believe 'these Orders of Ministers in Christ's Church: Bishops, Priests and Deacons' to have come down to us from apostolic times; and we do not consider that the churches of the Anglican Communion have authority to change the historic tradition of the Church that the Christian ministerial priesthood is male.

It must be added that at Pentecost 1988 significantly more bishops signed a message describing the ordination of women as vital to the Church. The Pentecost message was initiated by the bishop of Brisol (chairman of the Advisory Council for the Church's Ministry) and the bishops of Manchester and Southwark. Other signatories included the bishops of Durham and Lichfield. Whereas the Ash Wednesday statement included bishops from all over the world the Pentecost statement was largely confined to 'first world' bishops.

History is littered with the corpses of people who have stood firm and called the Church to realize what obedience to our Lord means at times when it has succumbed to worldly voices and wordly judgements. What matters is not the values and standards of the world but the 'Mind of Christ'; not that which glitters and passes, but that which outlasts the universe itself. Leonard's own chosen way as a disciple of Jesus Christ is through that portion of the one holy Catholic Church which is *ecclesia Anglicana*, the ancient Catholic Church of England. The Church is moving away from Leonard, not Leonard from it. His choice has not meant a priesthood and episcopate of bliss. Choices carry consequences. His chosen path has often been gruelling, grievous and grave. The joy of fulfilment has

251

mingled with the tears of disappointment: both myrrh and incense.

Preaching at a service for the 20th anniversary of his consecration as bishop, in 1984, Leonard looked back with penitence and thanksgiving, with sadness and with joy, and made some words of St Francis Xavier his own prayer:

> My God, I love thee; not because
>   I hope for heaven thereby,
> Nor yet because who love thee not
>   Are lost eternally.
> Thou, O my Jesus, thou didst me
>   Upon the Cross embrace;
> For me didst bear the nails and spear,
>   And manifold disgrace.
> And griefs and torments numberless,
>   And sweat of agony;
> E'en death itself; and all for one
>   Who was thine enemy.

Graham Leonard has chosen to stand firm, for it is enough for him to hold fast to the truth he knows and to walk loyally in the path he sees.

In a television interview on 23 May 1988 the questioner caught Leonard completely by surprise and his reply was spontaneous: Hope Sealey: 'What, when you move on, when you arrive at the after life, what are the things you would like to think are in the merit book up there against your name?' Leonard: 'Oh dear, I would like to think that there was a recognition that I was actually prepared to seek forgiveness from God.'

Bibliography

This selective bibliography of Graham Leonard's writings only includes book reviews on subjects with which the bishop is personally concerned. Short articles, forewords, and his contributions to the *Cornish Churchman* have been excluded, but his contributions to *The Bishop of London's Newsletter* are given where they deal with matters of greater importance. The flavour and force of his teaching and concern for topical issues are found especially in the reports of the proceedings of General Synod and the House of Lords' Hansard.

Books
The Unity of the Faith (privately printed, 1967)
To every man's conscience . . . : Comments on the report of the Anglican–Methodist Unity Commission (privately printed, 1968)
with C. O. Buchanan, E. L. Mascall and J. I. Packer: *Growing into Union: Proposals for forming a united Church in England* (London: SPCK, 1970)
The Gospel is for Everyone (London: Faith Press, 1971, 2/1977)
God Alive: Priorities in Pastoral Theology (London: Darton, Longman and Todd, 1981)
Firmly I Believe and Truly (London: Mowbray, 1985)
Life in Christ (London: Mowbray, 1986)
ed.: *Faith for the Future: Essays on the Church in Education* [to mark the 175th anniversary of the National Society] (National Society, 1986)

Pamphlets
Science and Religion (Church Literature Association, 1958)
Reality (n.d.)
The Thorsen Film [speech to the General Synod, 8 Nov 1976] (Ch. Lit. Assn, 1976)
The End of Anglicanism, Dolphin Paper no. 9 (Ch. Lit. Assn, 1978)
with P. Boulton and O. W. H. Clark: *The Covenant: a reassessment*, Dolphin Paper no. 12 (Ch. Lit. Assn, 1981)

Genesis and the Christian Gospel [St Paul's Lecture, 27 Oct 1983] (Council for Christian–Jewish Understanding, 1983)

Mary and the Body of Christ (Walsingham, 1985)

The Council of 381 and Article XXI [The Fifth Constantinople Lecture, 28 Nov 1983] (Anglican and Eastern Churches Assn, 1986)

Contribution to composite books

'Prayer', in *The Christian Religion Explained* (London: Mowbray, 1960)

'The Agreed Statements and the Eucharistic Traditions of the Church', in *A Critique of Eucharistic Agreement* (London: SPCK, 1974)

'The conductor's use of method', and 'The conductor's use of liturgical practices', *Retreats Today* (APR, 1962)

chapter in D. Stacey, ed.: *Is Christianity credible?* (London: Epworth, 1983)

'A Fragile Peace', *The Cross and the Bomb* (London: Mowbray, 1983)

'The Morality of Nuclear Deterrence', *Unholy Warfare: The Church and the Bomb* (Oxford: Blackwell, 1983)

'Christian Decision-making', P. Moore, ed.: *The Synod of Westminster* (London: SPCK, 1986)

'Desecularizing the Social Gospel', W. Oddie, ed.: *Beyond the Deluge* (London: SPCK, 1987)

Selected articles

'Some to be Teachers', *Church Observer* (May, 1956)

'Birthday of a Community' [Community of the Glorious Ascension], *Church Illustrated*

'The Church and her Schools', *Home Words* (Jan, 1959)

'The New Education Act', *Church Observer* (Oct, 1959)

'Spiritual direction in the second half of the 20th century', *Home Mission News* (Sept, 1961)

'The Christian and Modern Education' *Church of England Newspaper* (6 Oct 1961)

'Apostolic Ministry' [sermon at the annual festival of the Additional Curates' Society], *Home Mission News* (summer, 1963)

review of M. Thornton: *English Spirituality, Home Mission News* (spring, 1964)

'Baptism and the Eucharist', *The Vision* (1964, no. 2)

'The Sacramental Life' [sermon at the Whit Monday Pilgrimage, Walsingham], *The Server* (autumn, 1966)

'St Charles, king and martyr', *Church and King* (May 1967)

'Episcopal care of ordinands', *Ministry* (autumn, 1967)

'The Church and the World', *Eastern Churches Newsletter* (Dec 1967)

'One Lord, one faith, one baptism', *The Times* (13 July 1968)

'Catholics and Evangelicals', *Church Observer* (autumn, 1972)

'A Right Balance', *Cross Swords* (Jan 1973)
'The task of *diakonia* in the Church of England', *Diakonie* (Aug–Sept 1977)
'These views cannot be ignored', *Sunday Independent* (21 Oct 1979)
'The meaning of Christmas', *Illustrated London News* (Dec 1981)
'A book that has been important in my life' [C. Gore: *Belief in God*], *Spectator* (30 Jan 1982)
'Planning for a lifelong marriage', *Brides* (autumn, 1982)
'Why we must not ban the bomb', *News of the World* (7 Nov 1982)
'The defence of the bomb', *Reader's Digest,* (April 1983)
'The Oxford Movement and the Commissioners', *The Franciscan* (May 1983)
'A vision for the future' [address at the Loughborough Conference], *Church Observer* (summer, 1983)
'The Christian and politics', *Crucible* (July–Sept 1983)
'The Morality of Nuclear Deterrence' [sermon at St Lawrence Jewry, 3 Nov 1982], *Icto–Cahier* (Aug 1983)
'Marriage', *Church of England Newspaper* (1983)
review of J. M. R. Tillard: *Authority in the Church: the bishop of Rome, Insight* (Dec 1983)
'Christmas' *Women and Home* (1983)
'The Ordination of Women: theological and biblical issues', *Epworth Review* (Jan 1984)
review of A. Kilmister: *When will ye be wise?, The Daily Telegraph* (2 Jan 1984)
'Personal view' [on the life to come], *Church of England Newspaper* (27 Jan 1984)
'Real priorities for Christians to tackle evil', *Guardian* (6 Feb 1984)
'A new creation', *Spectator* (12 April 1984)
review of M. Perry: *Psychic Studies: a Christian's view, the Christian Parapsychologist* (March 1984)
'Spiritual direction today', *Mowbrays Journal* (spring, 1984)
review of P. Cornwell: *Church and Nation, Theology* (May 1984)
'The Morality of Wealth', *Lombard Street Letter* (July 1984)
'The woman gave to me . . . and I did eat', *Jesus* [Italian White Fathers] (Sept 1984)
'The coherence of the life of Jesus', *The Times* (15 Sept 1984)
'Where the Church should not tread', *Mail on Sunday* (14 Oct 1984)
'Why women priests would be divisive', *Guardian* (12 Nov 1984)
'Why isn't life any easier for Christians?', *Church of England Newspaper* (21 Dec 1984)
'We can't decide, truth on a show of hands', *Mail on Sunday* (10 Feb 1985)
'Holy orders and women', *Faith and Worship* (autumn, 1985)

'If he be not risen', *St Mary's Bourne Street Annual* (1986)

'A tension within society' [on broadcasting], *Airwaves* (spring, 1986)

review of C. Moore. A. N. Wilson and G. Stamp: *The Church in Crisis, Spectator* (18 Oct 1986)

'AIDS, promiscuity and moral cowardice', *Daily Mail* (13 Dec 1986)

'Christmas: the meaning of the mystery', *The Times* (24 Dec 1986)

'Why I am prepared for the break-up of the Church of England', *Daily Mail* (19 Feb 1987)

'The splendour of chastity', *Viewer and Listener* (summer, 1987)

'Authority v. Autonomy', *Faith and Worship* (summer, 1987)

'Looking to the Future', *Anglican Free Press* (29 Sept 1987)

'The bishop running the Church towards disorder' [on Bishop Spong of Newark, USA], *Daily Mail*, (18 July 1988)

The Bishop of London's Newsletter

'The vocation of the laity' (Jan 1983); 'Penitence – the basis for renewal' (Feb); 'The gift of wisdom' and 'The conduct of public worship' (May); 'The Christian and Politics' (June); ('Communicating the faith') (July); 'Prayer' (Aug); 'Prayer' (Sept); ('Life as *The Divine Comedy*') (Oct); ('Functions of a bishop') (Nov); ('Belief') (Jan 1984); ('Spiritual direction') (Feb); ('The reality of death and Faith and life in Christ' [sermon at memorial service for those who died in the Harrods bombing] (March); ('Marriage and divorce') (April); ('Bearing reality') (June); ('Holiness and Christian morality') (July); ('A bishop in the Church of God') (Aug–Sept); 'A book for our time' [review of A. N. Wilson: *How can we know*] (March 1985); 'Pastoral reorganization' (May); 'Seek ye first the kingdom of heaven' (June); 'Synodical government' (July); Questions for Anglicans' (Aug); 'Remarriage after divorce when former spouse still living' (Sept); 'Ordination of women to the preisthood and episcopate' (Oct); 'Ordination of women' (Nov); 'Interpretation of the creed' (Dec); 'Synodical government' (Jan 1986); 'Teaching and communicating the faith' (Feb); 'Repentance' (Aug); 'A prayer for Advent' (Nov); 'The creed of Athanasius' (Dec); 'Epiphany: gold frankincense and myrrh' (Jan 1987); 'Women deacons' [charge given on 18 March 1987] (April); 'Education' (March); 'A whole Christian' [address at thanksgiving Requiem for Tim Darton] (July); ('Homosexuality') (Dec)

Appendix

Bishops of London used to live at Fulham Palace, which despite being geographically inconvenient and too large for financial comfort had a living historic feel to it. Now the bishop lives at London House, Barton Street, Westminster: geographically central, cramped, with a window box for a garden, and no parking outside. It was possible to make a home at Fulham Palace. But London House is working premises with the resident occupant pushed into a flat upstairs like some ecclesiastical janitor. However, go down to the small basement chapel and you are at an oasis of holiness, a haven of beauty. Priscilla Leonard is primarily responsible for the beauty. She is one of the very best ecclesiastical embroiderers and her work is there to kneel on and to gaze at: examples of the holiness of beauty.

Priscilla has been responsible for some of her husband's vestments, notably several mitres. Leonard's first mitre was made of cloth of gold and was given to him by a parish in the Willesden area. After a few years a new one was needed and Priscilla decided to make one herself. She has made two plain ones; one genuine cloth of gold and one of gold lurex. She has also made two embroidered ones. She used canvas embroidery (needlepoint), the hardest wearing type, and enriched the design with metal threads and beads. The first of the embroidered ones, the 'creation' mitre, carries a symbolic design of the cosmos; the front design symbolizes recreation in Christ; the cross bursting the tomb. (This mitre is illustrated in Beryl Dean's book on church embroidery). The second is a mitre for our Lady: the Archangel Gabriel of the Annunciation on the back, and our Lady crowned in a mandorla on the front. Priscilla's very good friend Sylvia

Green, to whom she looks as a mentor in embroidery, drew the designs for both these mitres.

Leonard has four pectoral crosses. The period between his appointment as bishop of Willesden in August and his consecration in September was short. He needed a pectoral cross, and had no time to have one made. When he was made deacon he had been given a beautiful cross by Priscilla's oldest friend which hung above his prie-dieu ever since. Could this be adapted? As it was cleaned it became clear that it was not as they thought, gun metal, but rather silver over copper. They took it to be replated as it was mostly copper but were advised to have it gilded, which was done. It is of beautiful proportions. Being copper, it cannot have been mass-produced. No one whom Leonard has consulted, either in England, Greece or Russia, can identify its provenance for certain but there is a general consensus that it probably comes from Mount Athos and may be quite ancient. The central panel is of the Baptism of our Lord. The panel above is of the Annunciation. Either side of the central panel are the Epiphany and the Presentation. The two panels below the central one cannot be identified; they may be of local saints – a fairly common practice.

Mr H. S. Swann (Priscilla's brother and a cabinet maker to the Queen) made a very beautiful cross of rosewood with a gold inlaid corona in the centre of which is a chi-rho monogram in ivory. Leonard wears this cross every day. The Society of Mary gave him a gold cross on his appointment to Truro. The grille on the cross covers a relic of St Matthias. Leonard also has a 19th century enamelled cross given to him by the pilgrims to Lourdes.

His 'best' pastoral cross was also made by Hugh Swann. It is made of South American rosewood inlaid all over with ivory chronological symbols and those of the apostles. Technically it is a masterpiece: the wood was split down the middle and cemented and plugged together again with the inset of a steel core.

Leonard has a true relic of St Philip Neri. It had a cleansing in the washing machine when he forgot to remove it from a pocket. That bit of St Philip Neri survived.

Index

INDEX

INDEX

Winter, Bishop C. O'B. (Damaraland-in-exile) 174–5
Wood, Bishop M. A. P. (Norwich) 4, 174

Wright, H. J. L. 16
Wynn, Bishop H. E. (Ely) 11

Yates, Bishop J. (Gloucester) 135